How To Draw Penguin For Kids

In 10 Different Ways
With 5 Simple Steps

By
Global Baby Care

Legal Notice:

This book is copyright protected. This book is only for personal use. You cannot amend, distribute, sell, use, quote or paraphrase any part, or the content within this book, without the consent of the author or publisher.

Disclaimer Notice:

Please note the information contained within this document is for educational and entertainment purposes only. All effort has been executed to present accurate, up to date, and reliable, complete information. No warranties of any kind are declared or implied. Readers acknowledge that the author is not engaging in the rendering of legal, financial, medical or professional advice. The content within this book has been derived from various sources. Please consult a licensed professional before attempting any techniques outlined in this book.

By reading this document, the reader agrees that under no circumstances is the author responsible for any losses, direct or indirect, which are incurred as a result of the use of information contained within this document, including, but not limited to, — errors, omissions, or inaccuracies.

Learn How To Draw

We all are familiar with drawing from our childhood. In this book I'll show you how to learn to draw. It will help you even if you are an absolute beginner. We follow the grid method of drawing which is used by all famous painter or artist over years to have perfect picture.

Just pick a sharp pencil and an eraser and follow the steps we suggest.

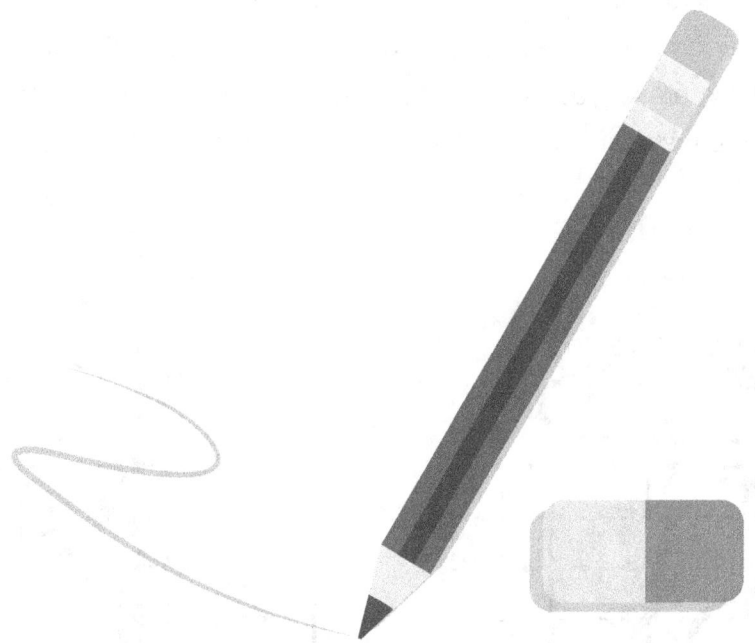

Steps to follow for Drawing:

1. At first hold your pencil correctly in order to maximize its utility. Then start drawing with soft lines and later on you can fix or erase if needed.

2. Remember you can learn a lot from looking at the ready picture. So focus before starting and capture in your mind before portraying.

3. Make sure you have drawn outlines for all the key parts of your drawing.

4. Practice makes a thing perfect. So don't expect perfection in your first attempt. The more you draw the more confident you'll become.

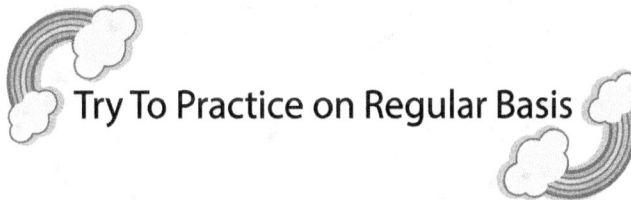

Try To Practice on Regular Basis

The Grid Copy Method:

     The grid method allows us to redraw a picture to absolutely any size. The grid basically divides the original image into smaller blocks so that you can more easily see what belongs where. The basic idea of the grid method is it divides your reference drawing up into equal squares. Choose the important side of the drawing. The grid copy is numbered along the one side and the other side is lettered, so you can focus to count those blocks and to read that value. By focusing on one square at a time, you end up drawing what you actually see.

While drawing the grid, make sure your lines are fine, straight and clear. Then try to mark the center intersection on the grid as a reference point. Draw the outlines for all the key parts of your image. Then carefully erase your grid lines, repairing outlines if needed.

Now you are ready to start shading and coloring your drawing. Take your time and practice.

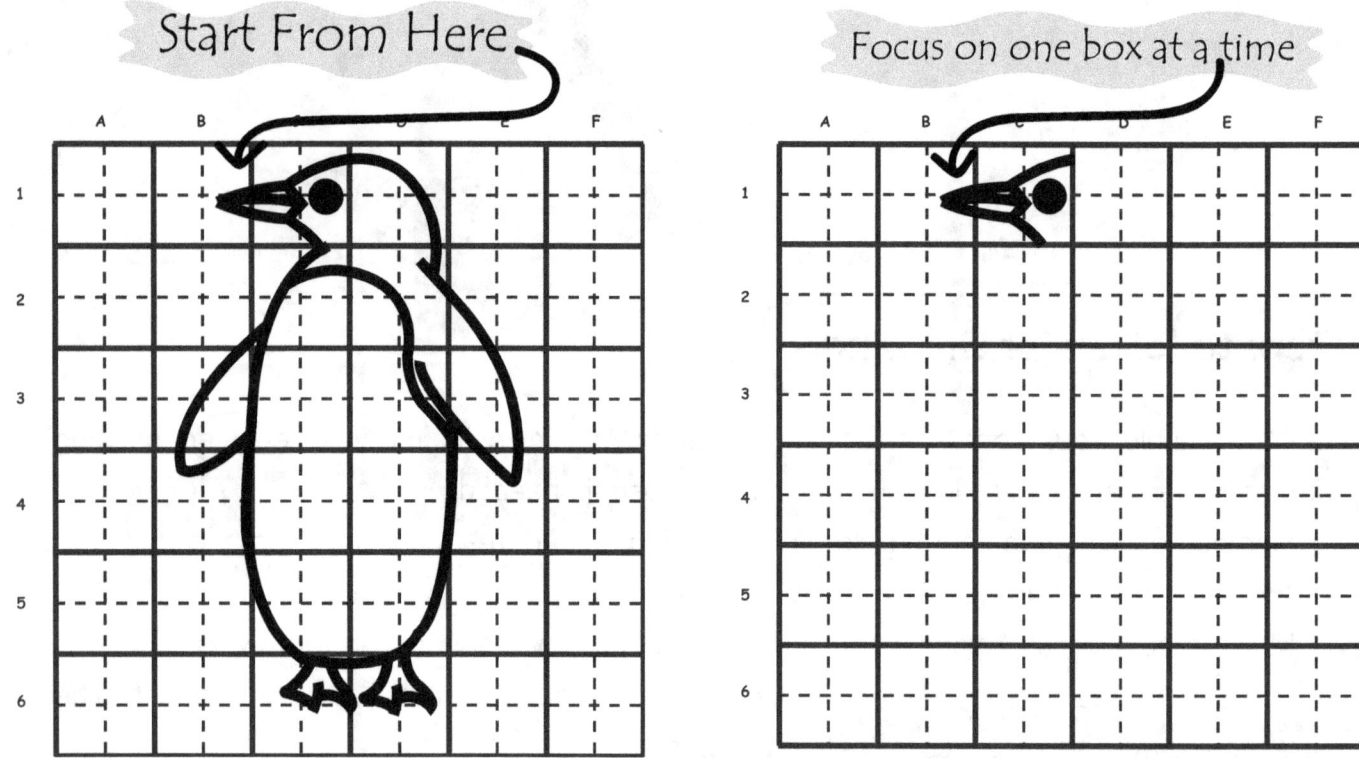

Penguin Art With Grid For Easy Way To Art

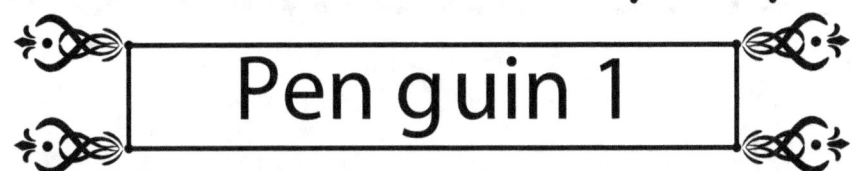

Pen guin 1

1 Draw the shape of the penguin

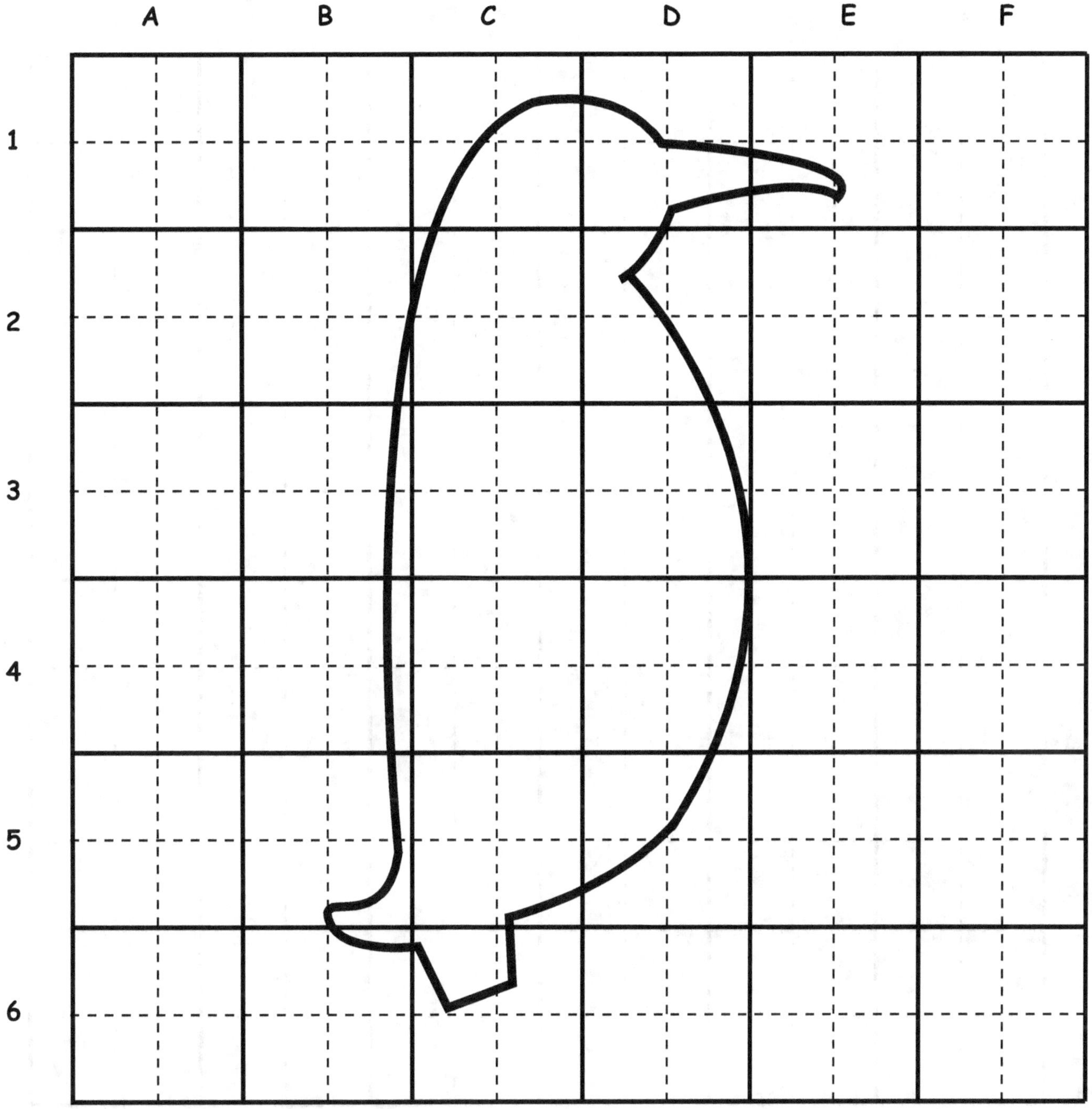

A B C D E F

1 2 3 4 5 6

Practice Here With Gride

Draw the shape of the penguin

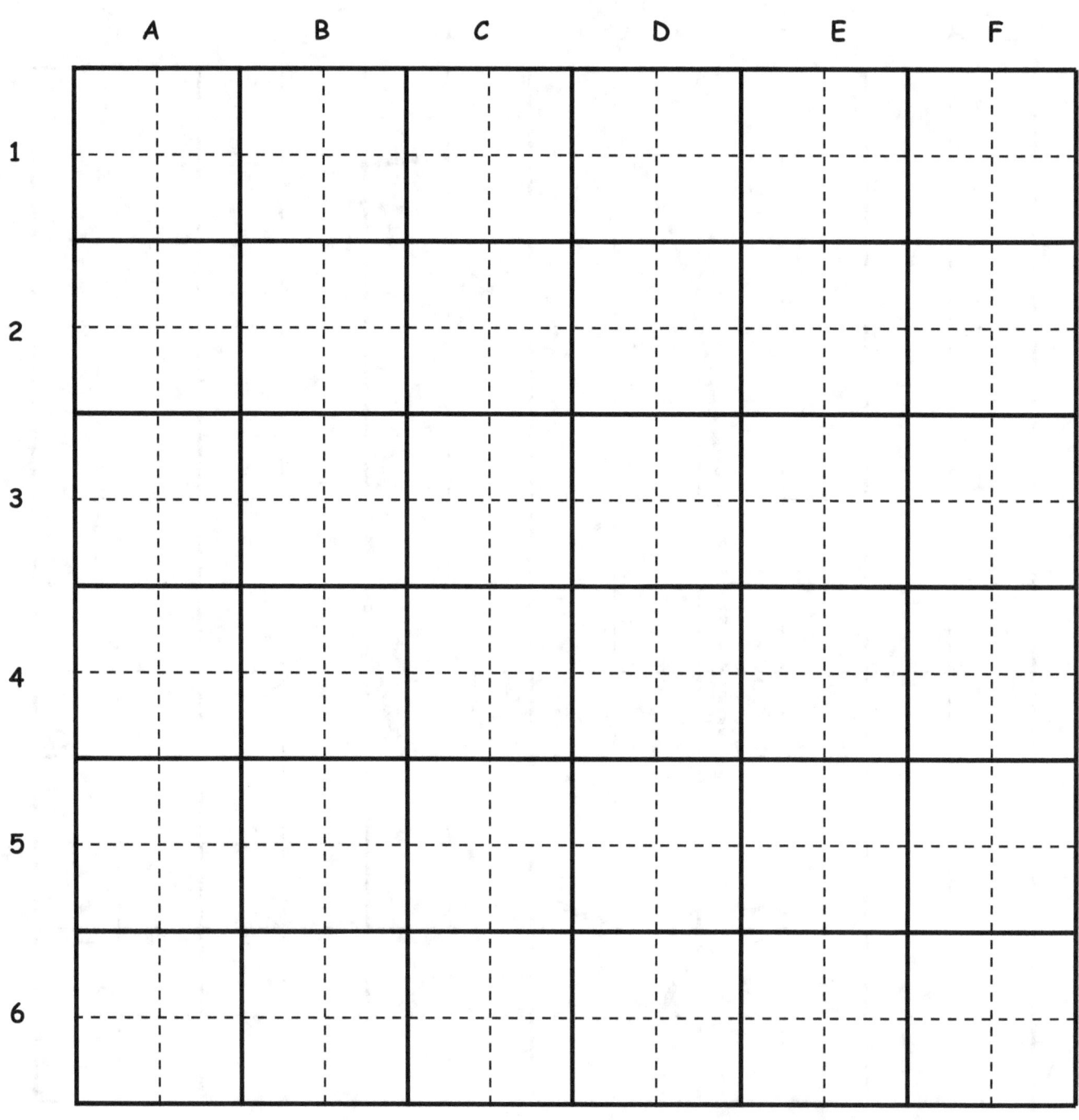

Penguin Art With Grid For Easy Way To Art

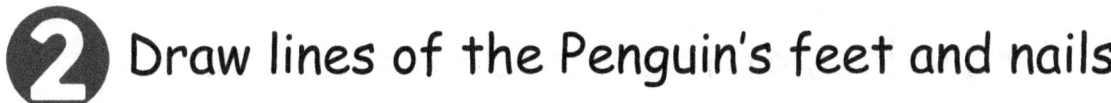 Draw lines of the Penguin's feet and nails

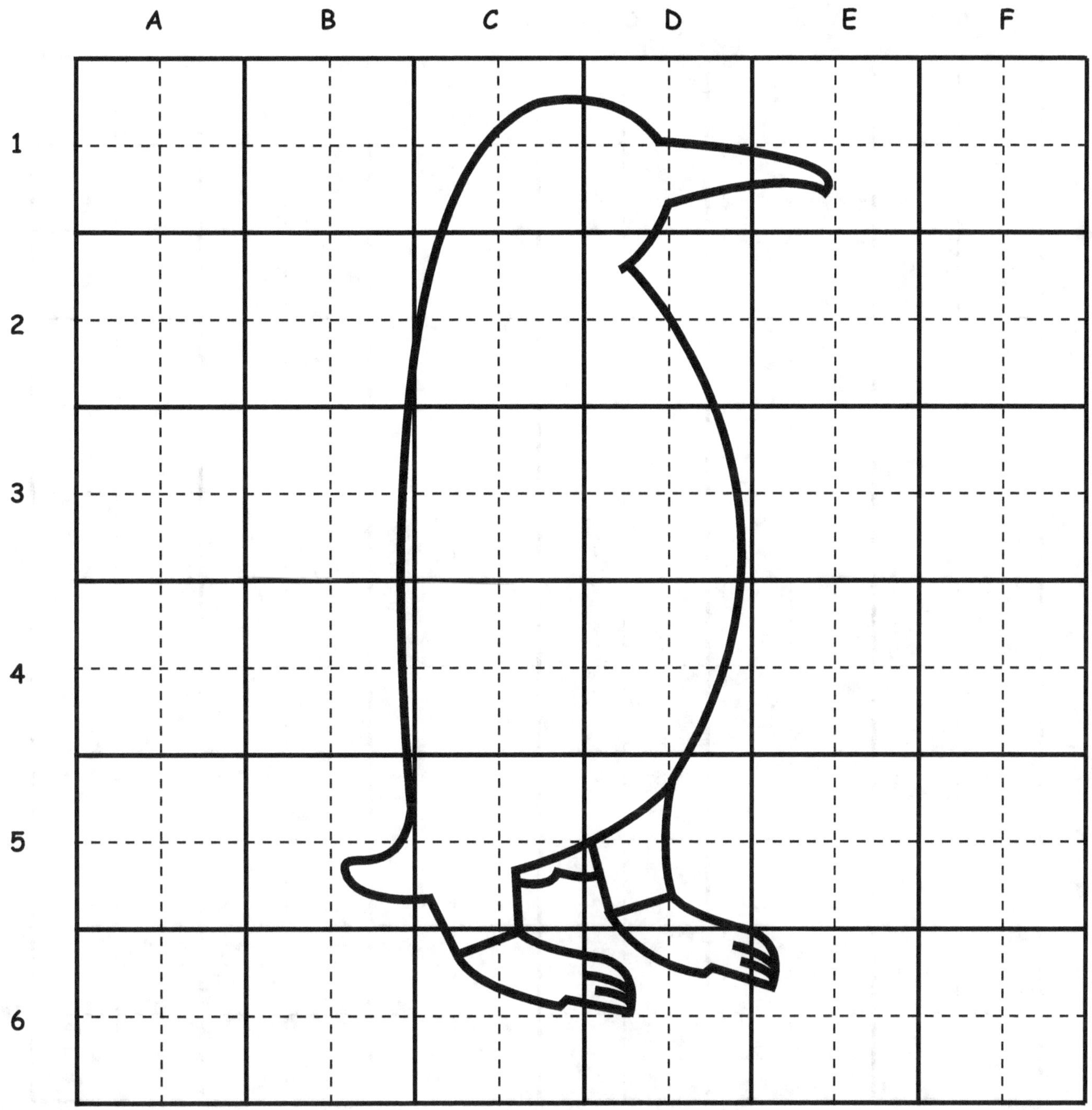

	A	B	C	D	E	F
1						
2						
3						
4						
5						
6						

Practice Here With Gride

Draw lines of the Penguin's feet and nails

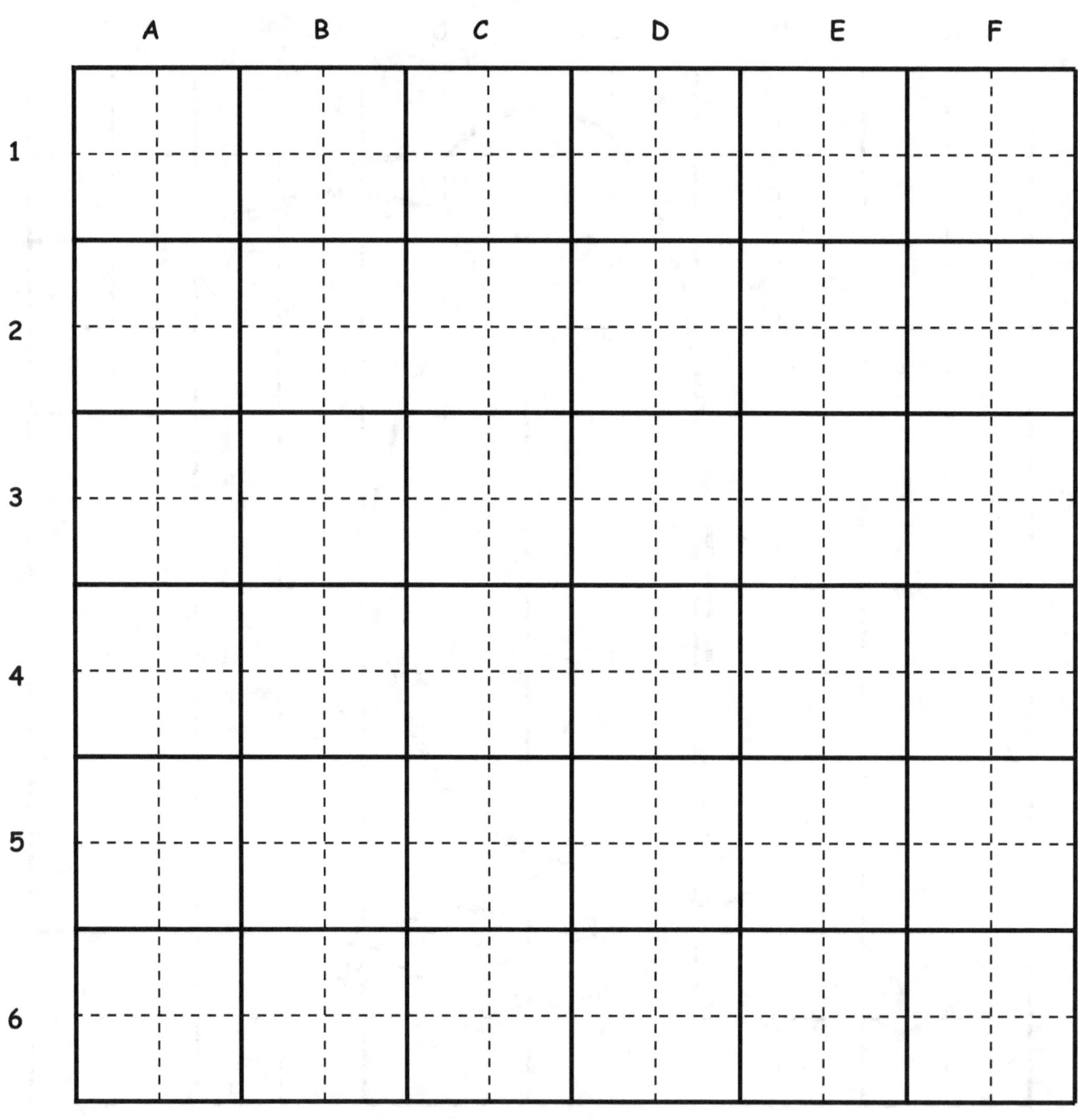

Penguin Art With Grid For Easy Way To Art

3 Draw shape of the Penguin's Ear

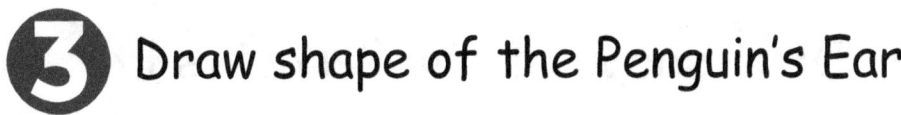

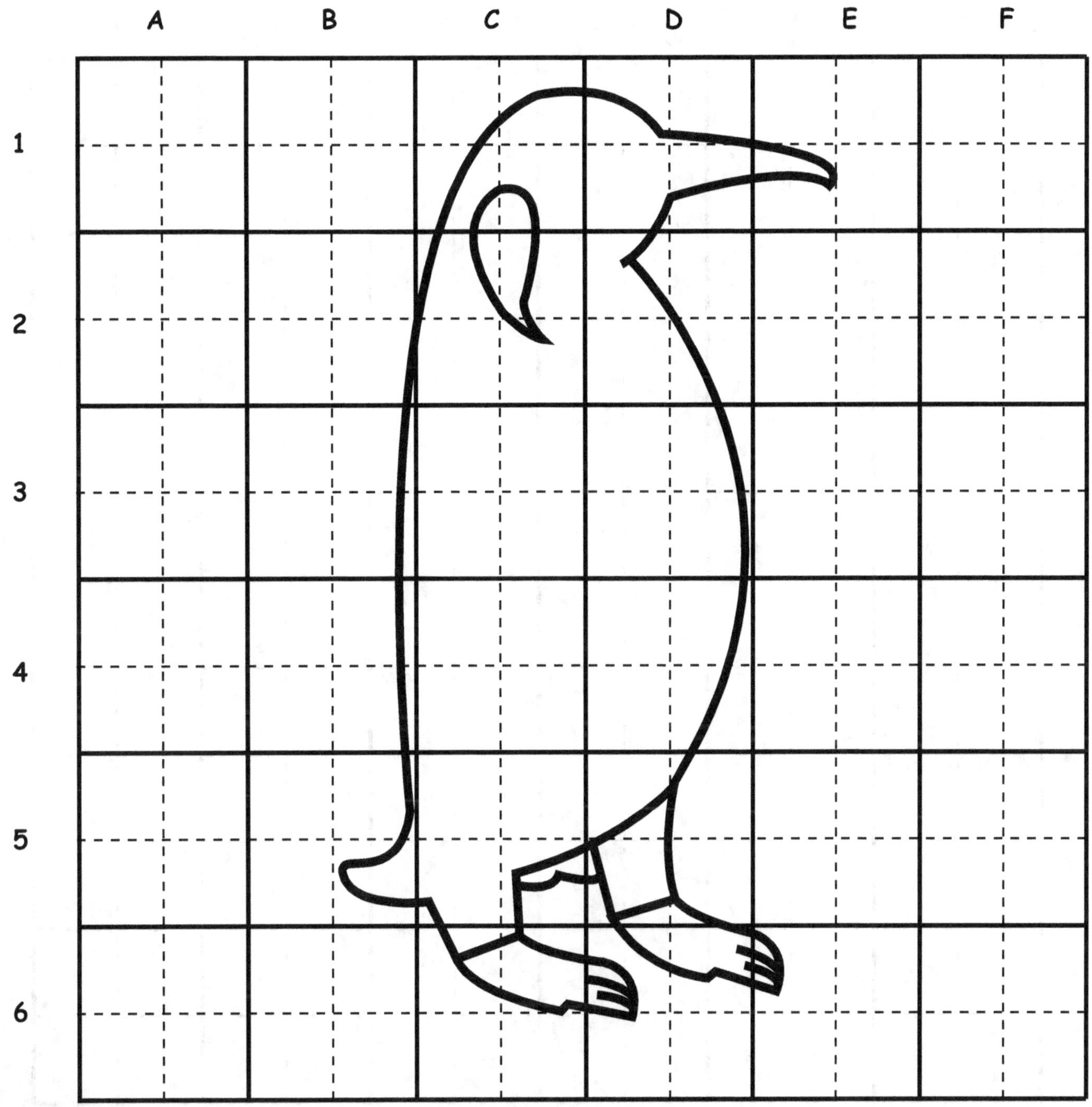

Practice Here With Gride

Draw shape of the Penguin's Ear

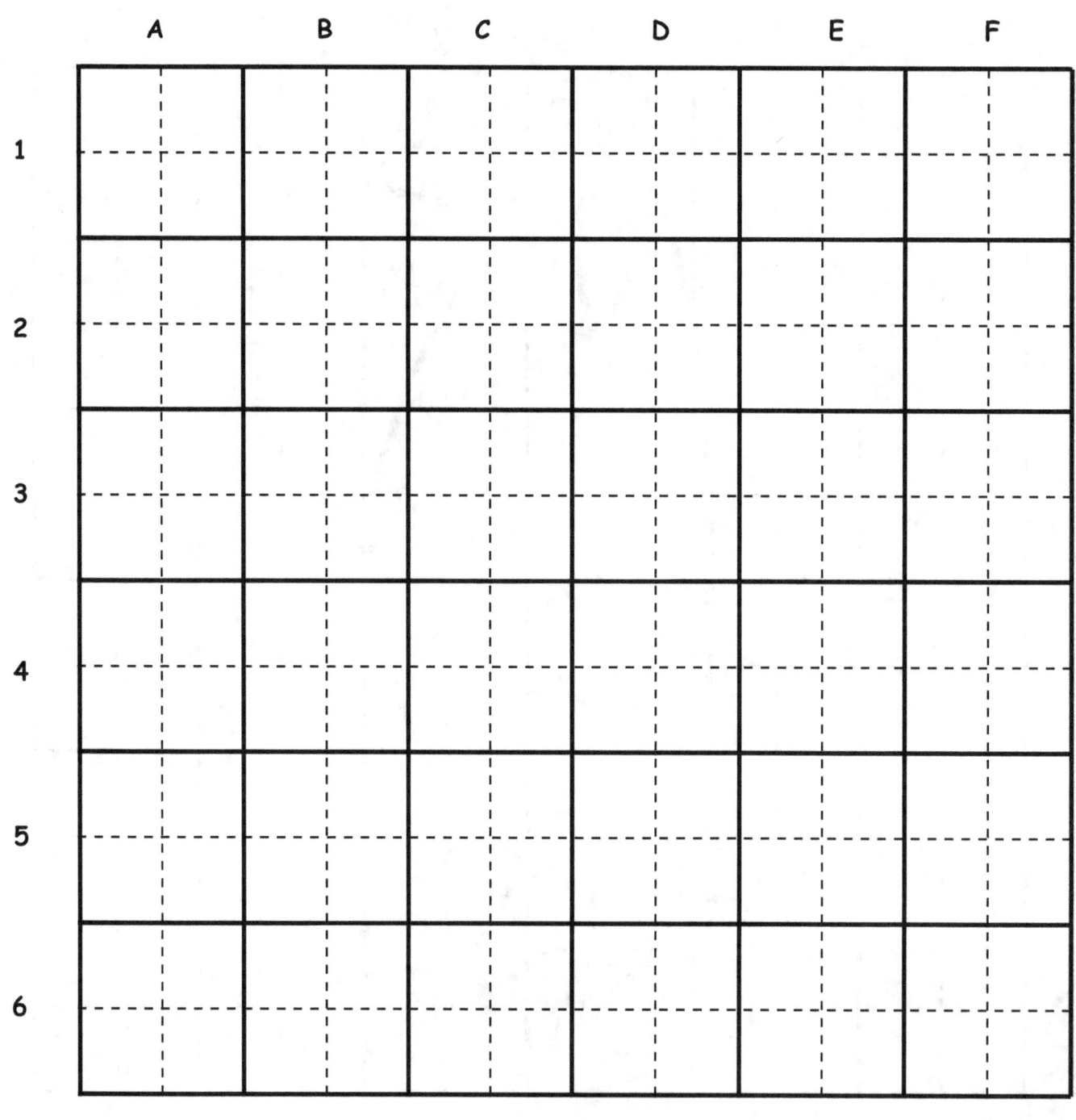

Penguin Art With Grid For Easy Way To Art

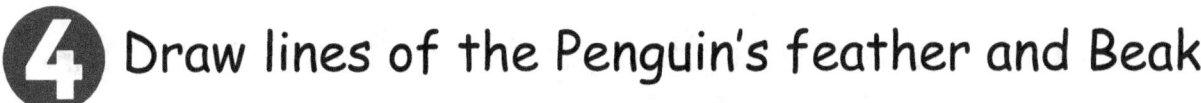

4 Draw lines of the Penguin's feather and Beak

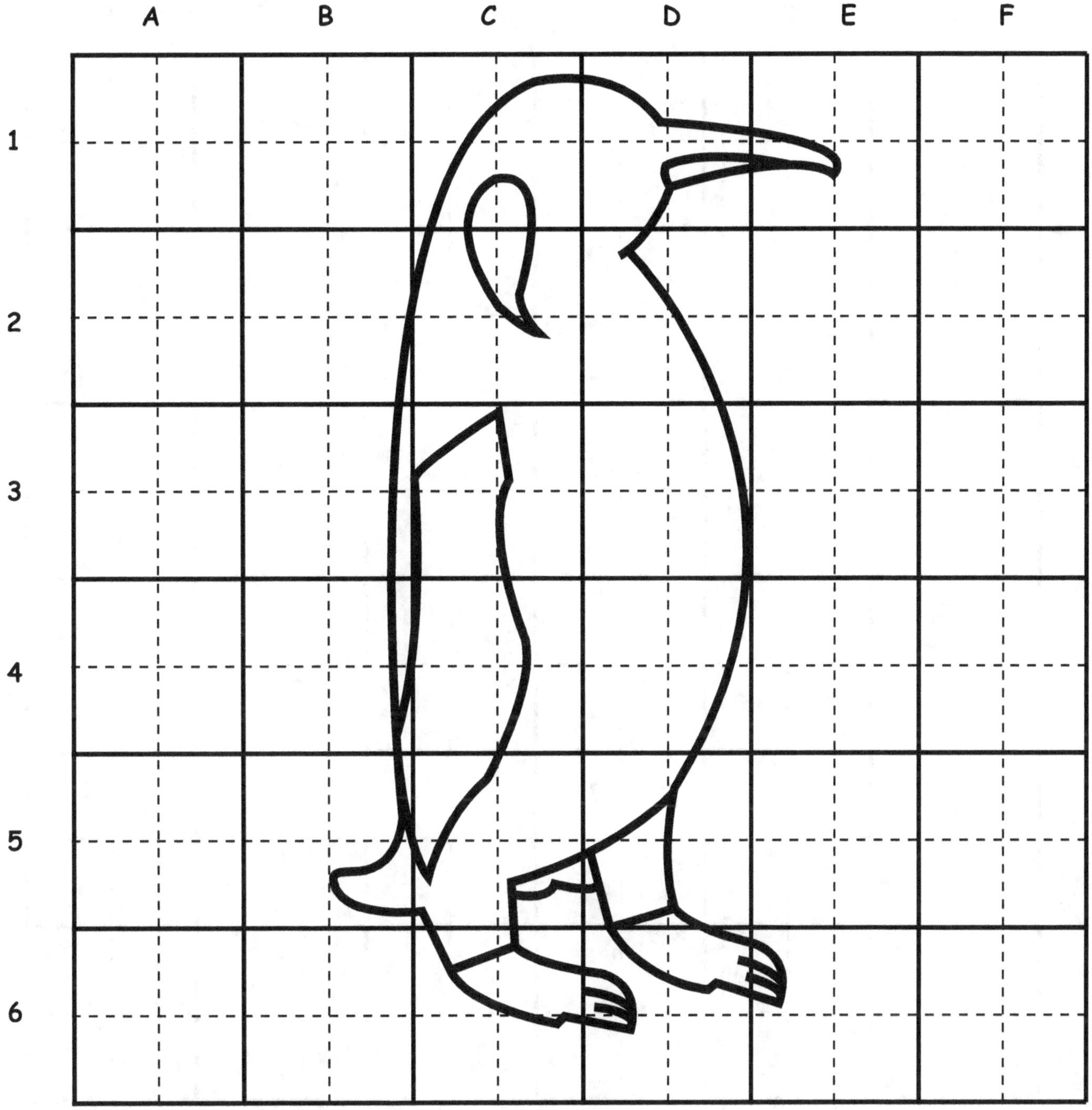

	A	B	C	D	E	F
1						
2						
3						
4						
5						
6						

Practice Here With Gride

Draw lines of the Penguin's feather and Beak

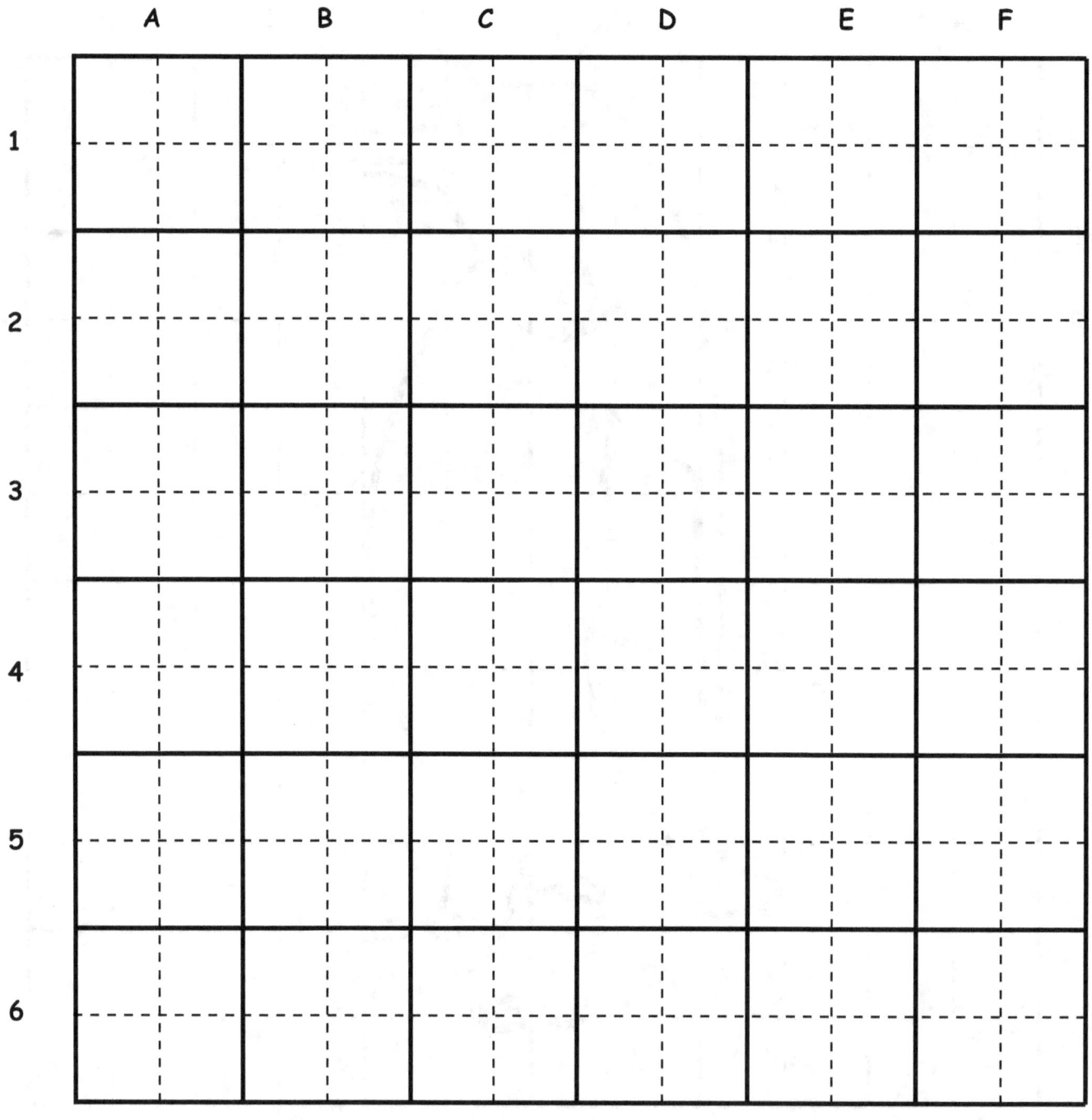

Penguen Art With Grid For Easy Way To Art

5 Draw lines of the Penguin's eye and body shape

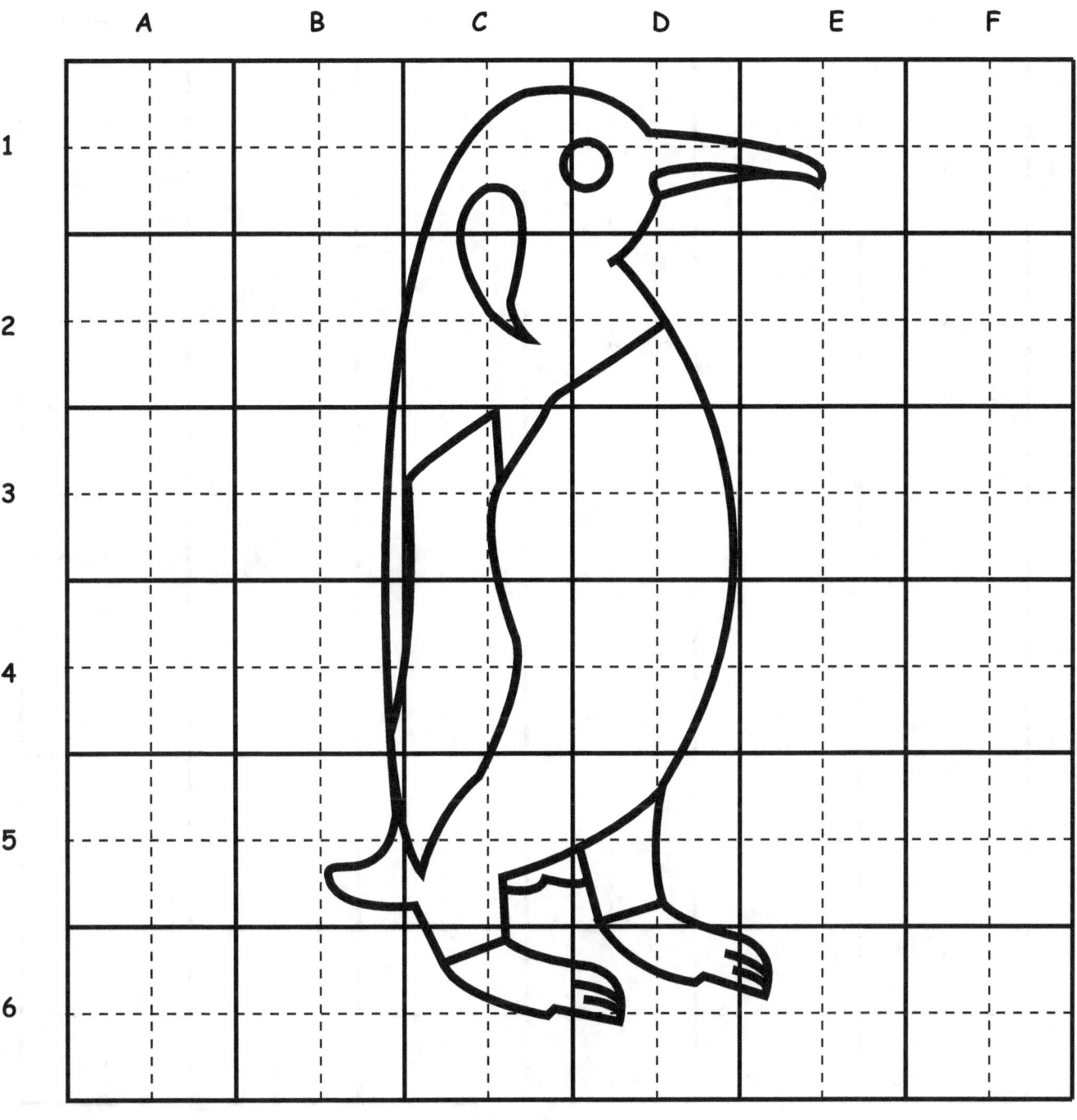

Practice Here With Gride

Draw lines of the Penguin's eye and body shape

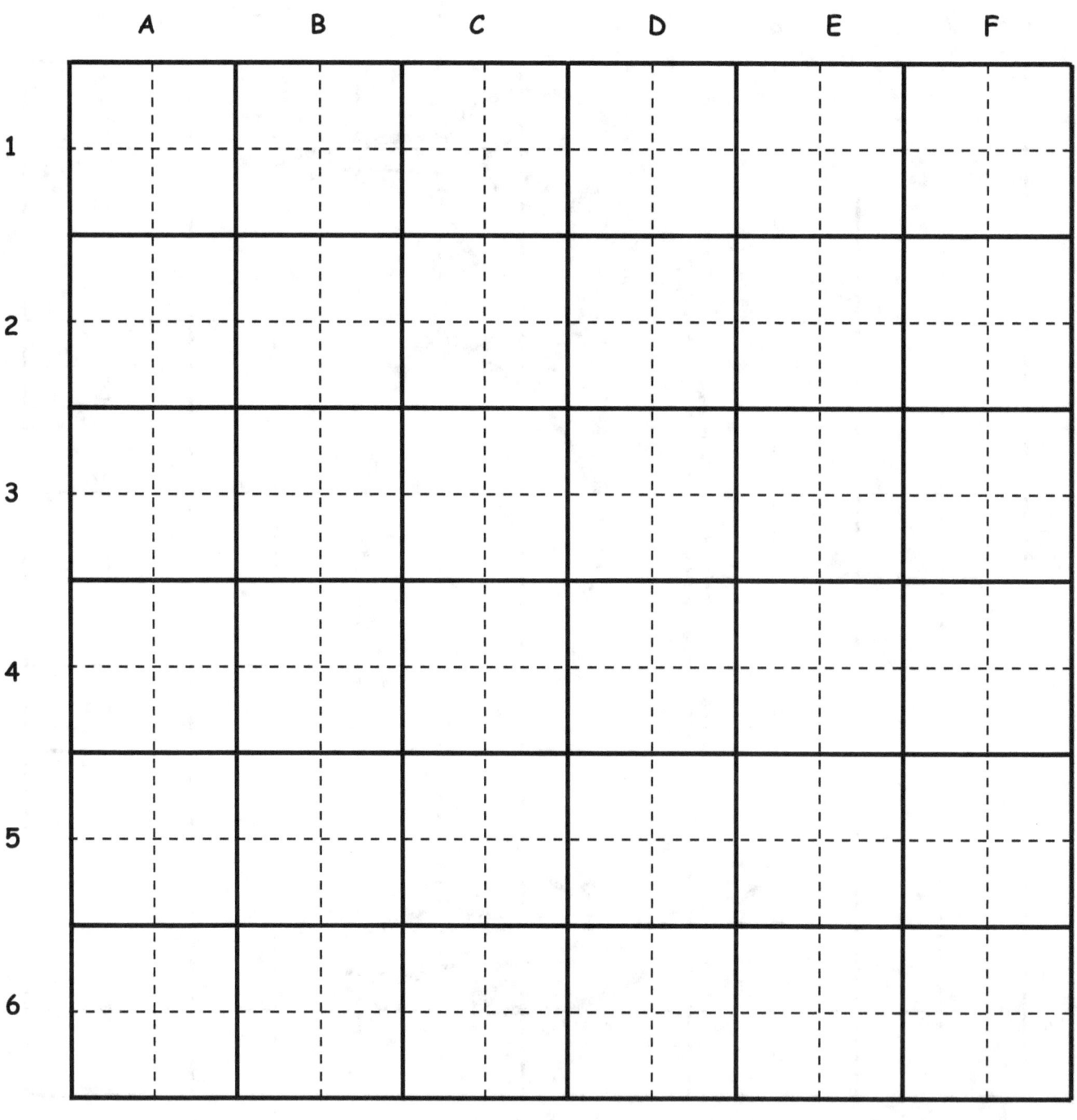

Your Penguin is Done!

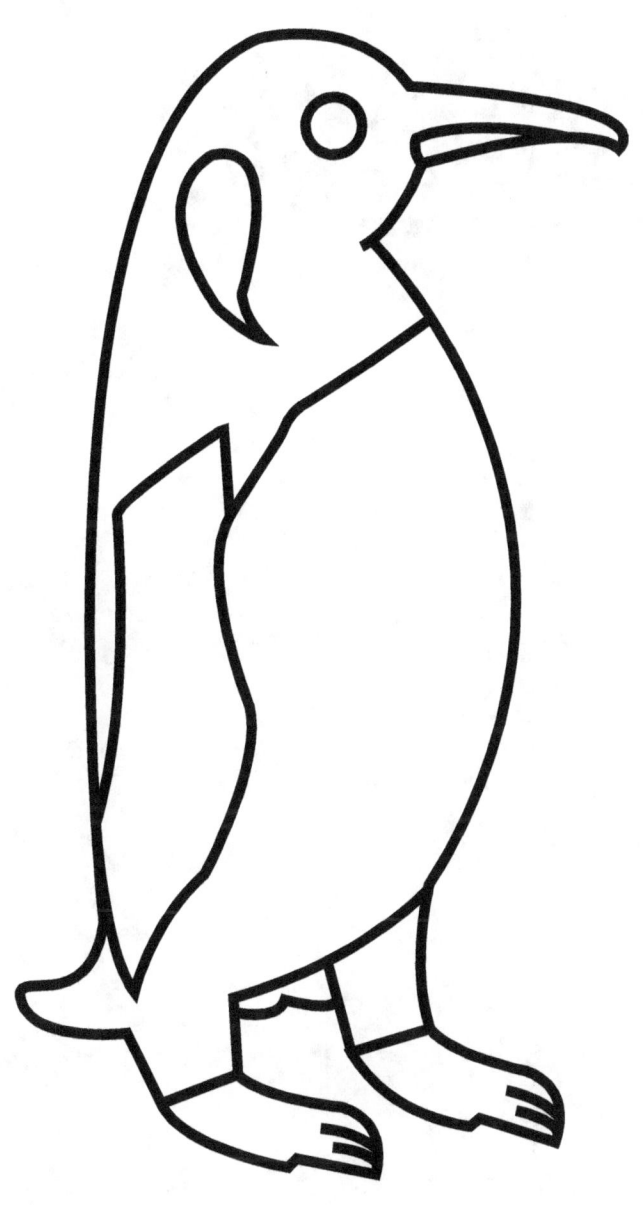

Practice Here Blind

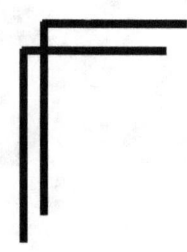

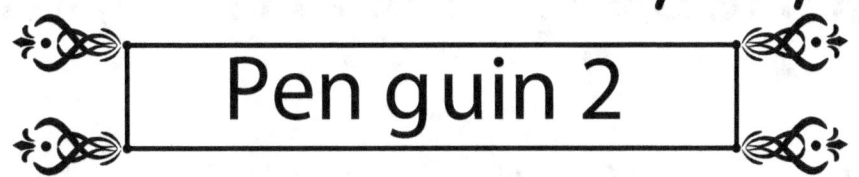

Pen guin 2

1 Draw two ovals for the body shape and head of penguin as shown

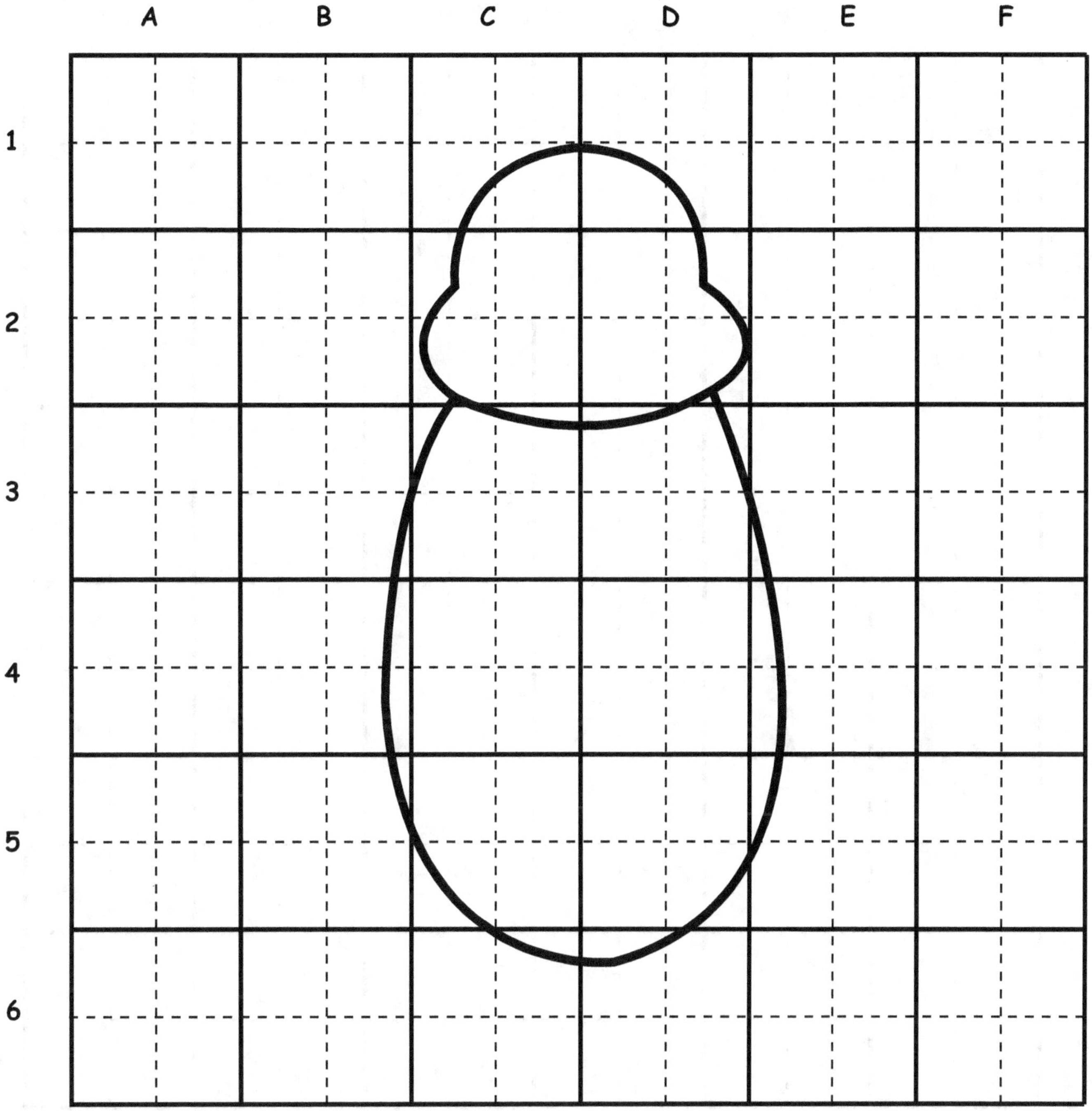

Practice Here With Gride

Draw two ovals for the body shape and head of penguin as shown

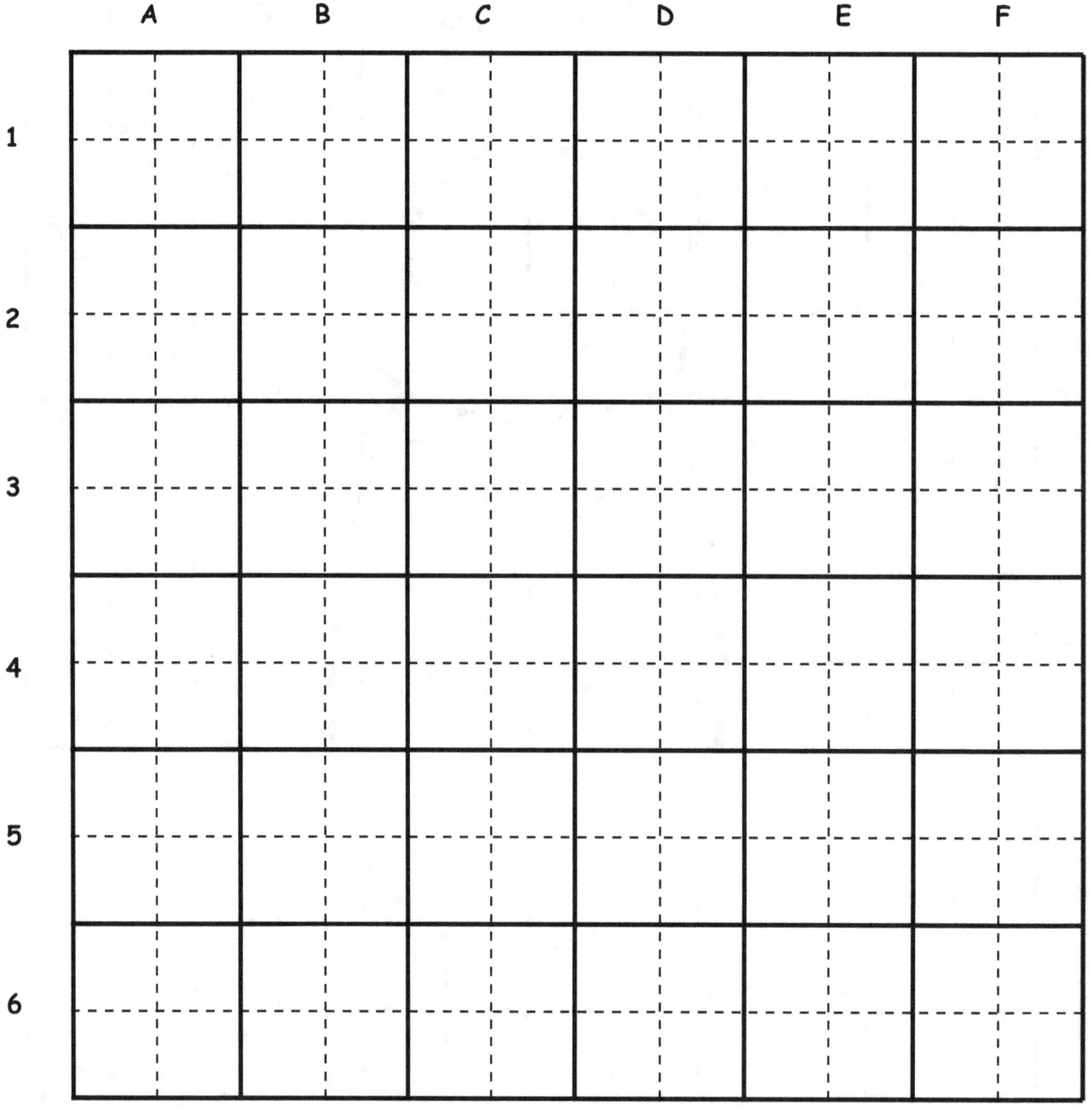

Penguin Art With Grid For Easy Way To Art

2 Draw lines of the Penguin's feather and feet

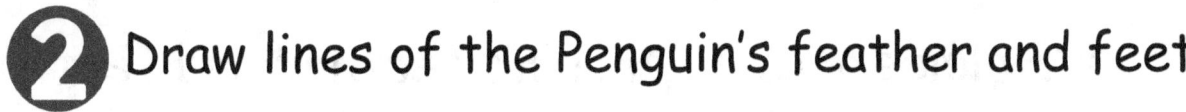

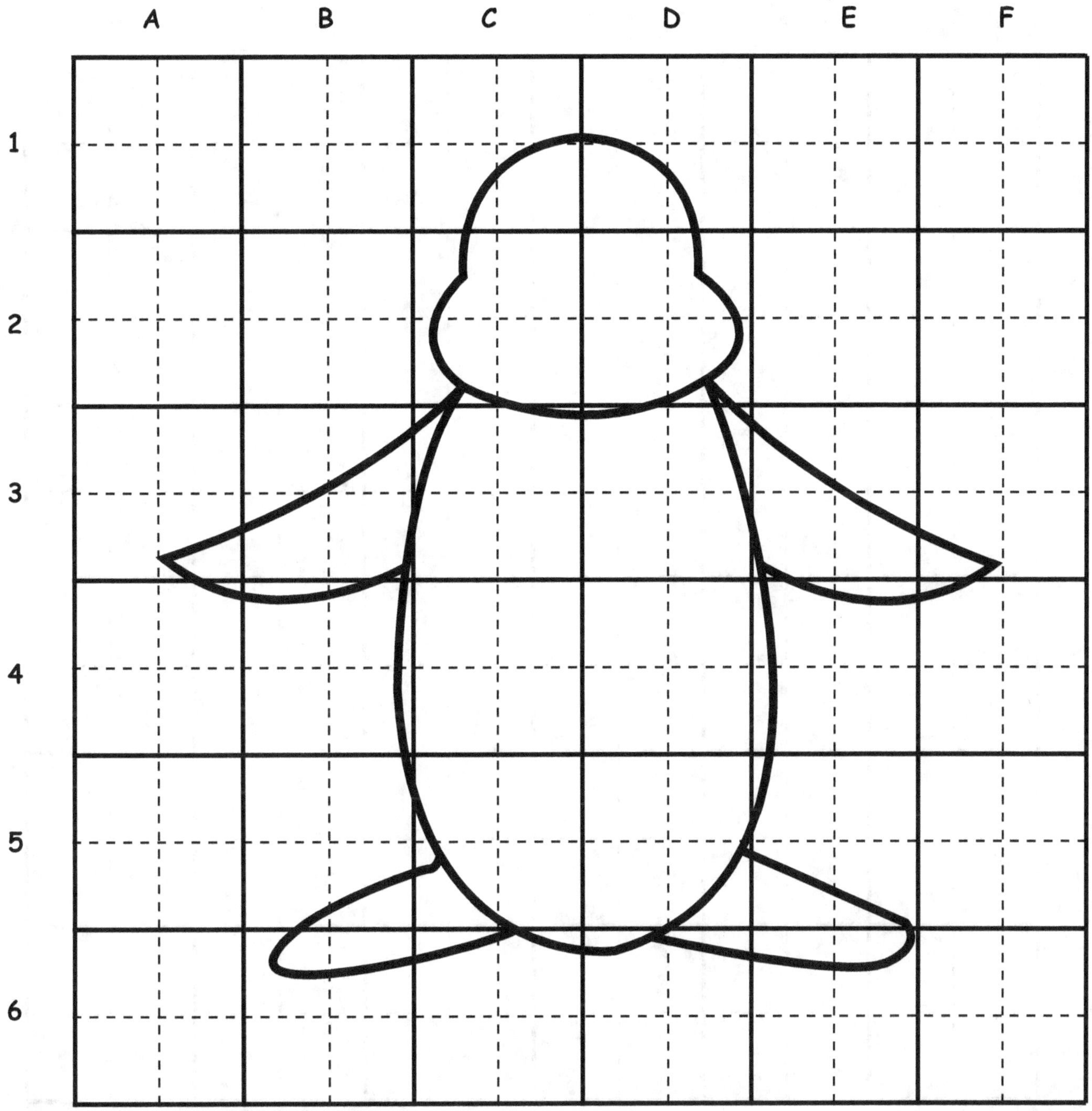

Practice Here With Gride

Draw lines of the Penguin's feather and feet

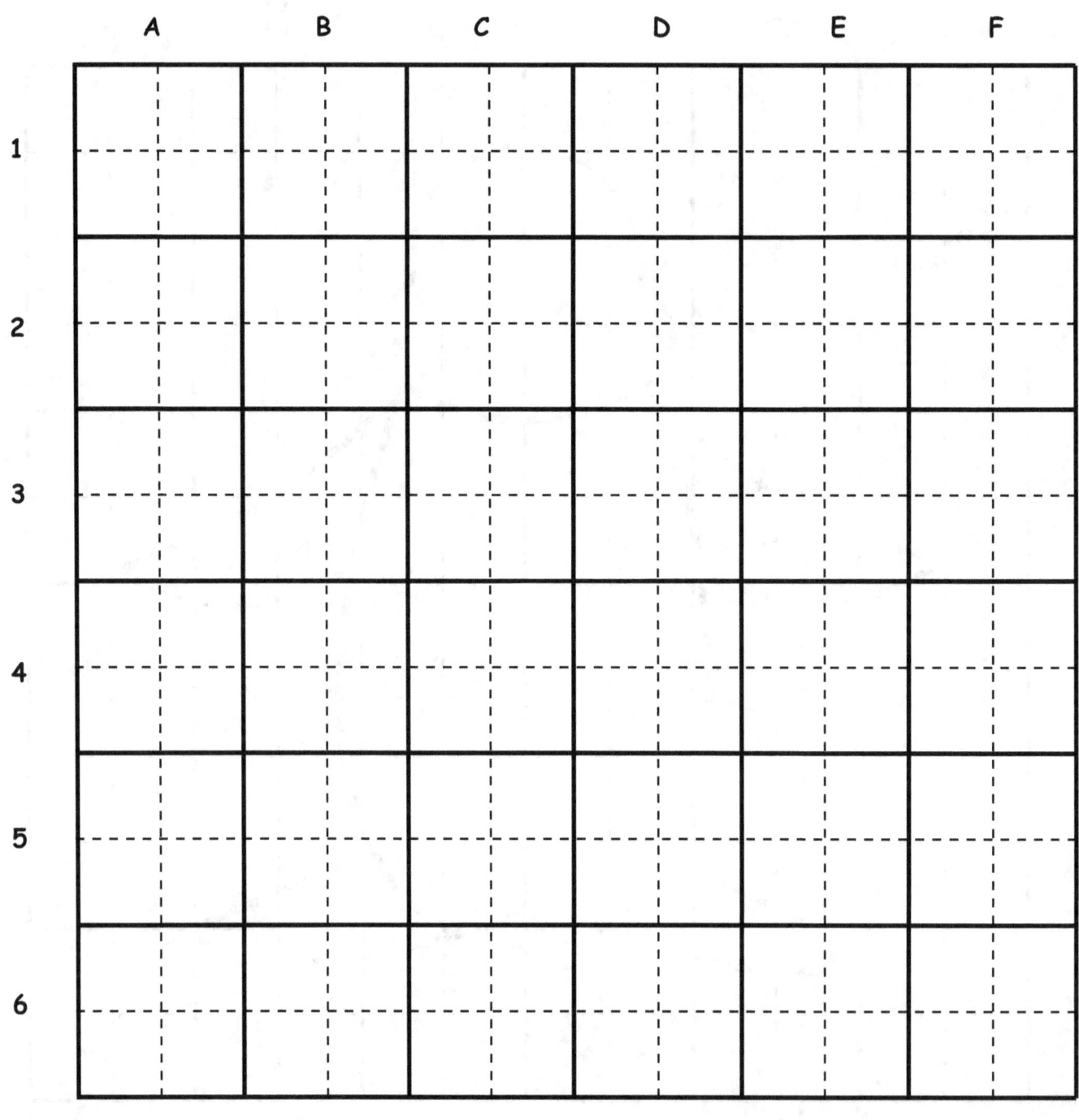

Penguin Art With Grid For Easy Way To Art

3 Draw the eyes as shown

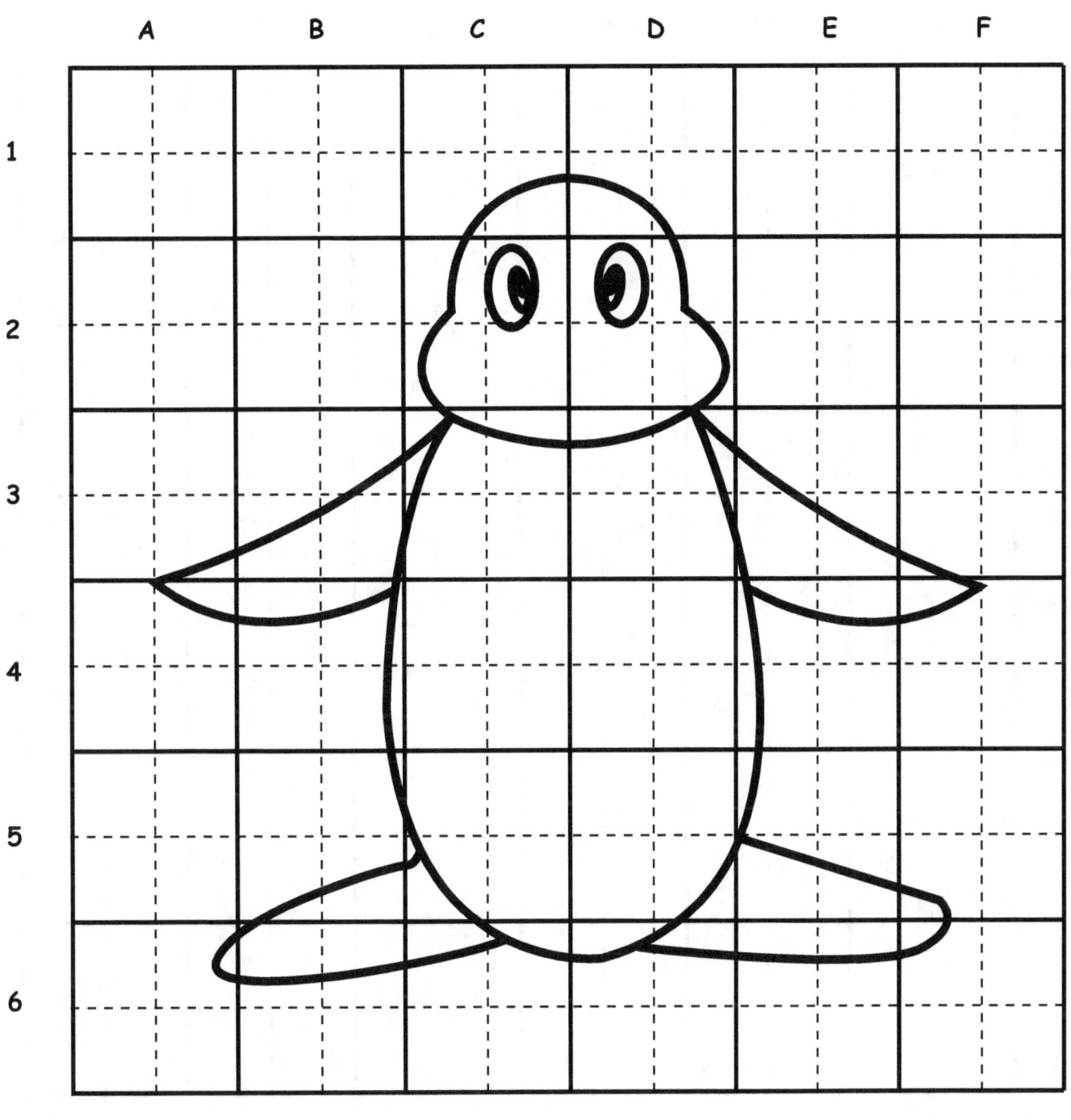

Practice Here With Gride

Draw the eyes as shown

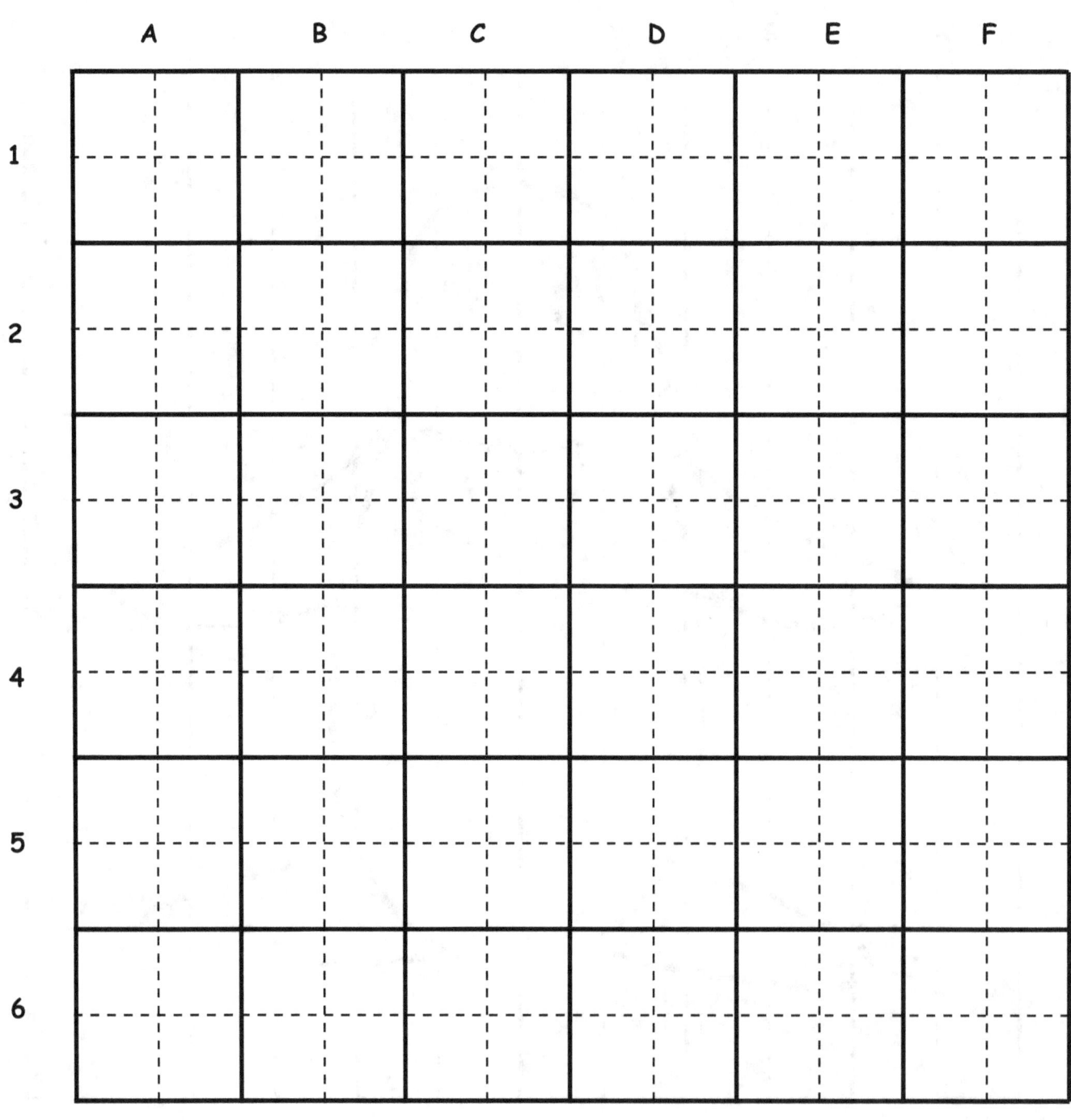

Penguin Art With Grid For Easy Way To Art

4 Draw the lines of the nose and other details

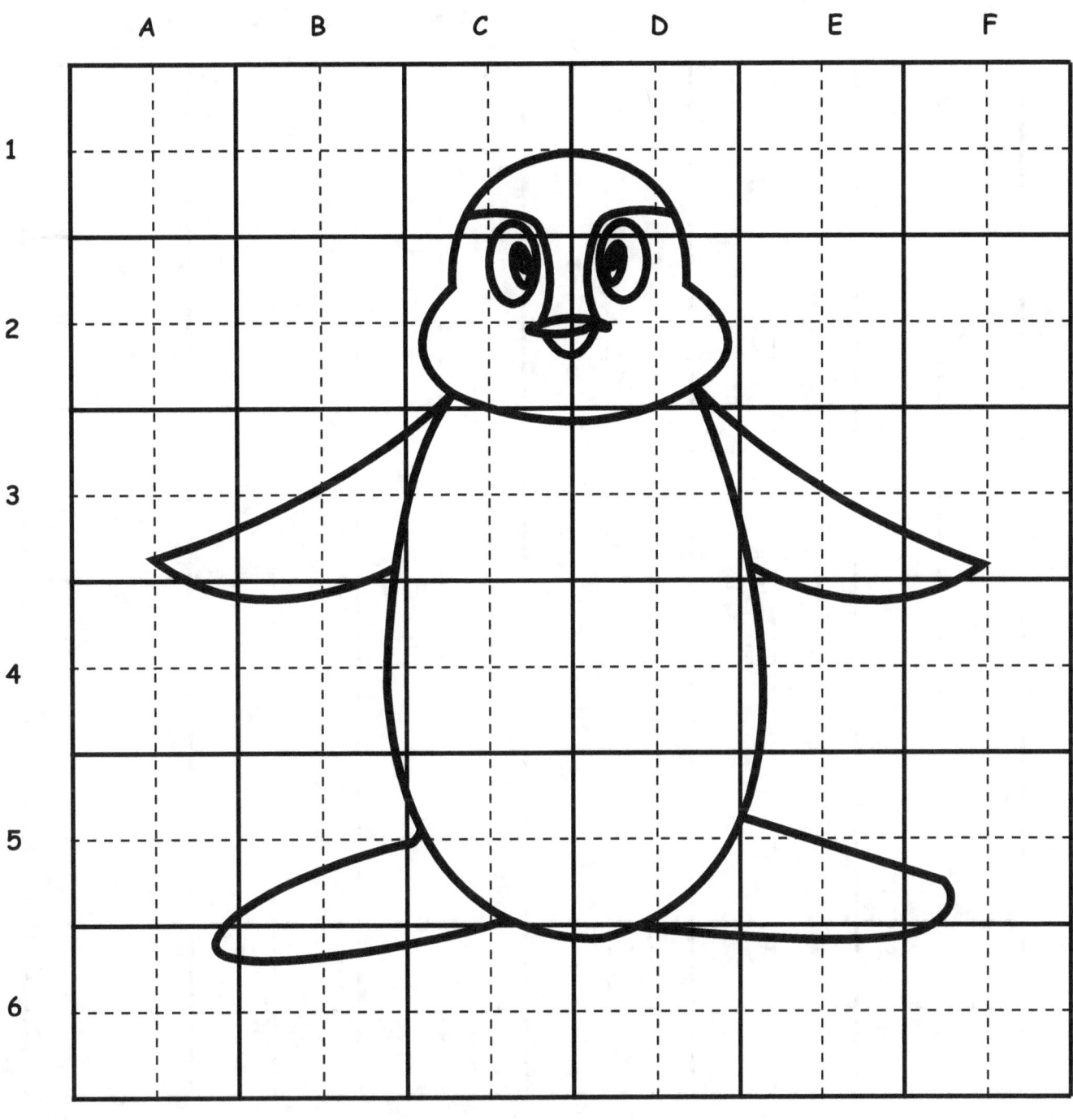

Practice Here With Gride

Draw the lines of the nose and other details

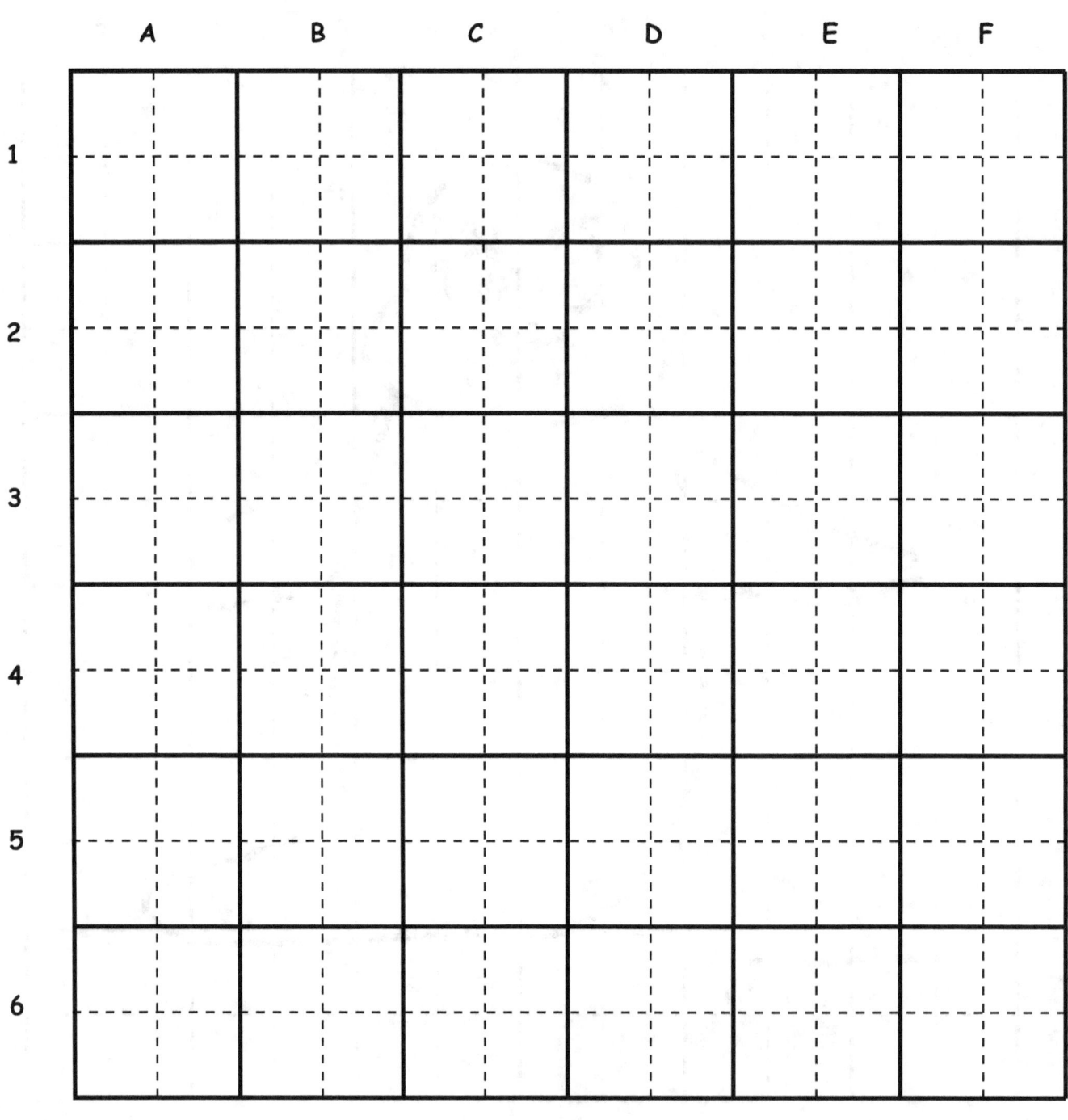

Penguin Art With Grid For Easy Way To Art

5 Draw the inner body shape lines as shown

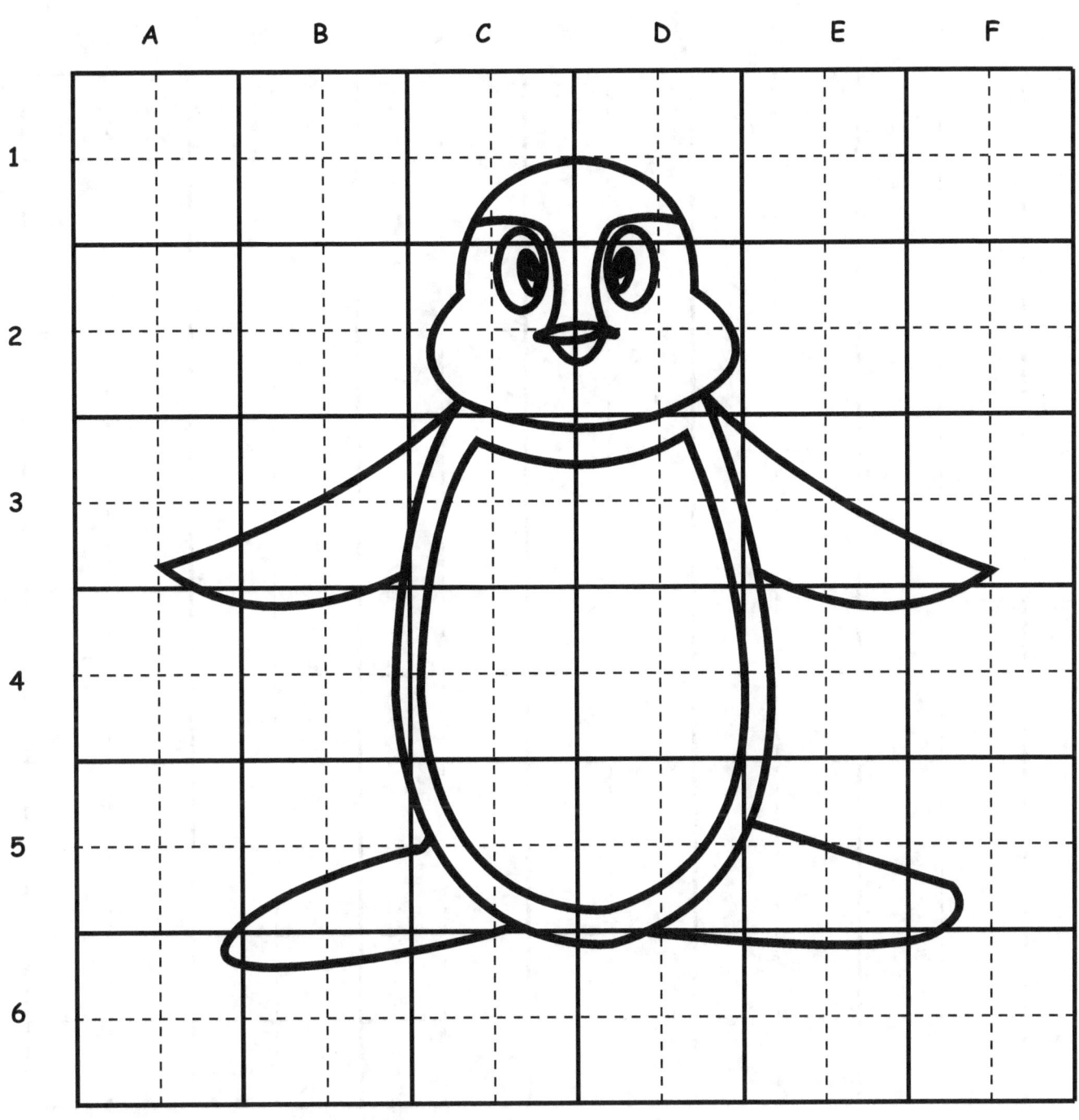

Practice Here With Gride

Draw the inner body shape lines as shown

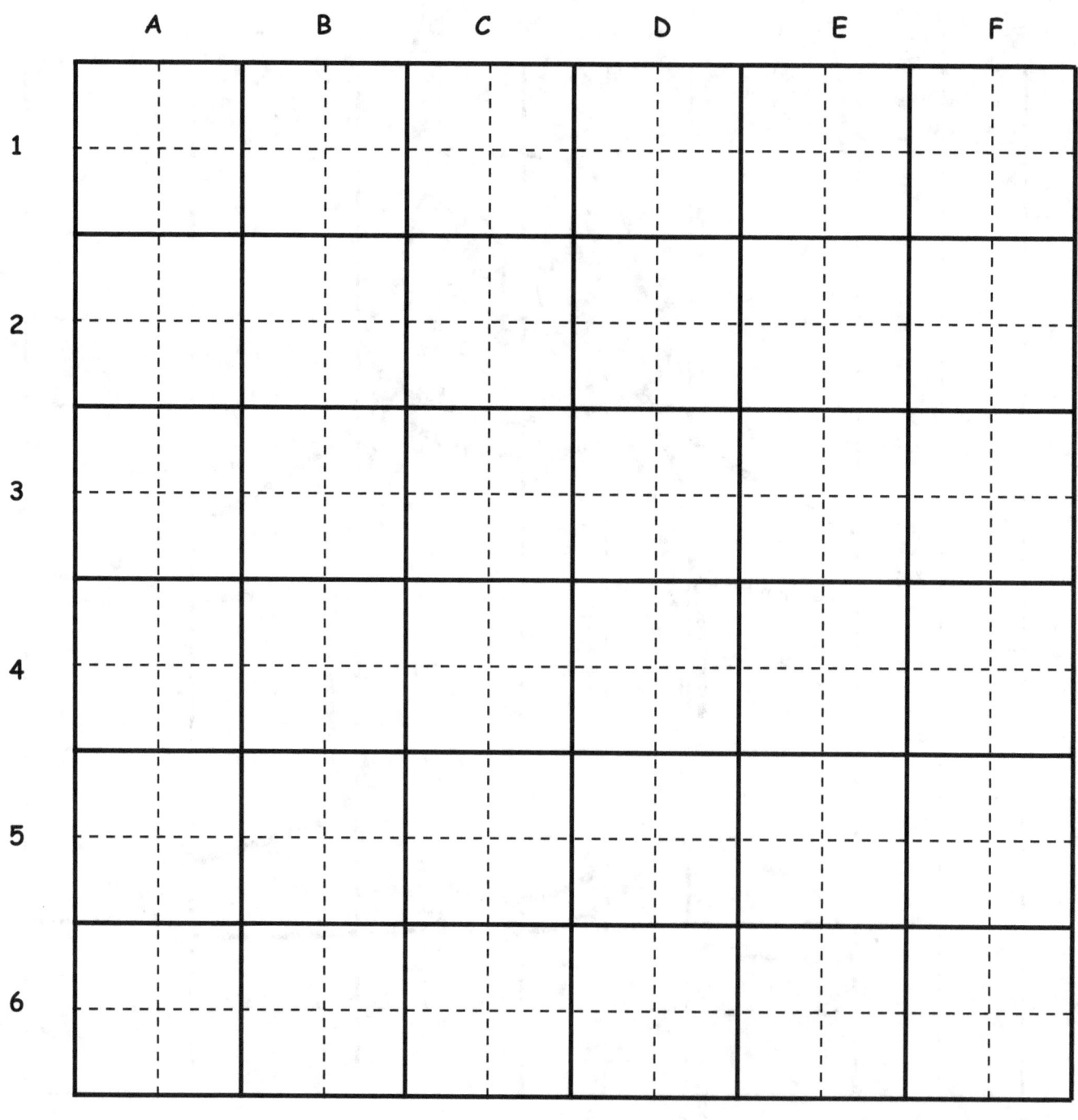

It's Finished! A penguin Done!

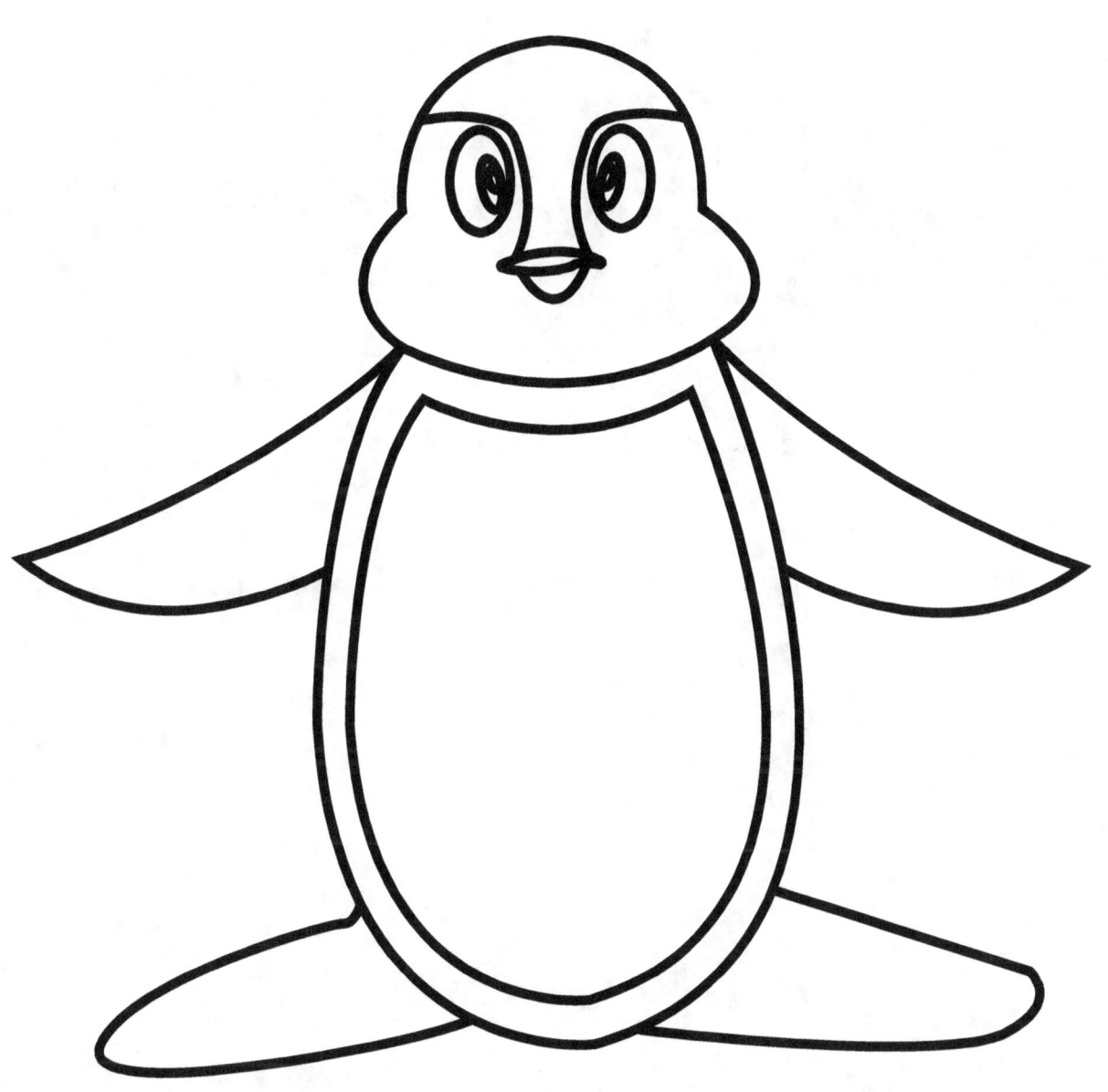

Practice Here Blind

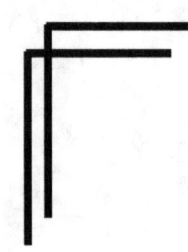

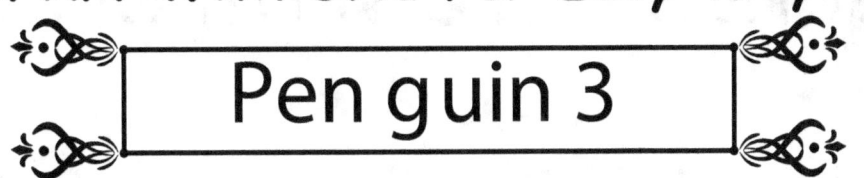

Penguin 3

1 Draw lines of the Penguin's body and feather

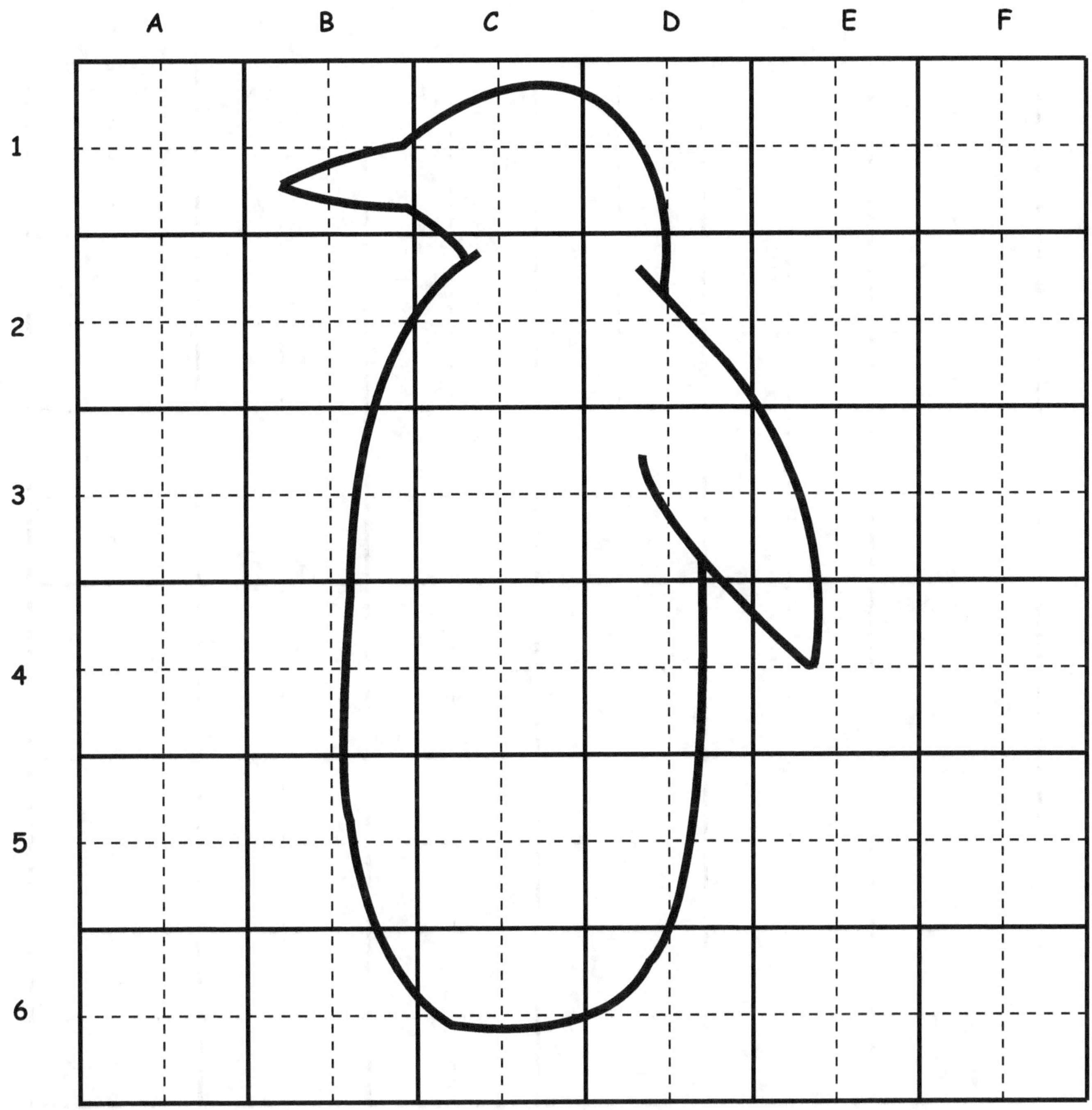

	A	B	C	D	E	F
1						
2						
3						
4						
5						
6						

Practice Here With Gride

Draw lines of the Penguin's body and feather

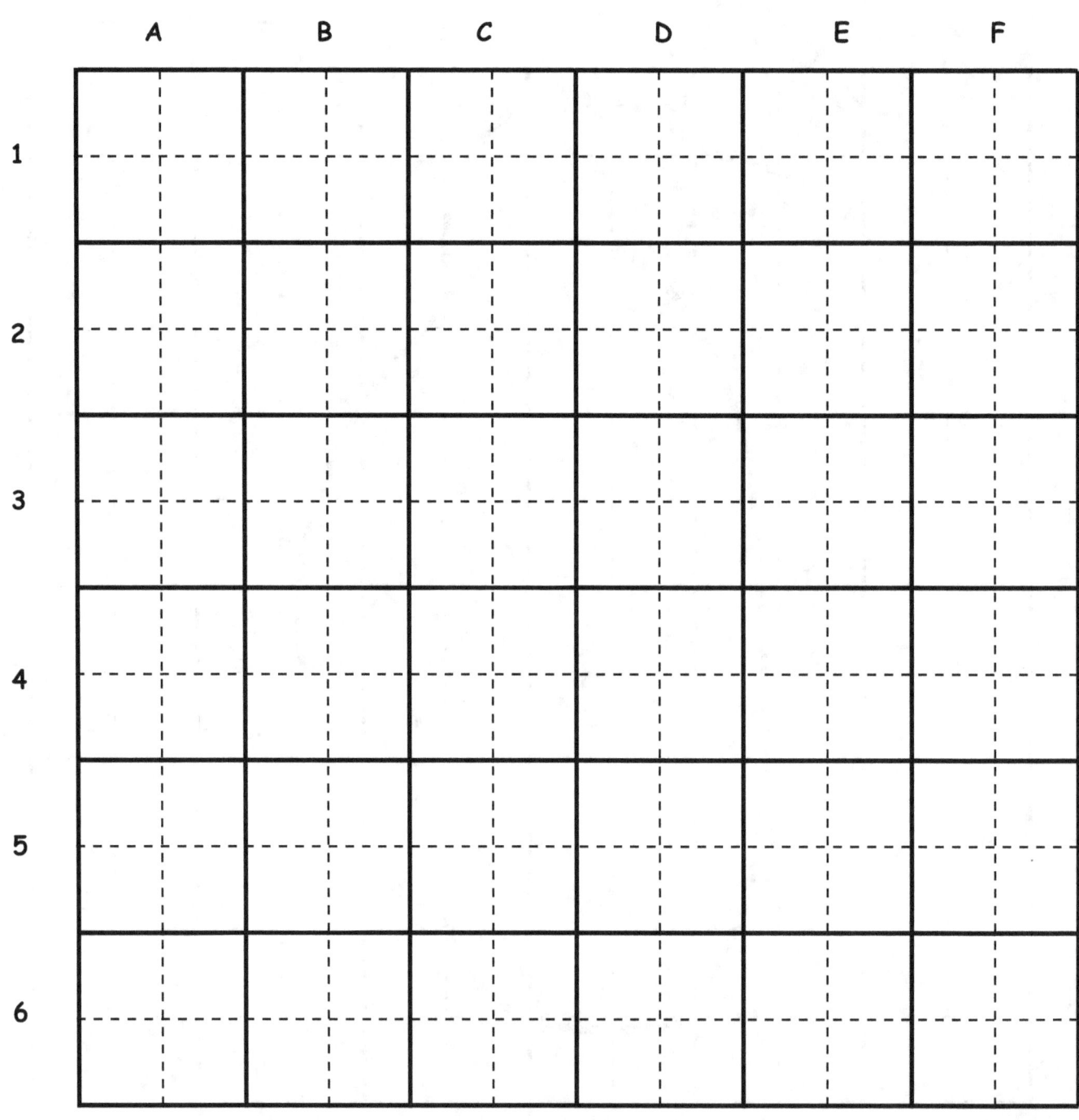

Penguin Art With Grid For Easy Way To Art

2 Draw a line through the Penguin's body as shown

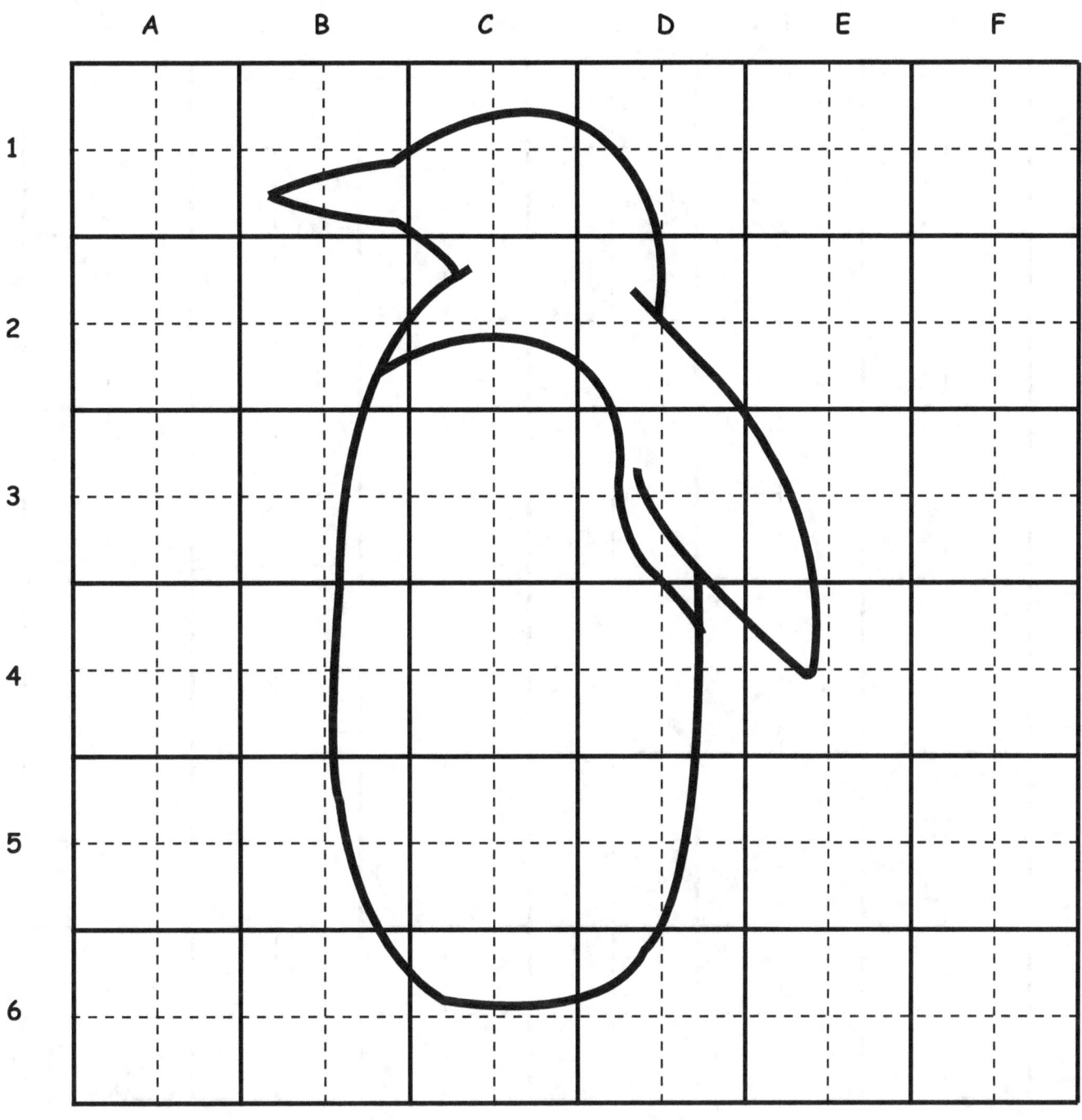

Practice Here With Gride

Draw a line through the Penguin's body as shown

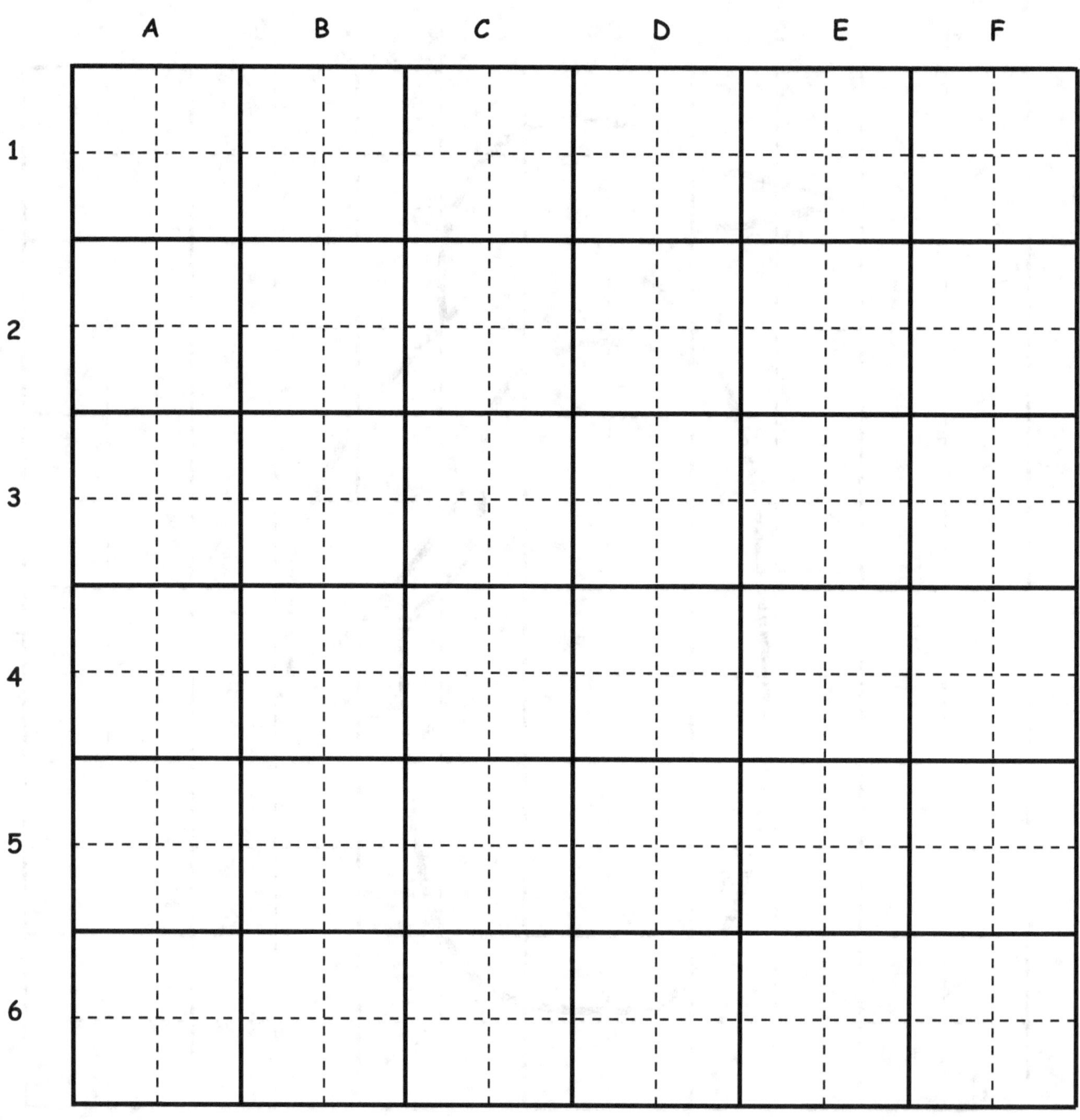

Penguin Art With Grid For Easy Way To Art

3 Add line for another penguin feather

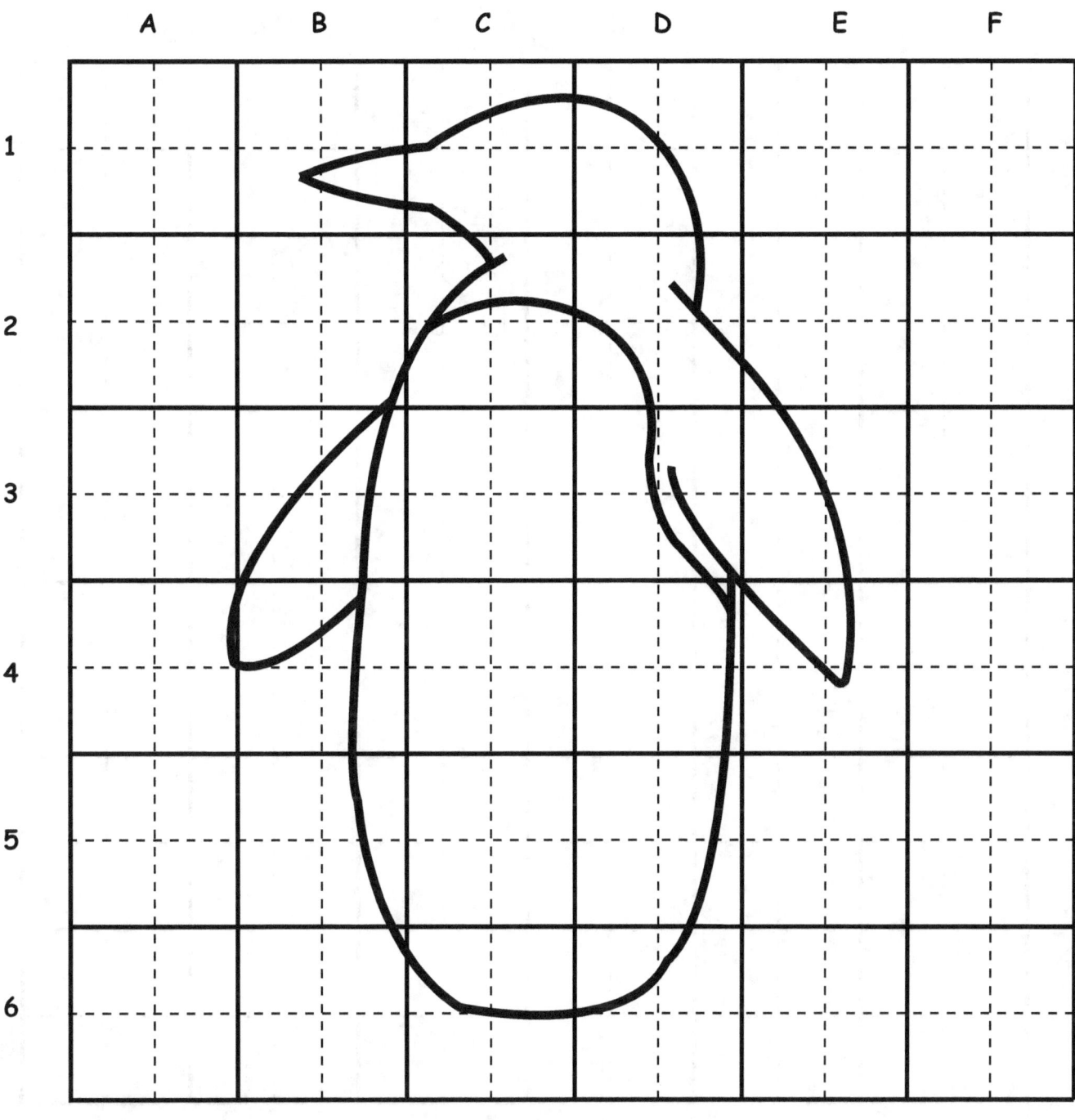

Practice Here With Gride

Add line for another penguin feather

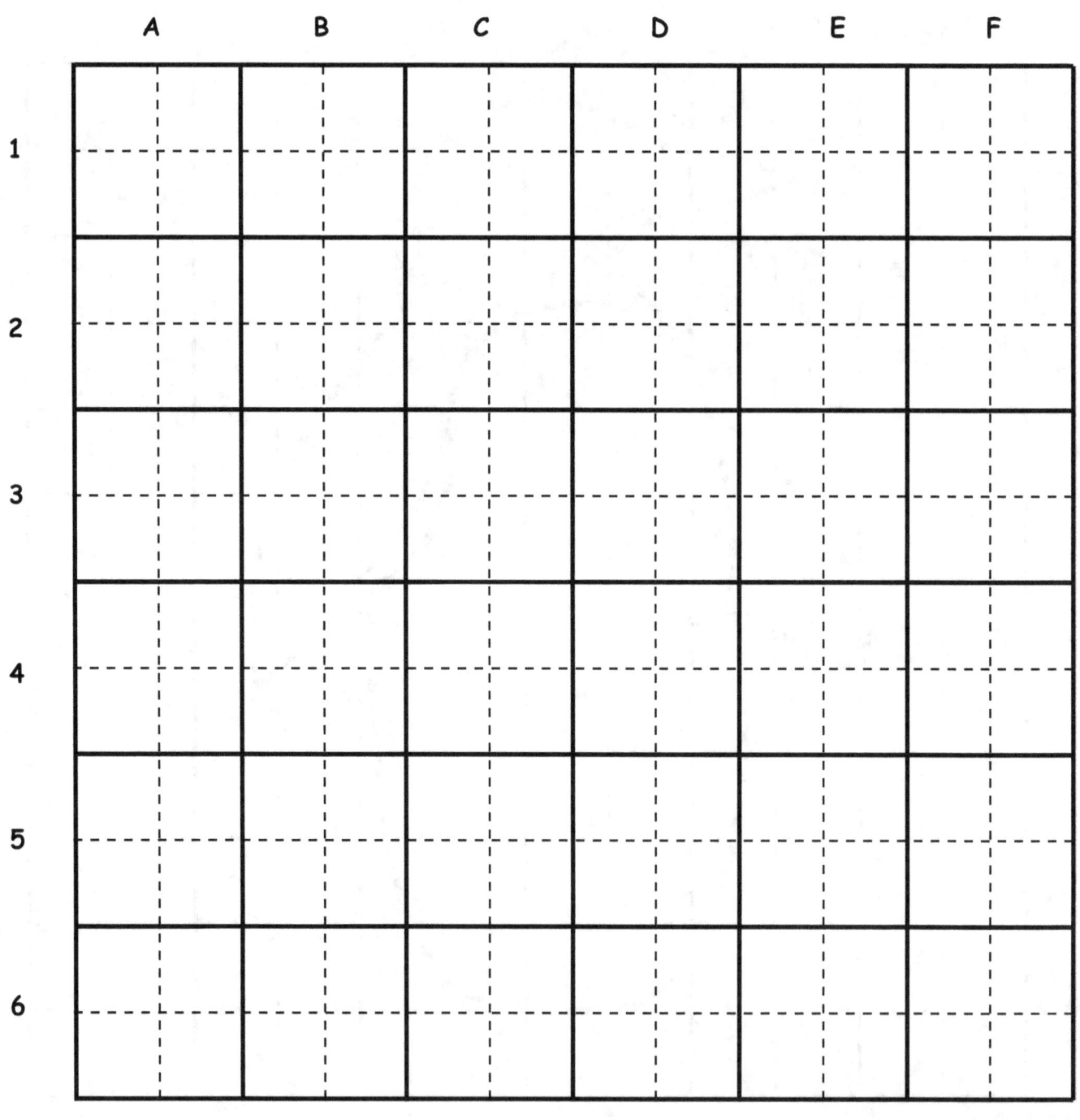

Penguin Art With Grid For Easy Way To Art

4 Draw lines of the Penguin's feet

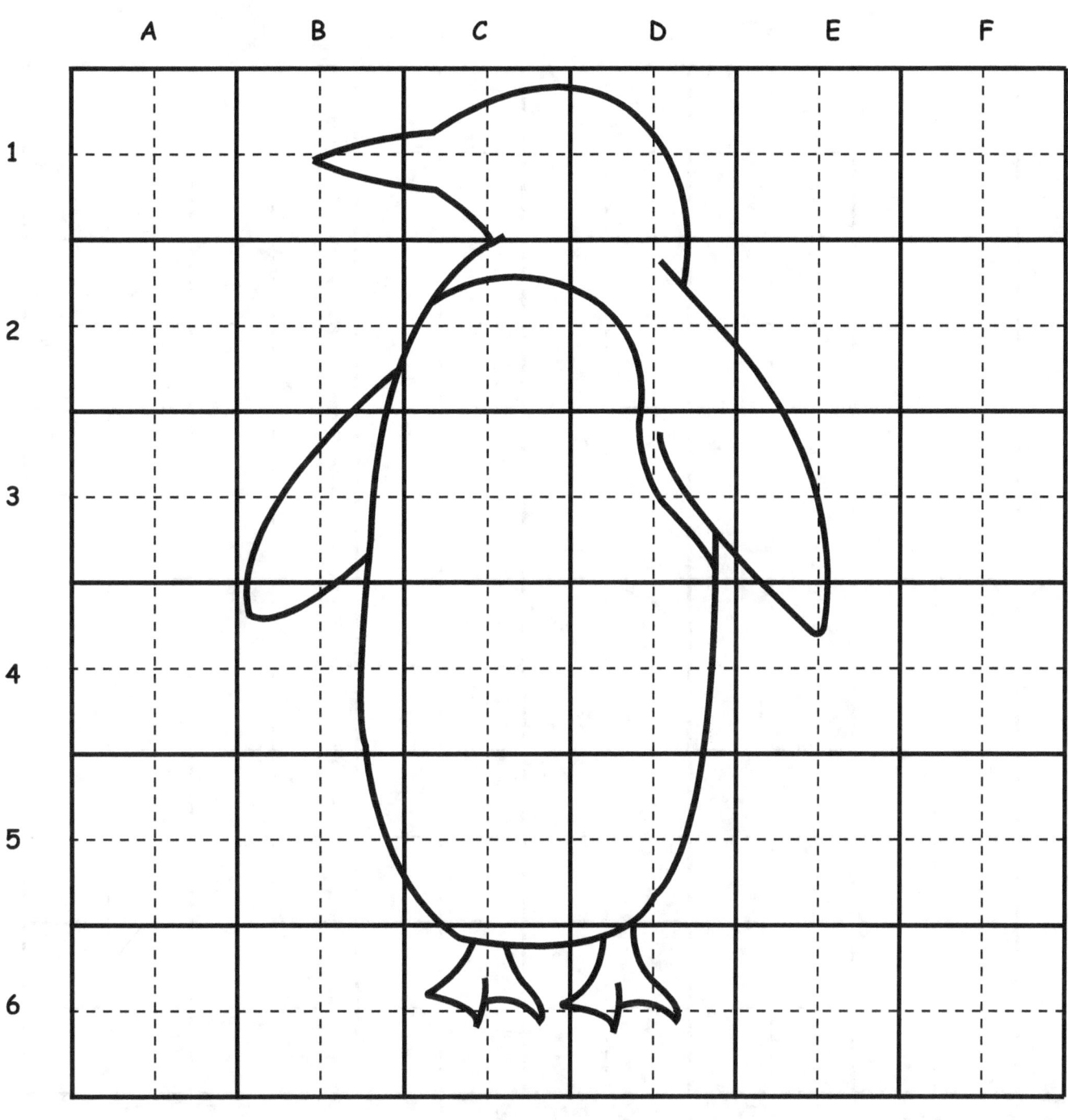

Practice Here With Gride

Draw lines of the Penguin's feet

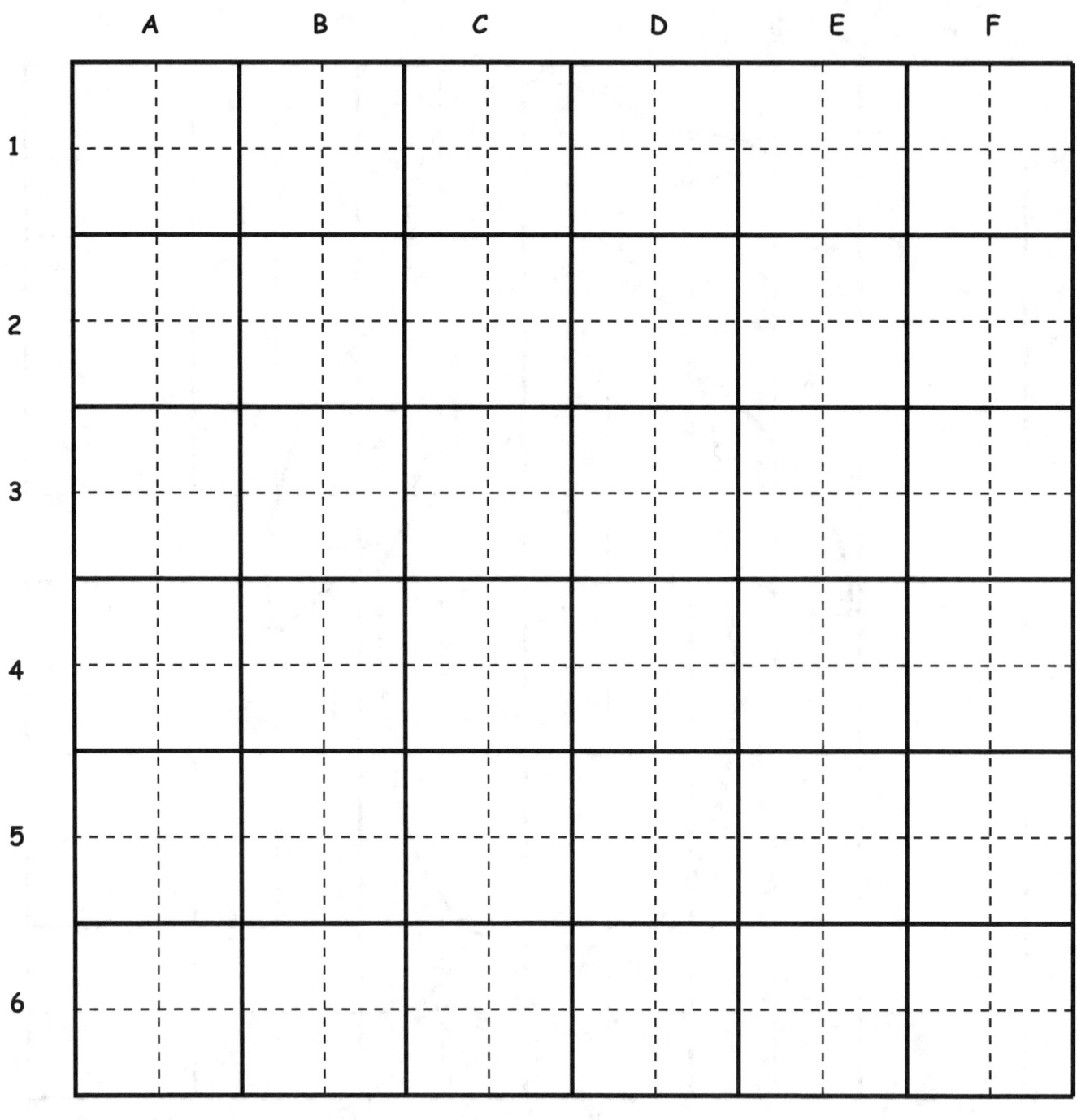

Penguin Art With Grid For Easy Way To Art

5 Draw lines of the Penguin's eye and Beak

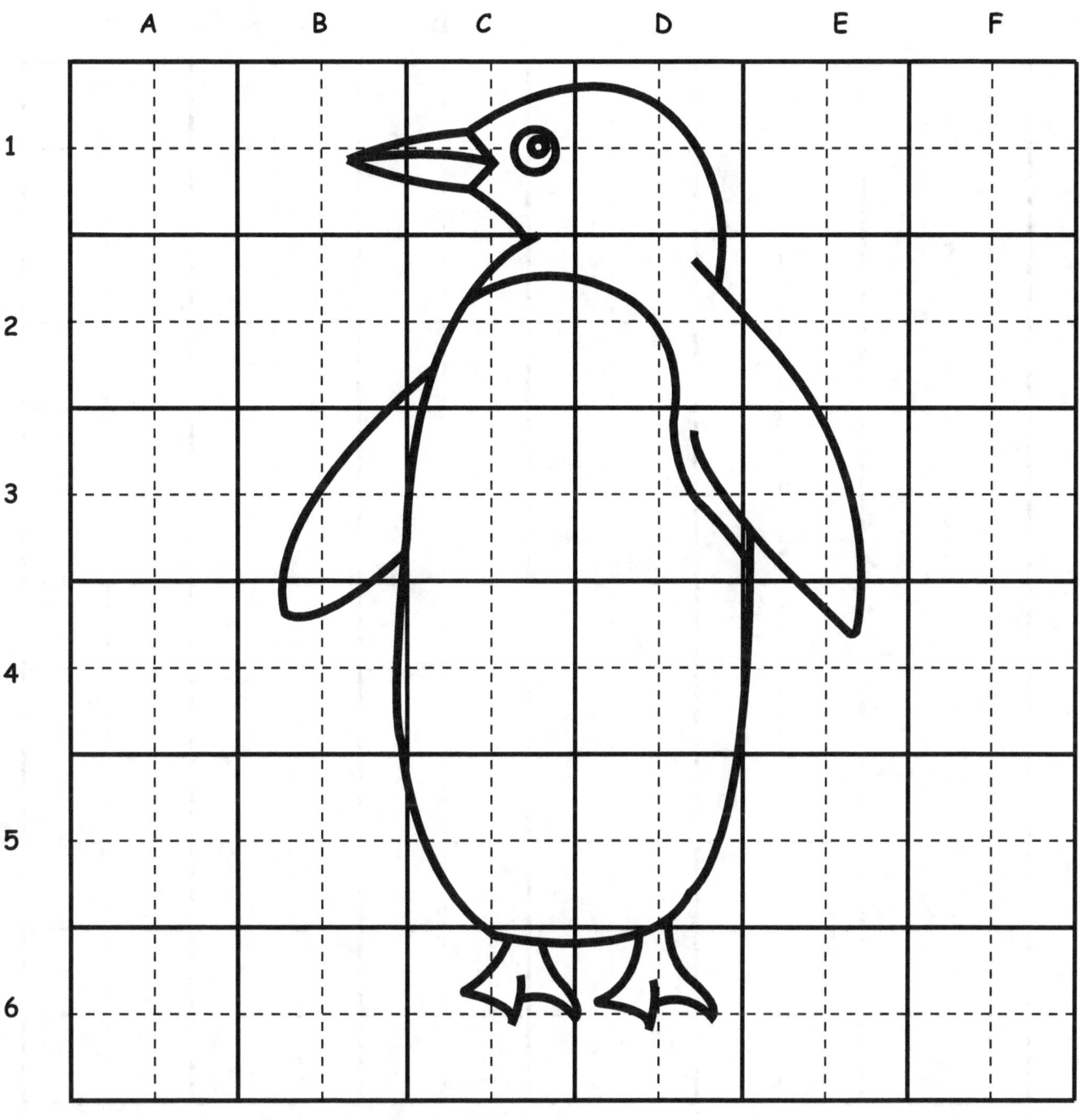

Practice Here With Gride

Draw lines of the Penguin's eye and Beak

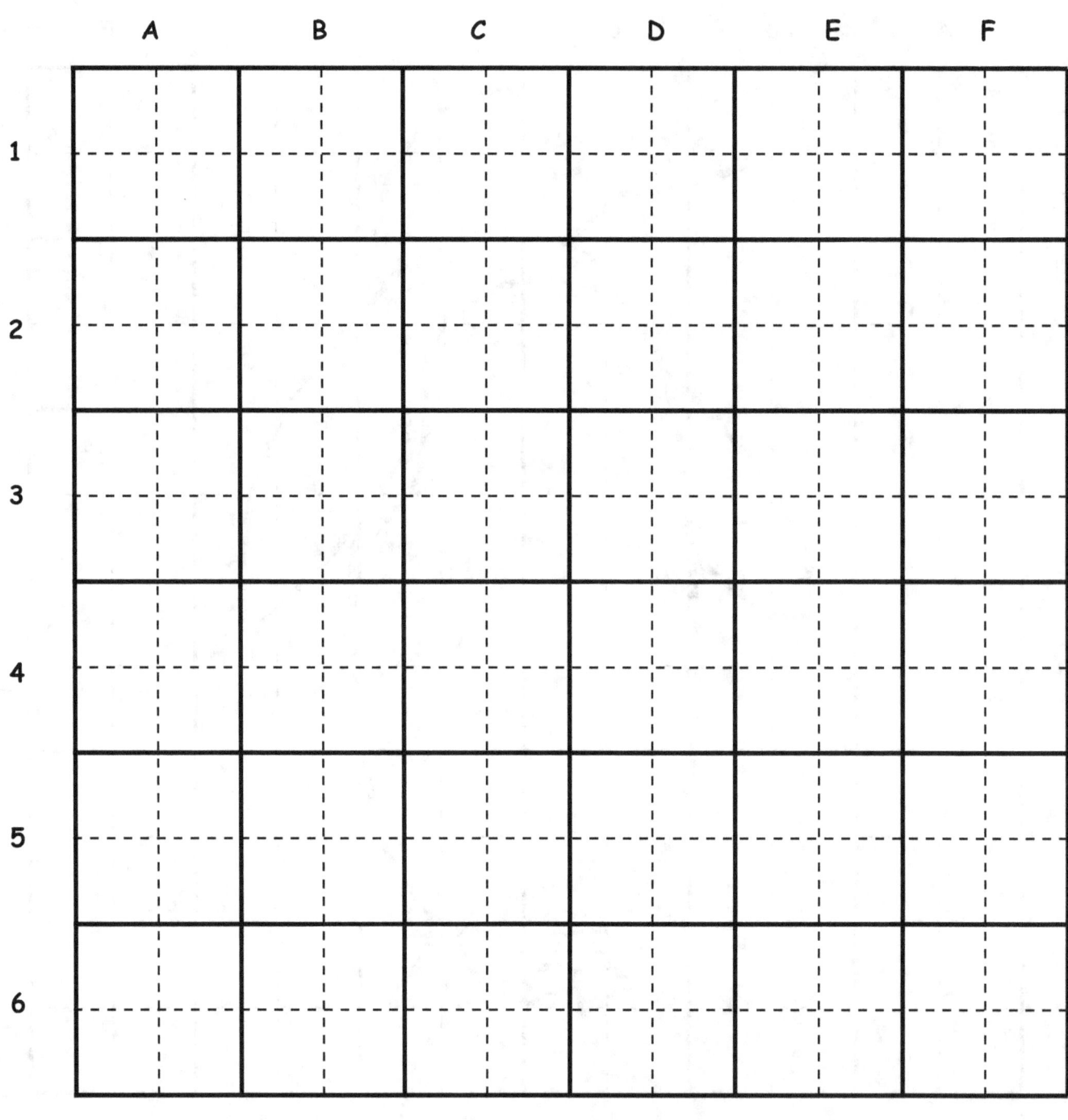

There is your ready Penguin.

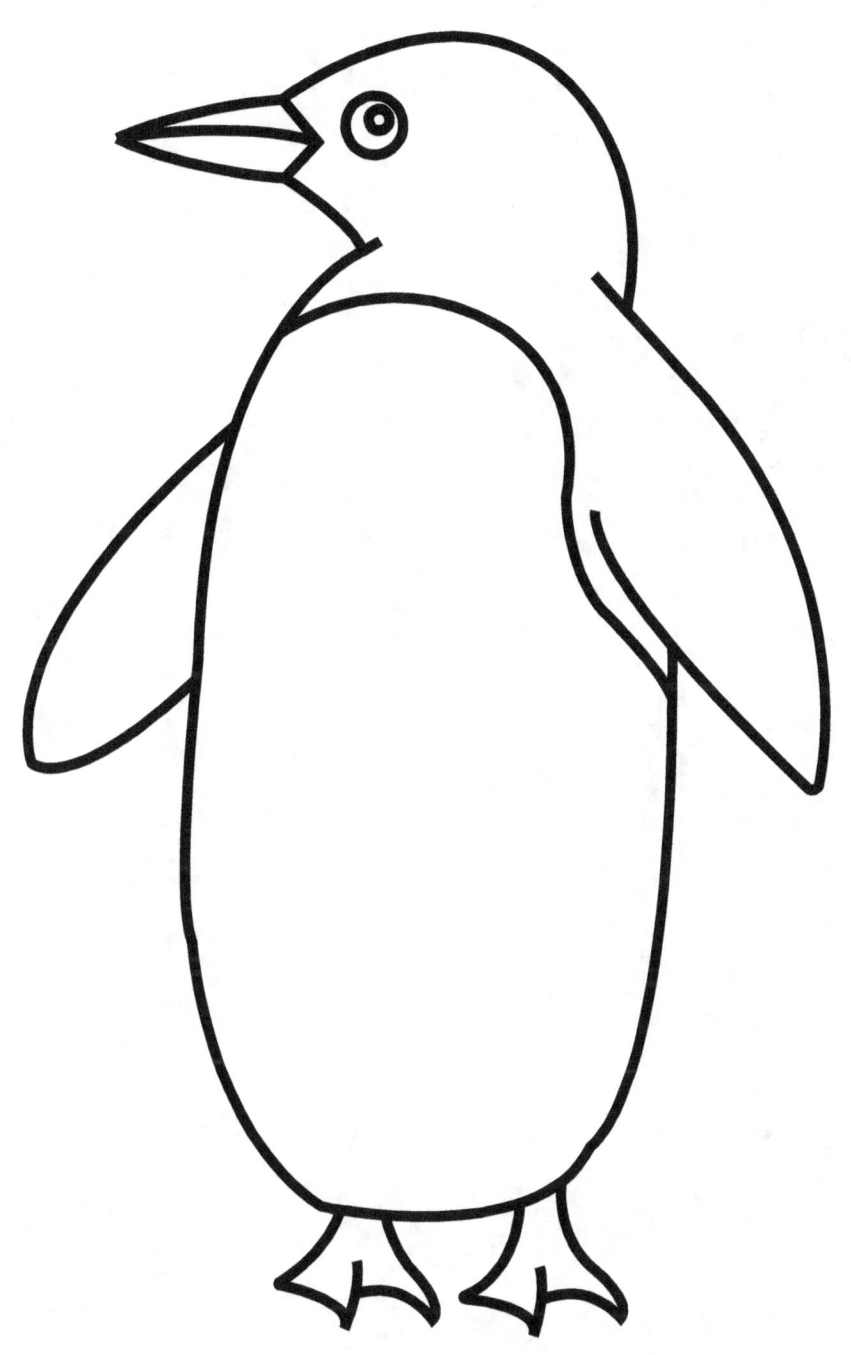

Practice Here Blind

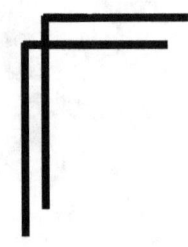

Penguin Art With Grid For Easy Way To Art

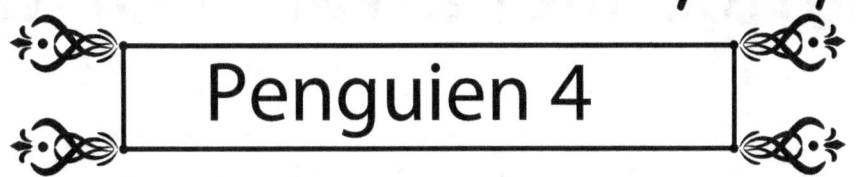

Penguien 4

1 Start by drawing the head

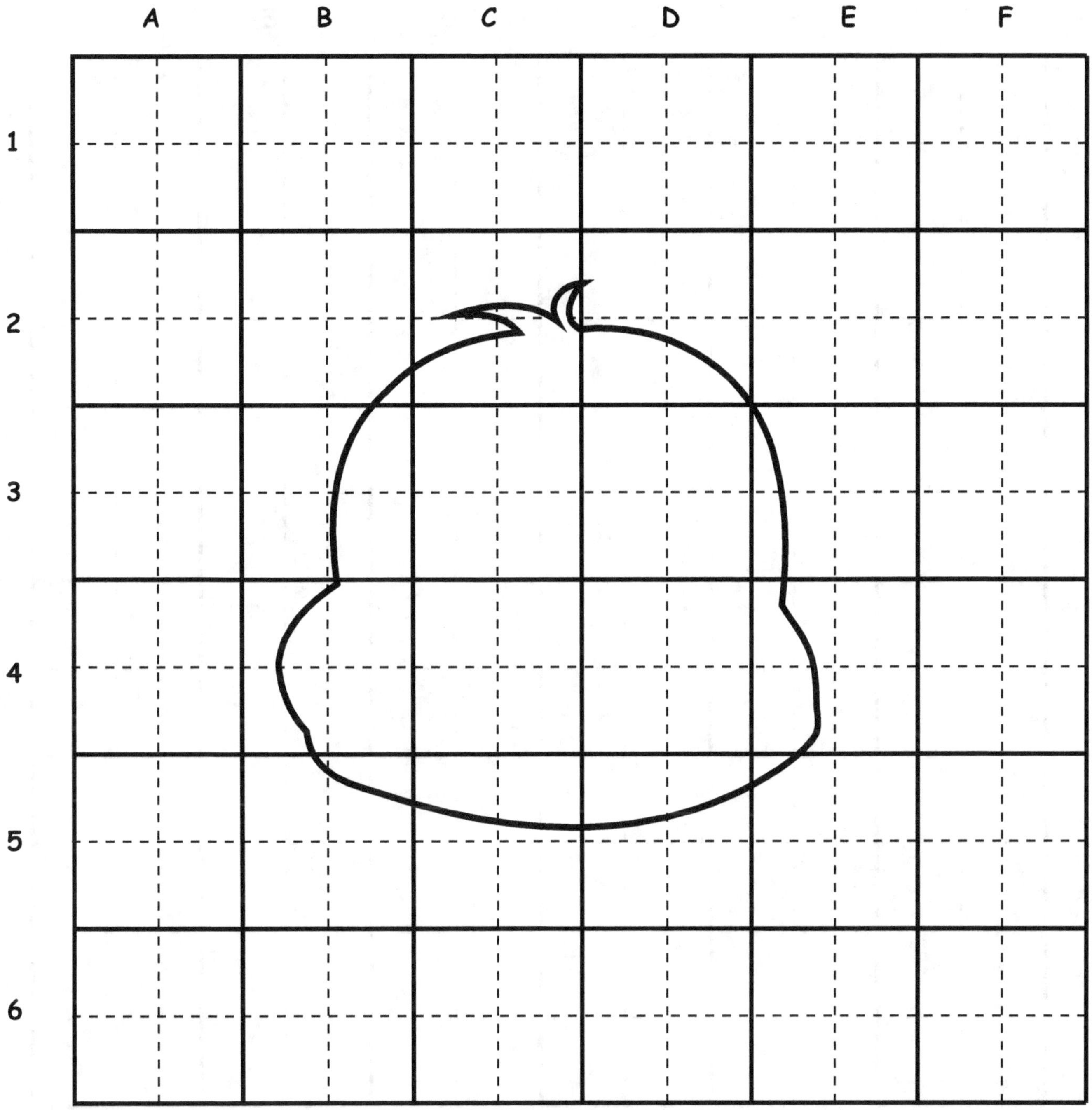

Practice Here With Gride

Start by drawing the head

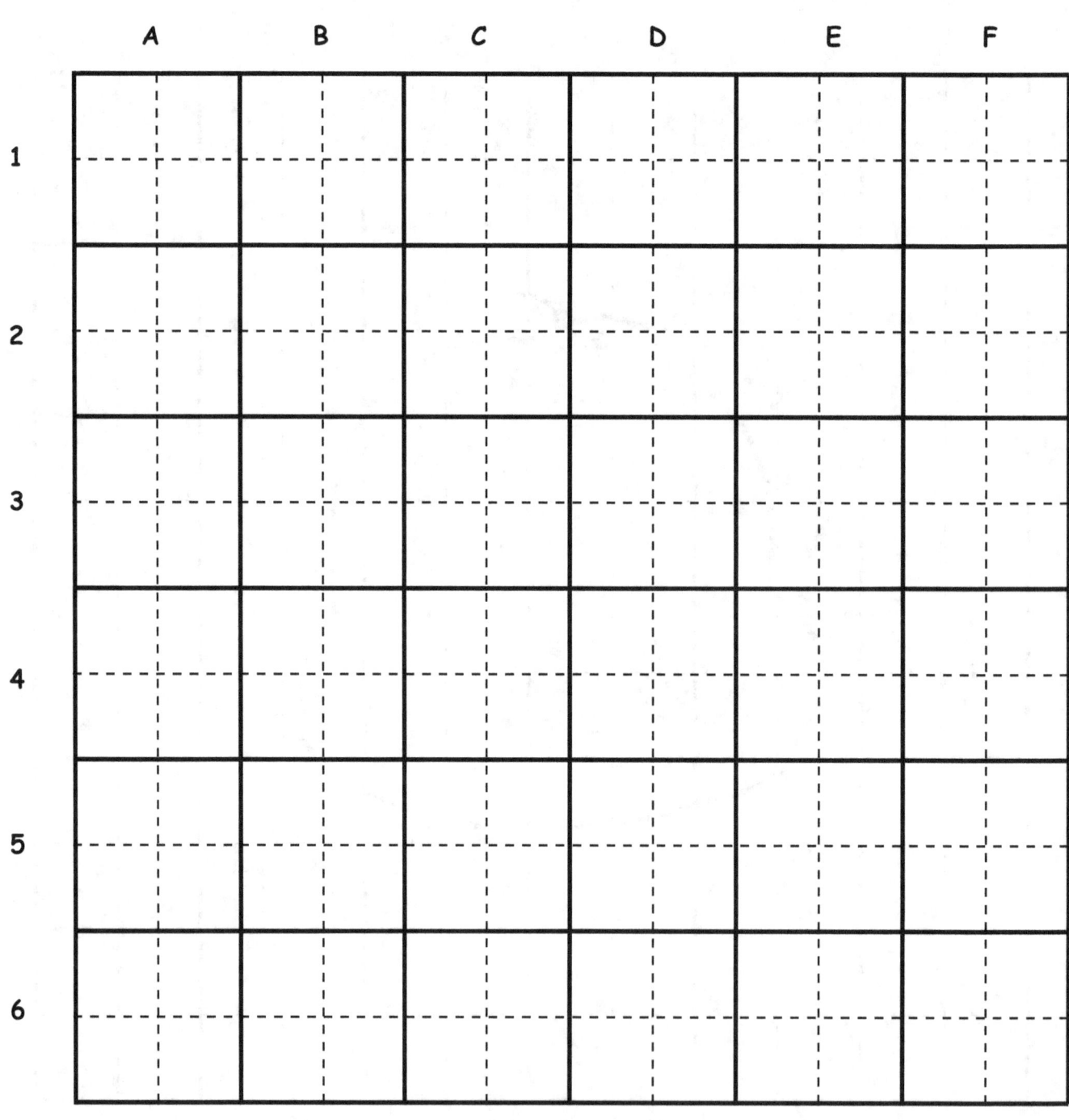

Penguin Art With Grid For Easy Way To Art

2 Draw lines of the Penguin's feather and body shape

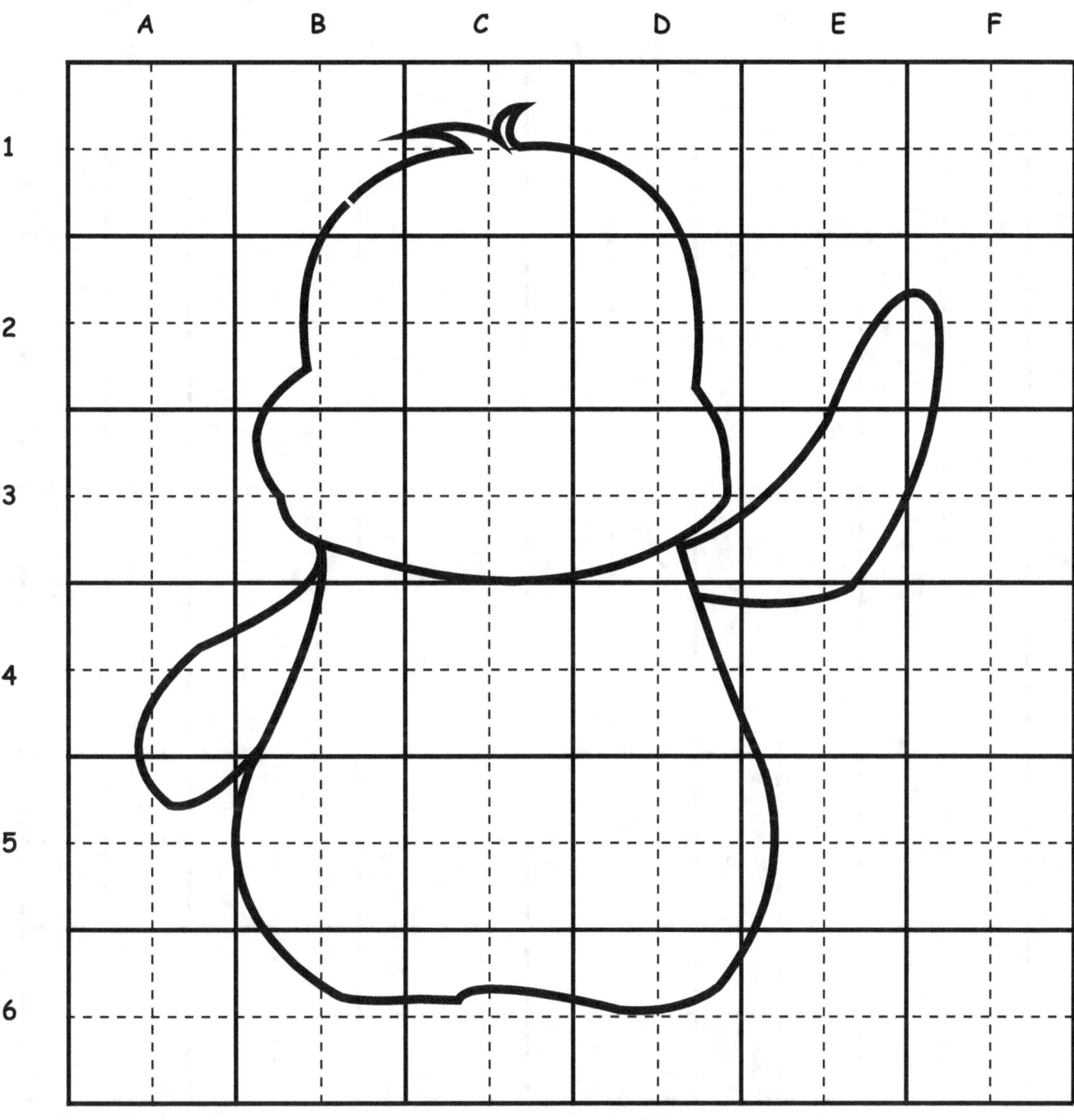

Practice Here With Gride

Draw lines of the Penguin's feather and body shape

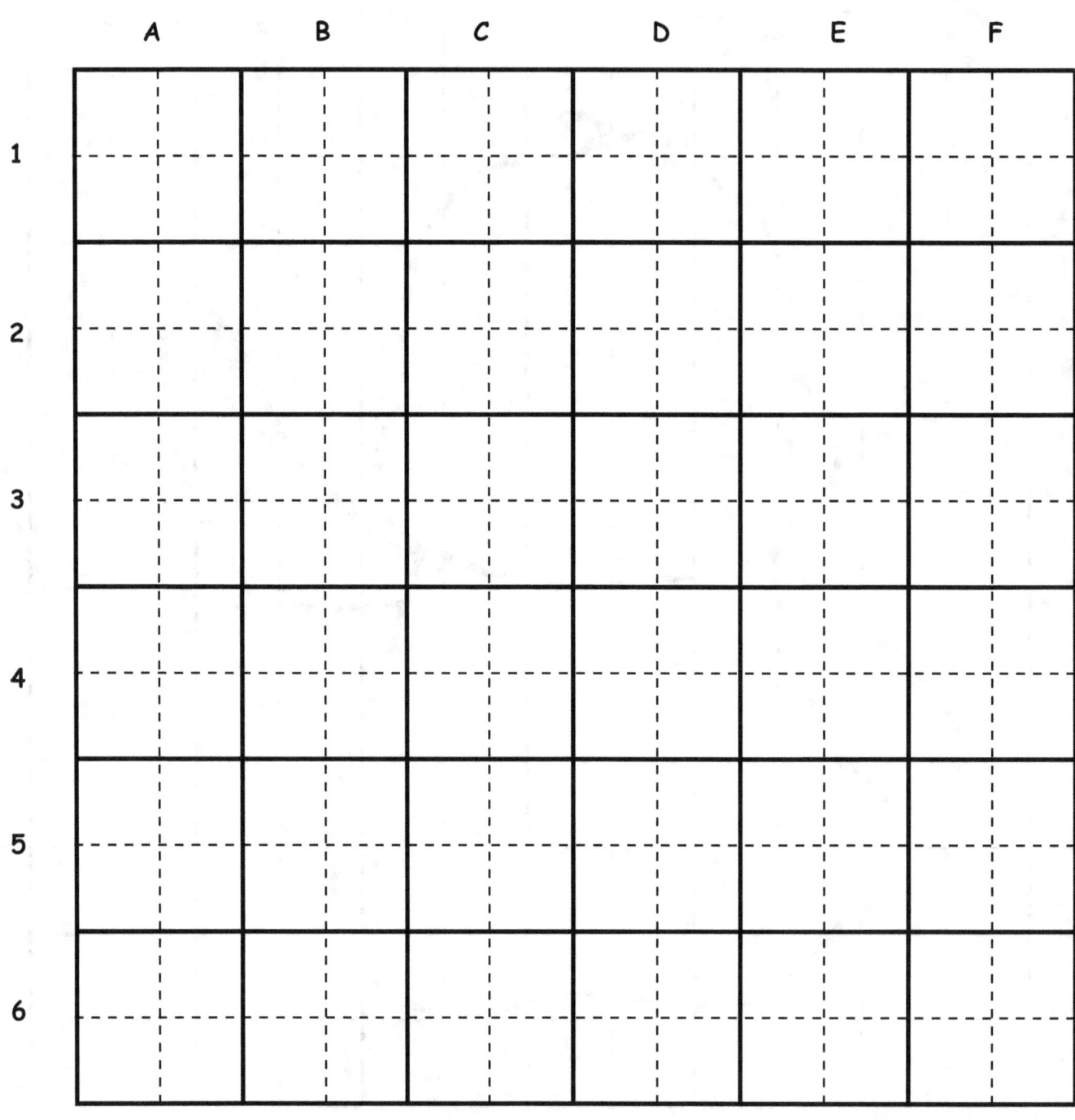

Penguin Art With Grid For Easy Way To Art

3 Draw lines of the Penguin's feet and the face nose details as shown.

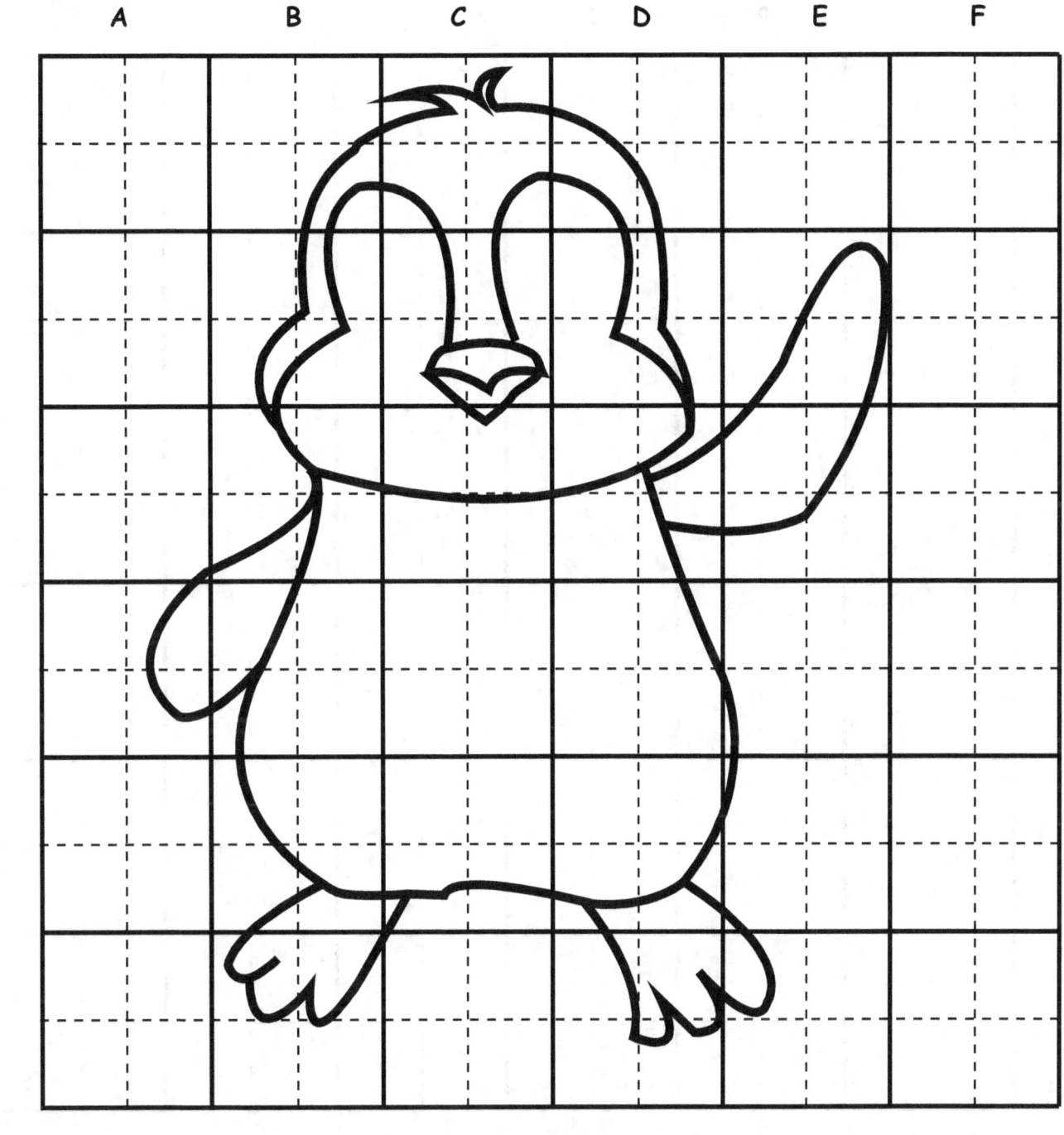

Practice Here With Gride

Draw lines of the Penguin's feet and the face nose details as shown.

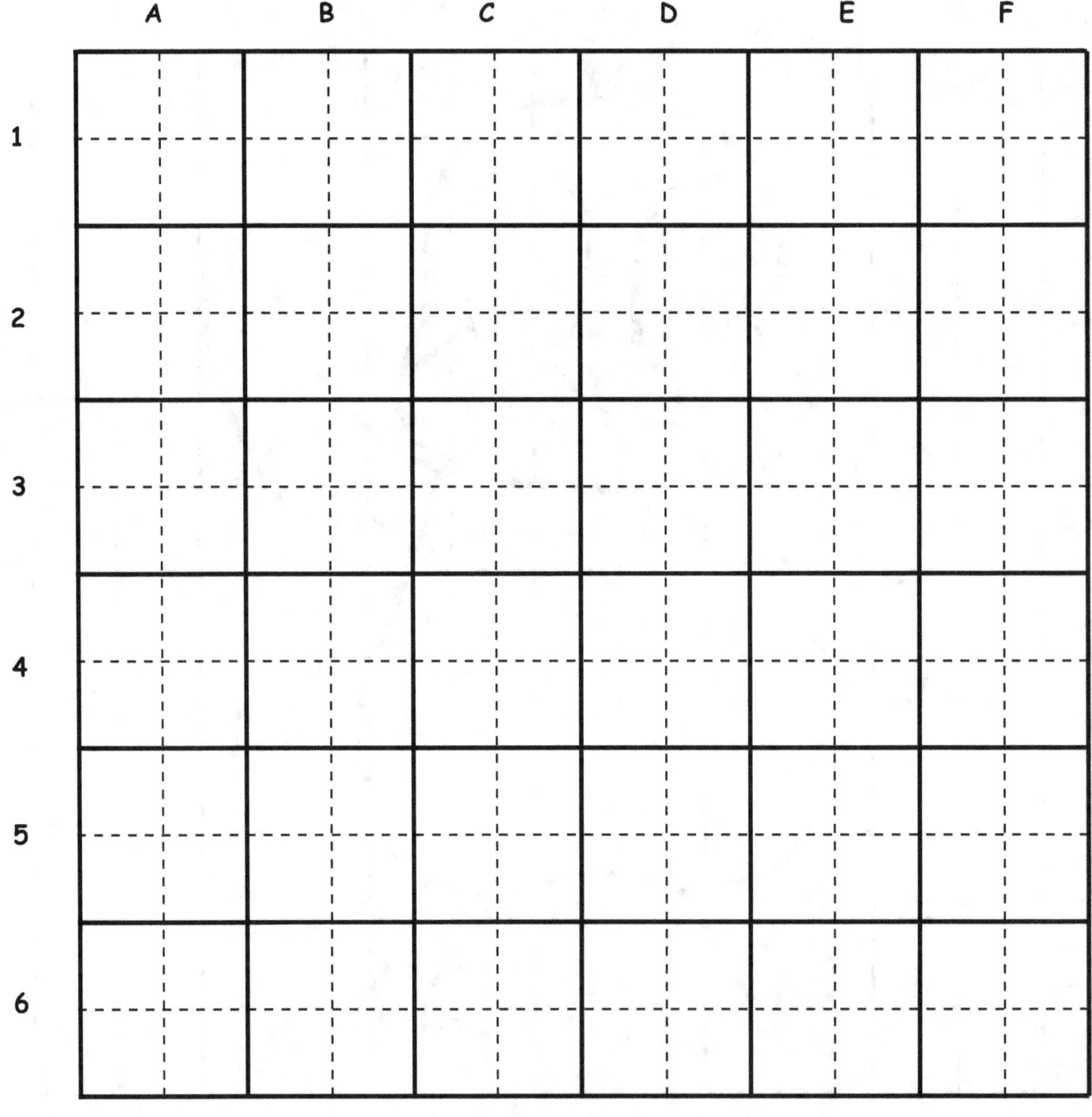

Penguin Art With Grid For Easy Way To Art

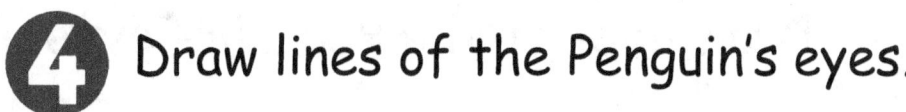 Draw lines of the Penguin's eyes.

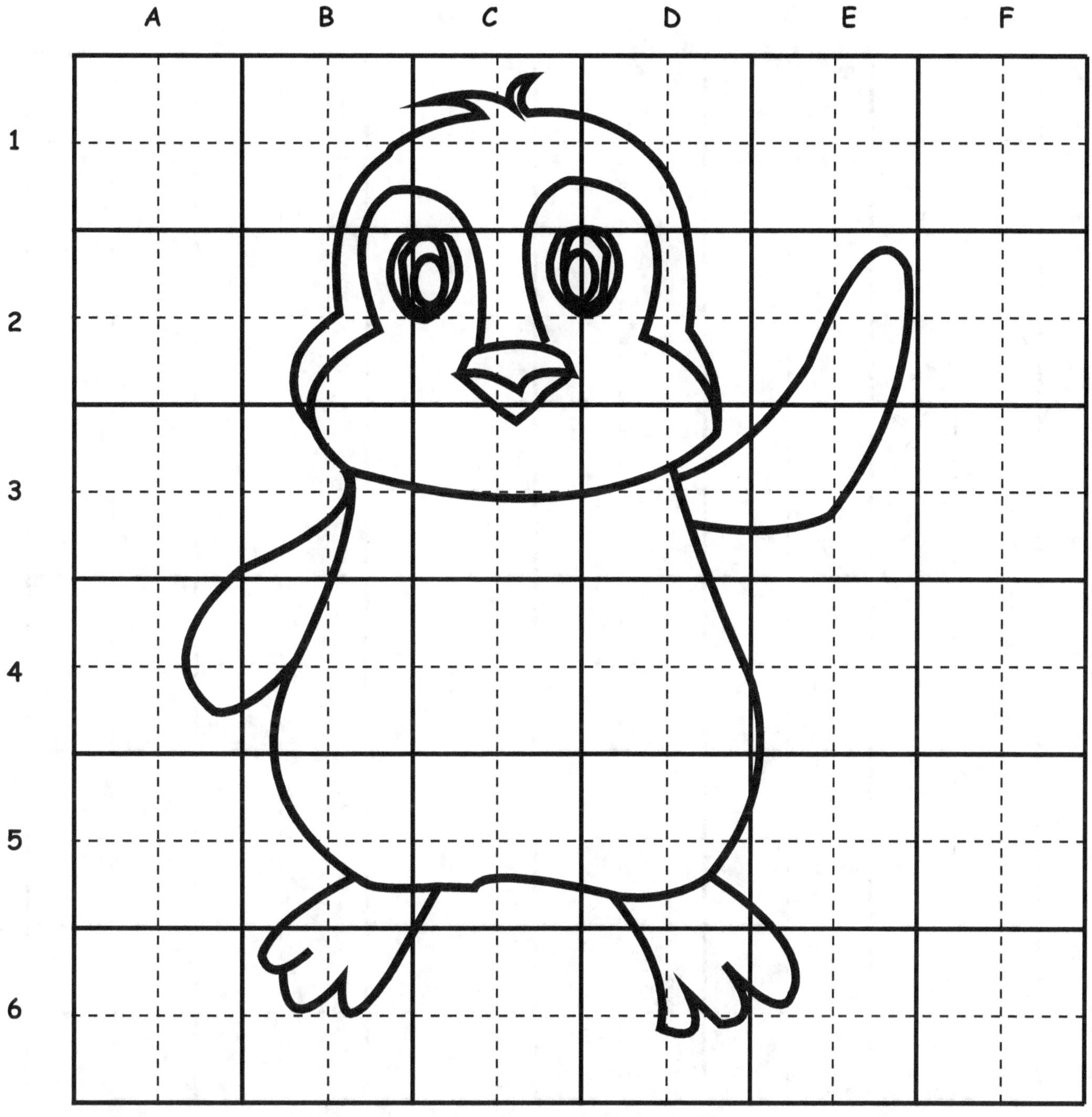

Practice Here With Gride

Draw lines of the Penguin's eyes.

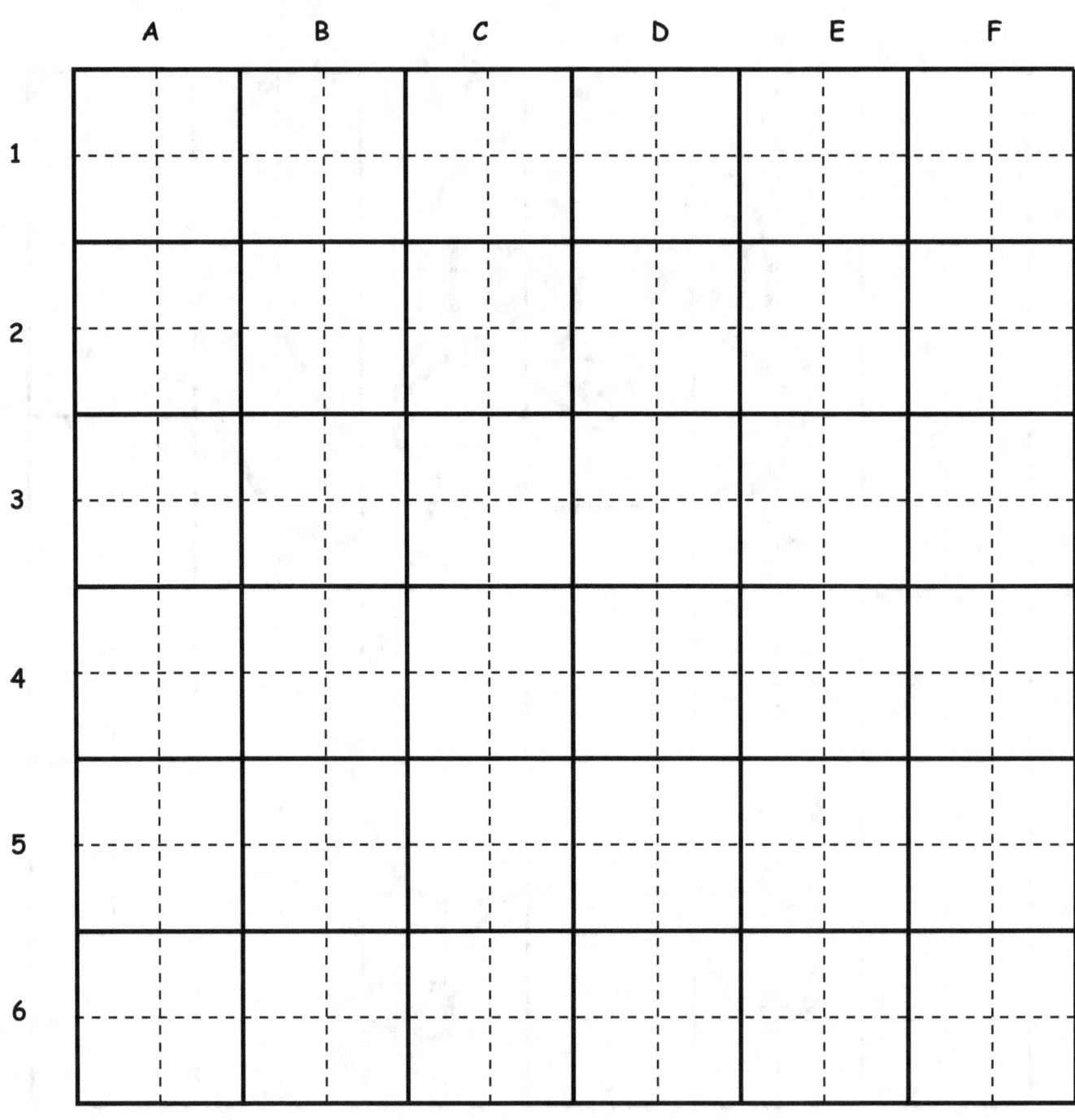

Penguin Art With Grid For Easy Way To Art

5 Add inner lines in body and feather as shown.

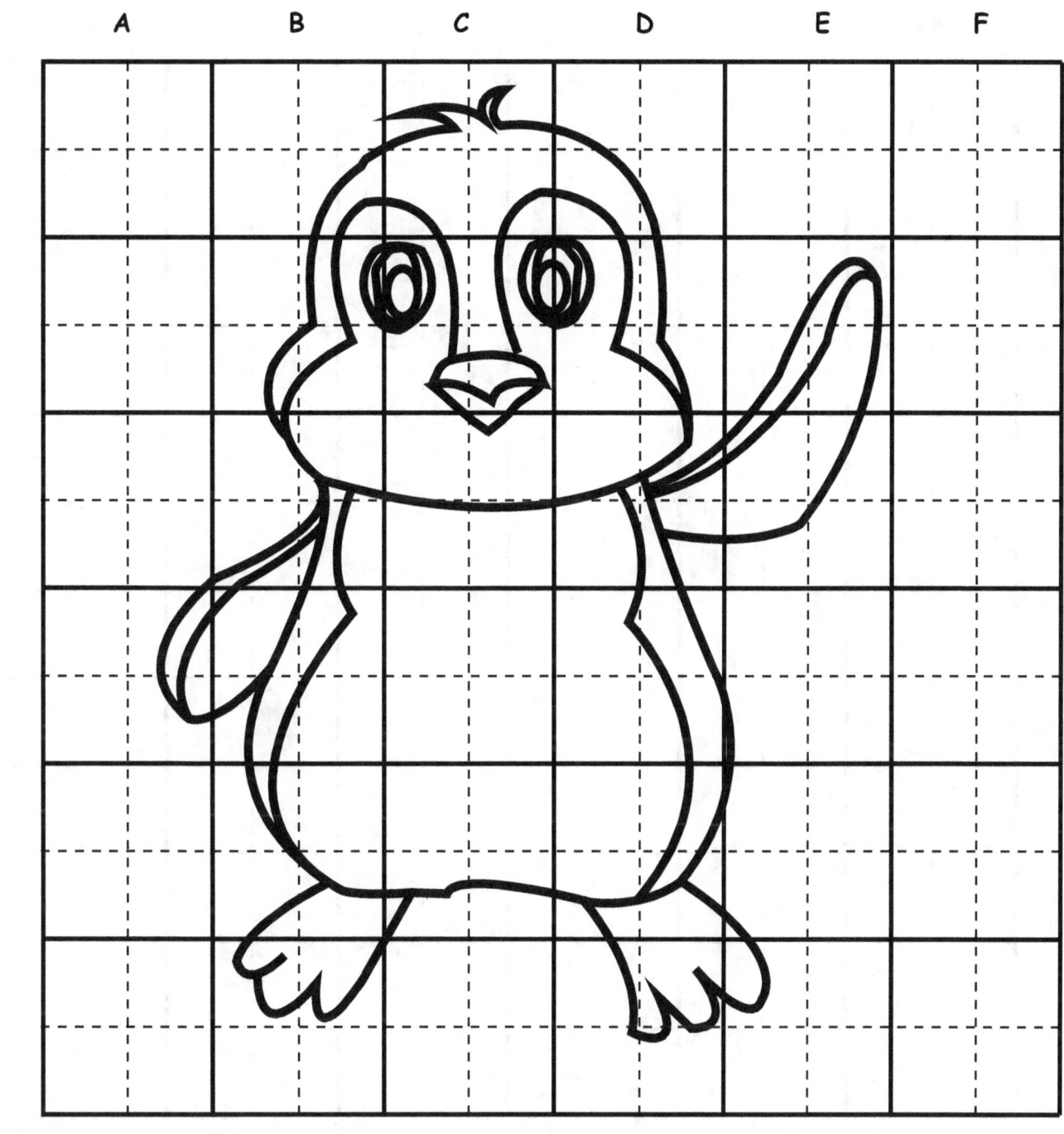

Practice Here With Gride

Add inner lines in body and feather as shown.

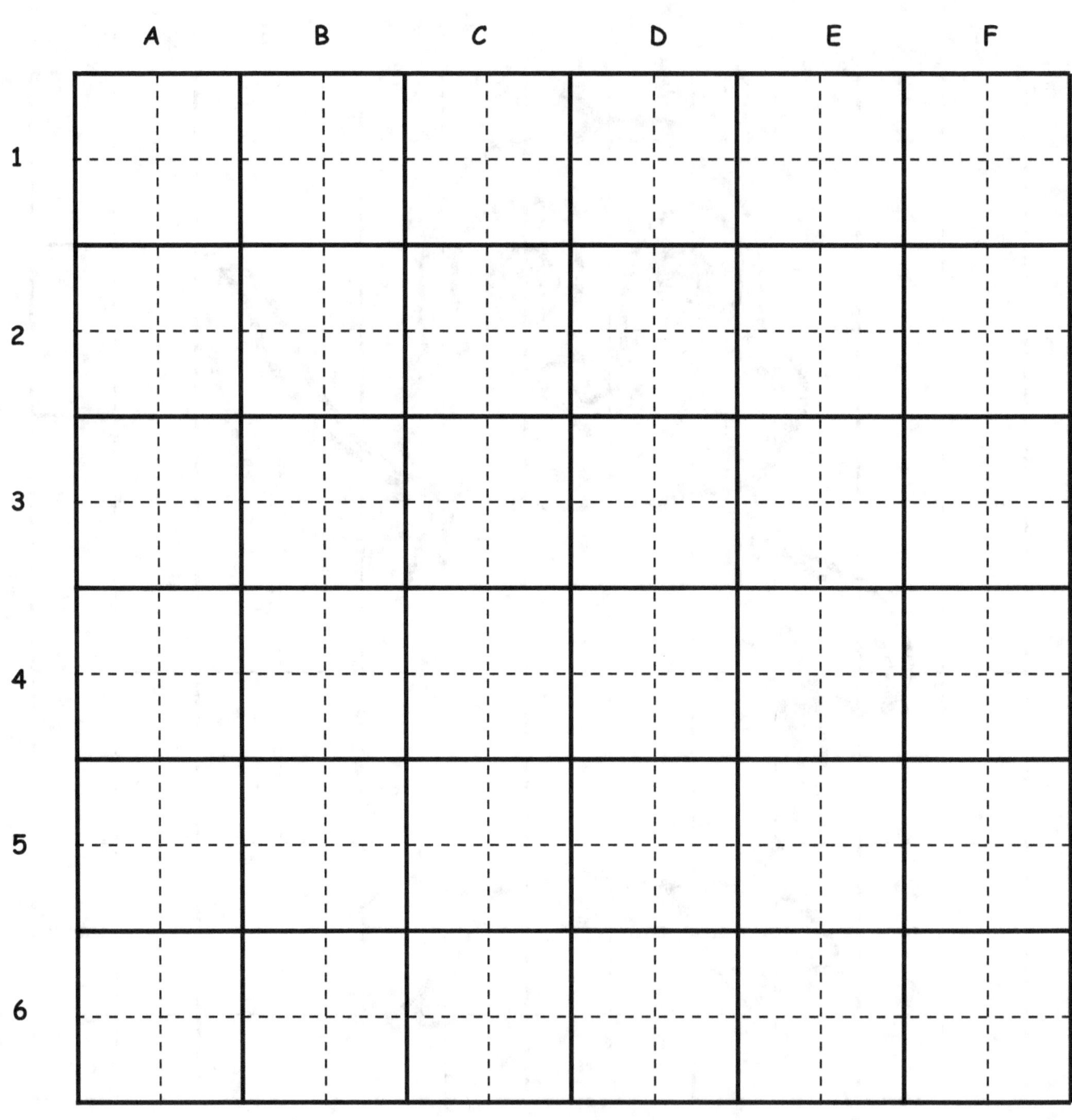

Your penguin is Done!

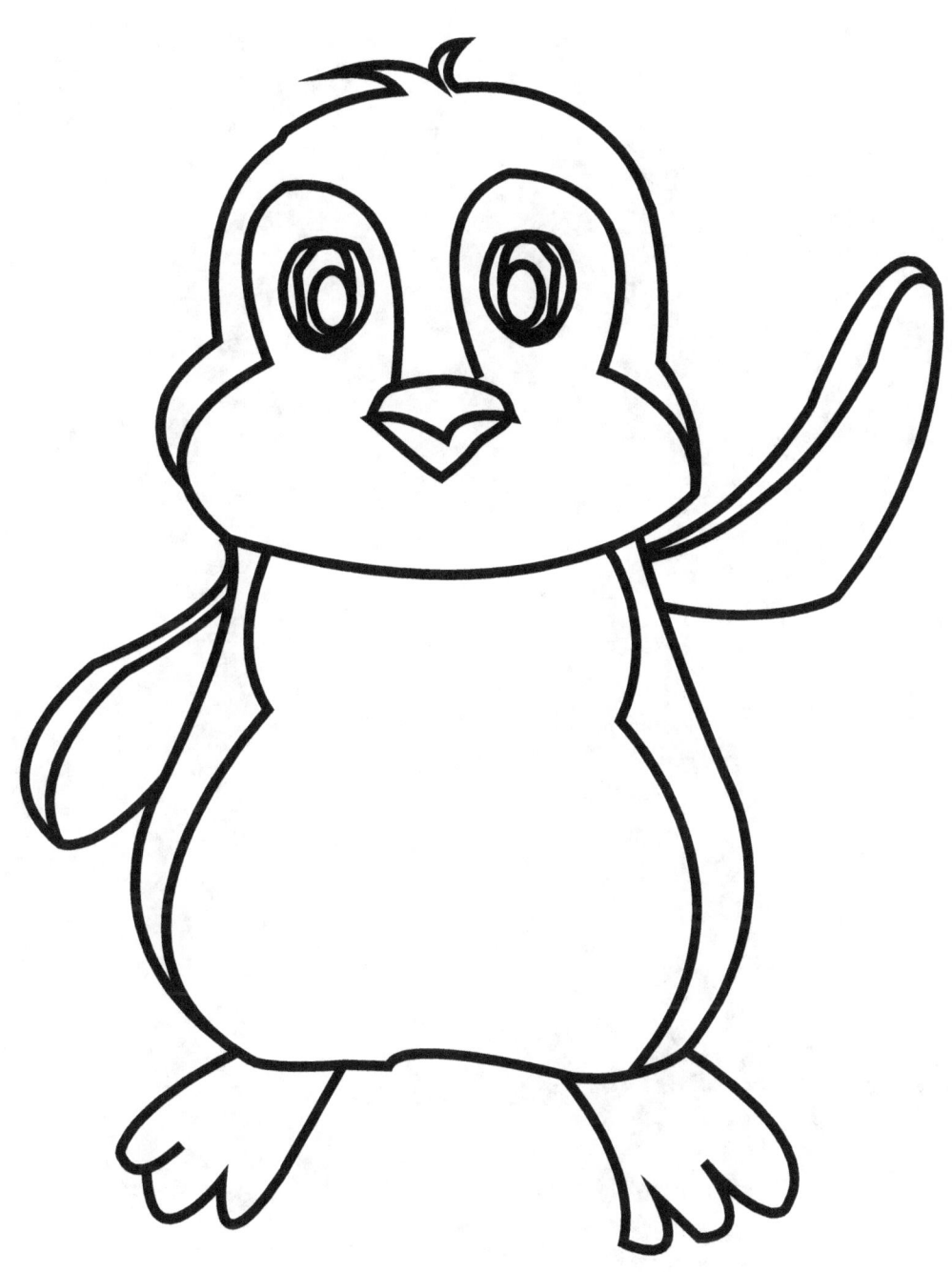

Practice Here Blind

Penguin Art With Grid For Easy Way To Art

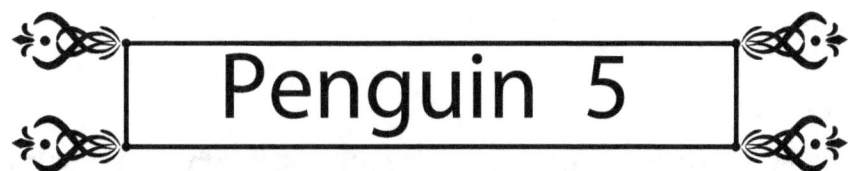

Penguin 5

1 Start by drawing the body shape as shown.

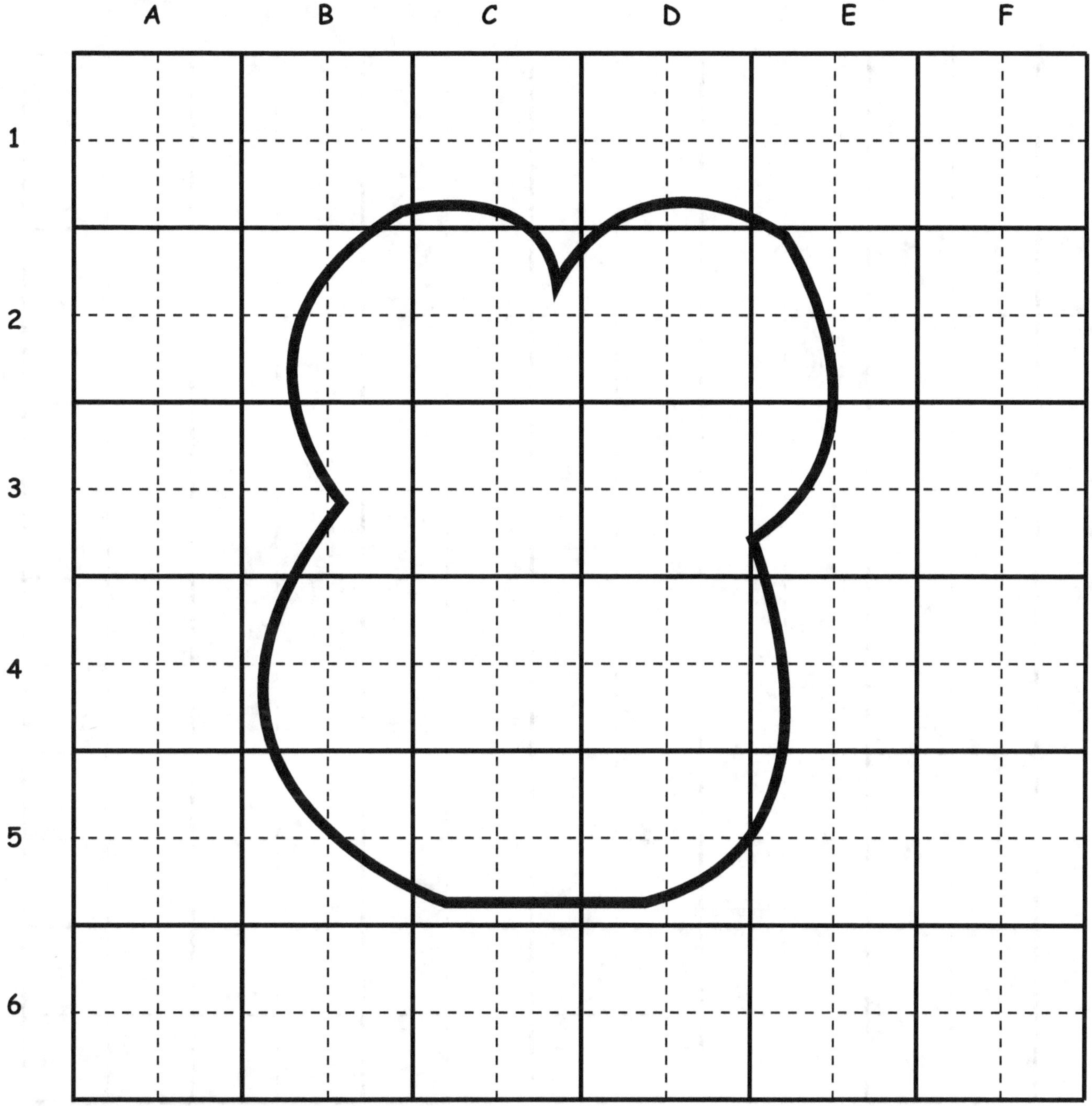

Practice Here With Gride

Start by drawing the body shape as shown.

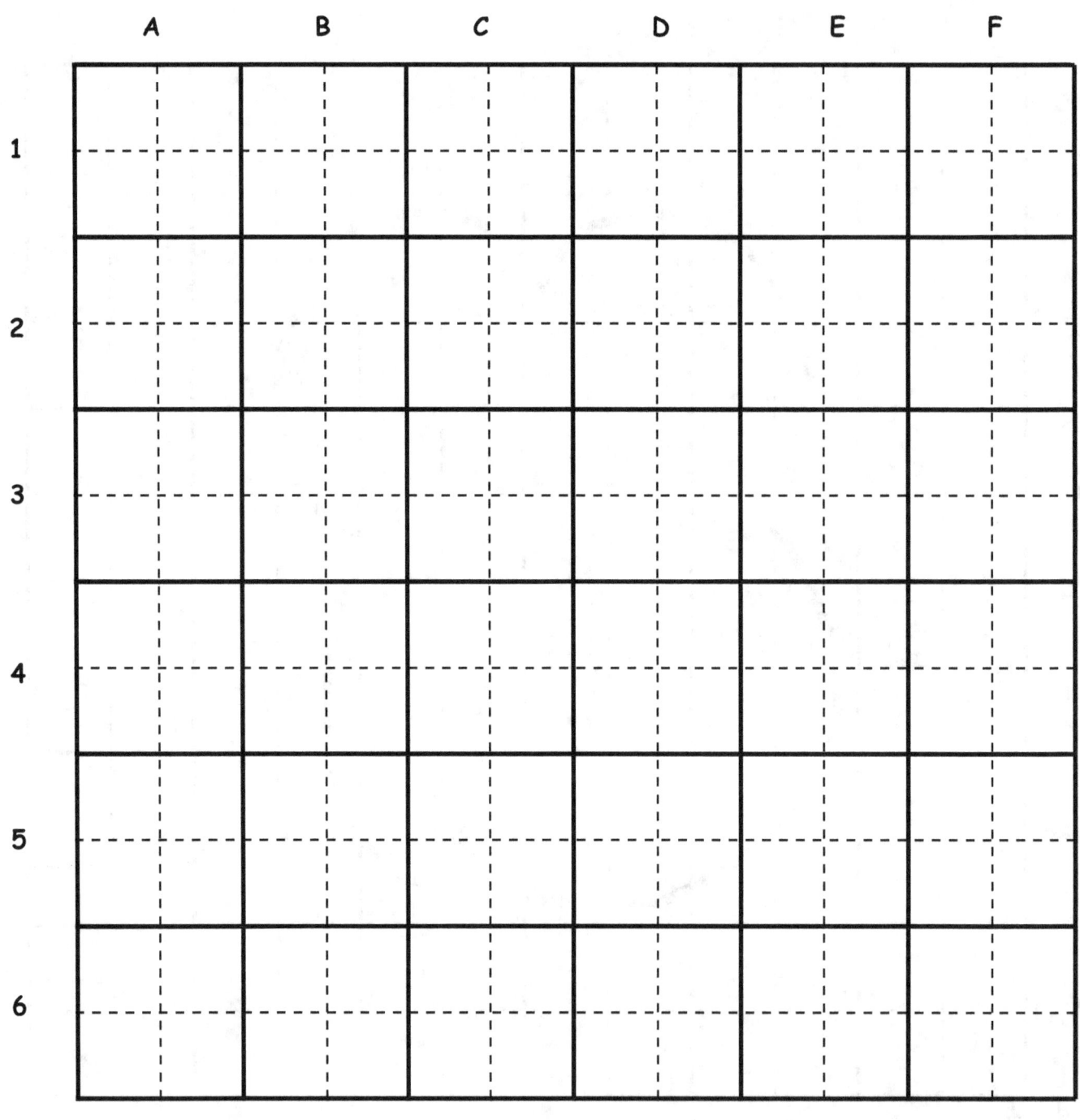

Penguin Art With Grid For Easy Way To Art

2 Draw another outer line with the Penguin's feather and body shape.

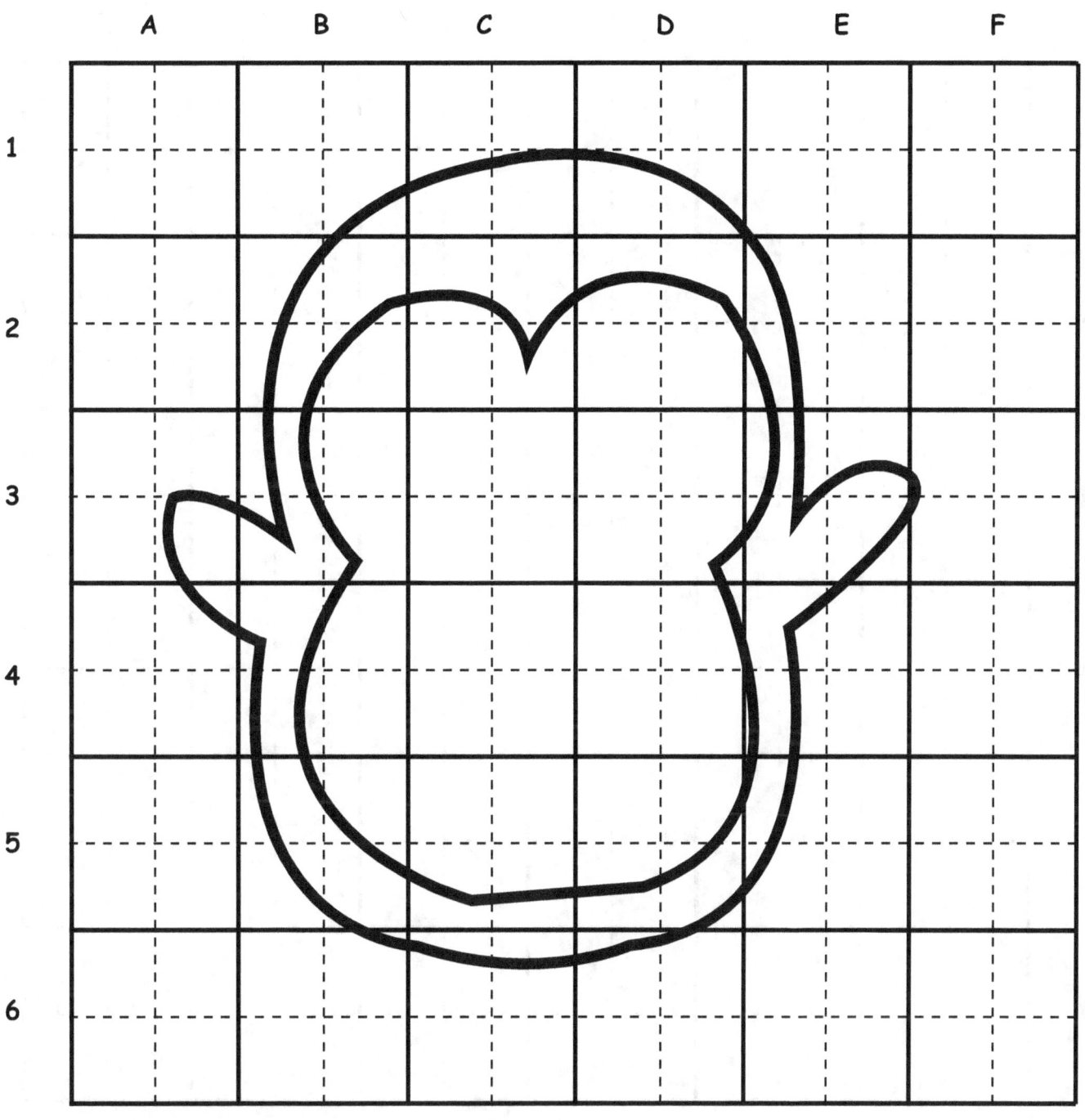

Practice Here With Gride

Draw another outer line with the Penguin's feather and body shape.

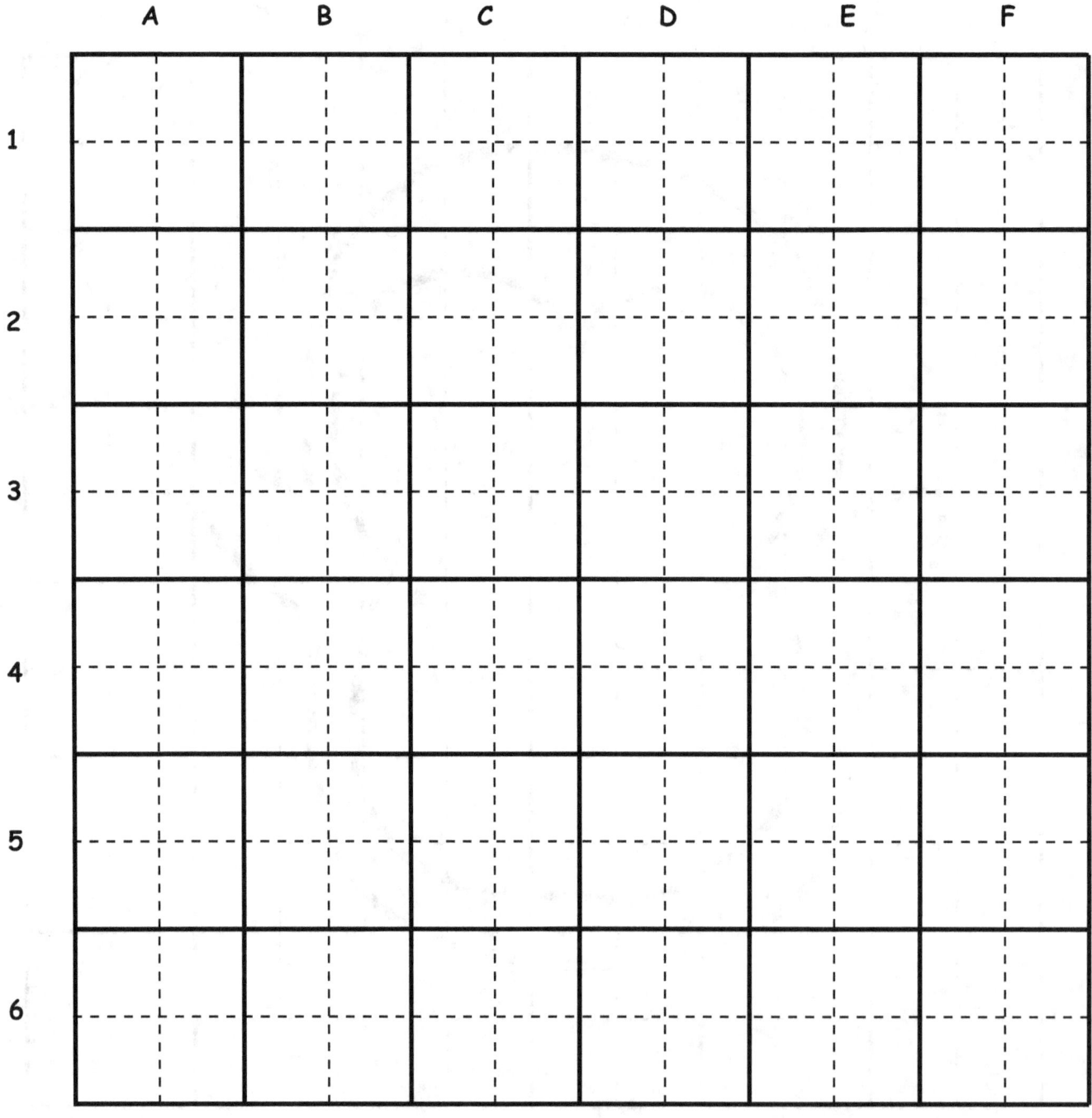

Penguin Art With Grid For Easy Way To Art

3 Draw lines of the Penguin's Beak and feet

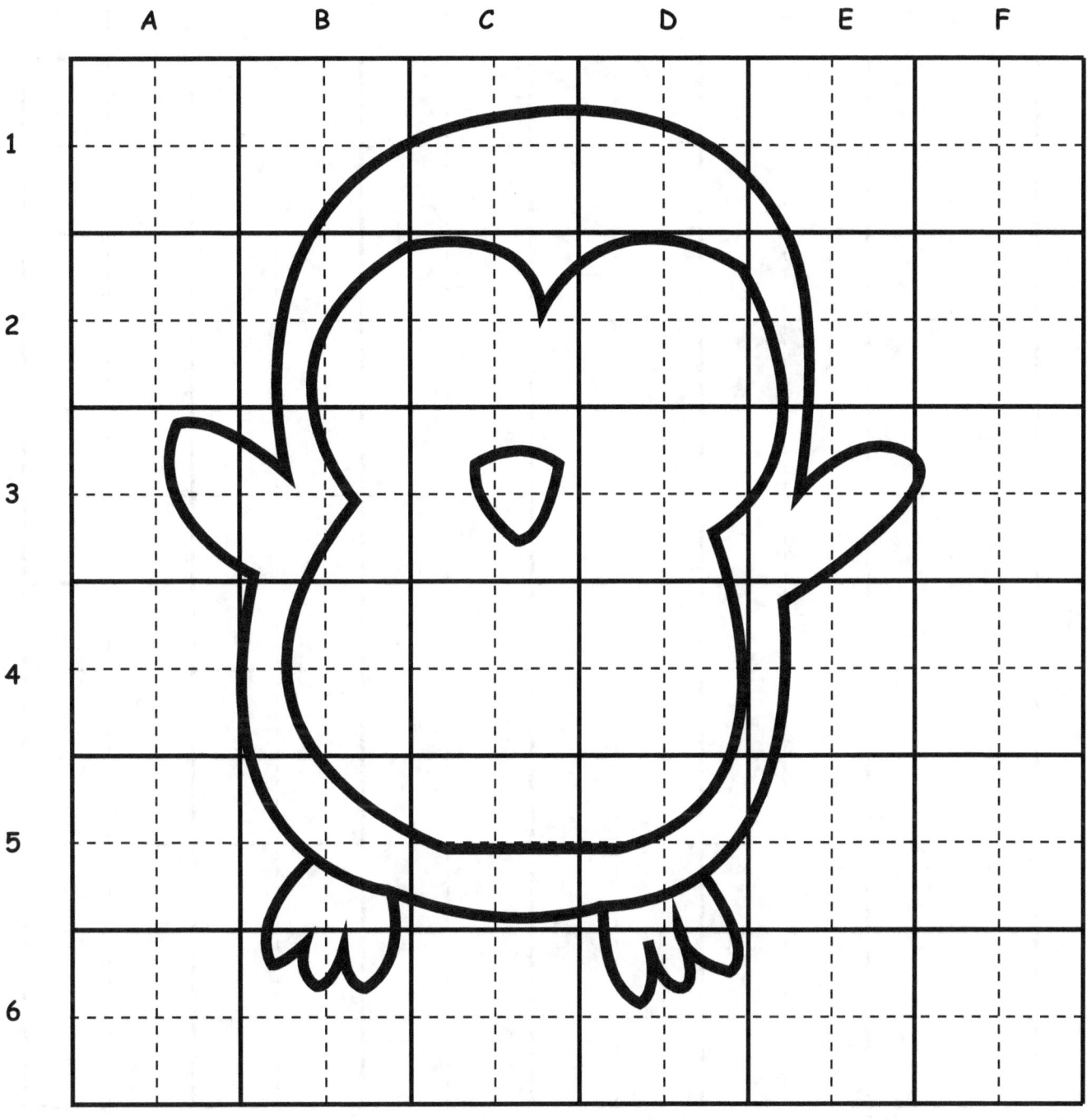

Practice Here With Gride

Draw lines of the Penguin's Beak and feet

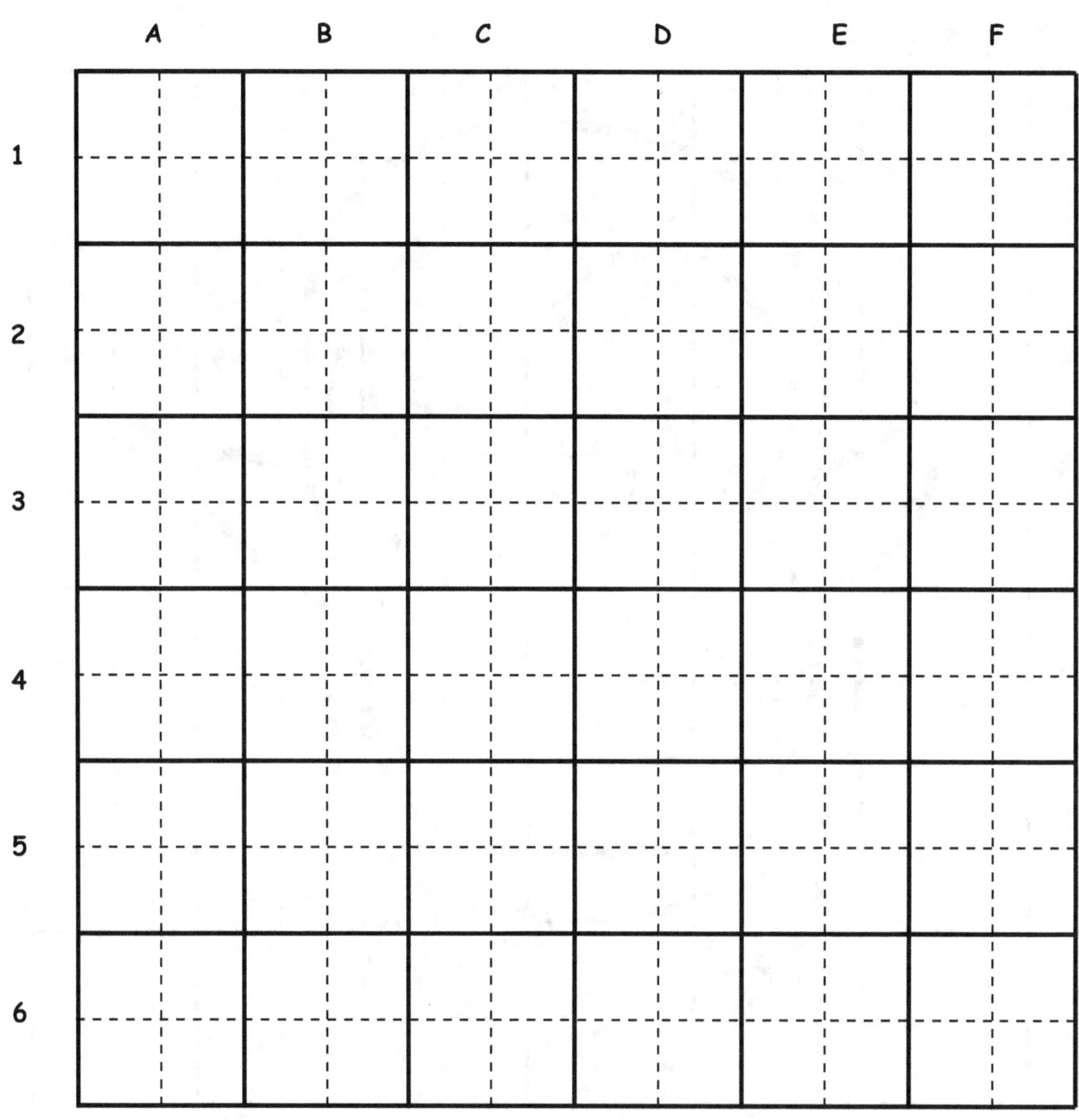

Penguin Art With Grid For Easy Way To Art

 Add few hairs on the top of the penguin's head.

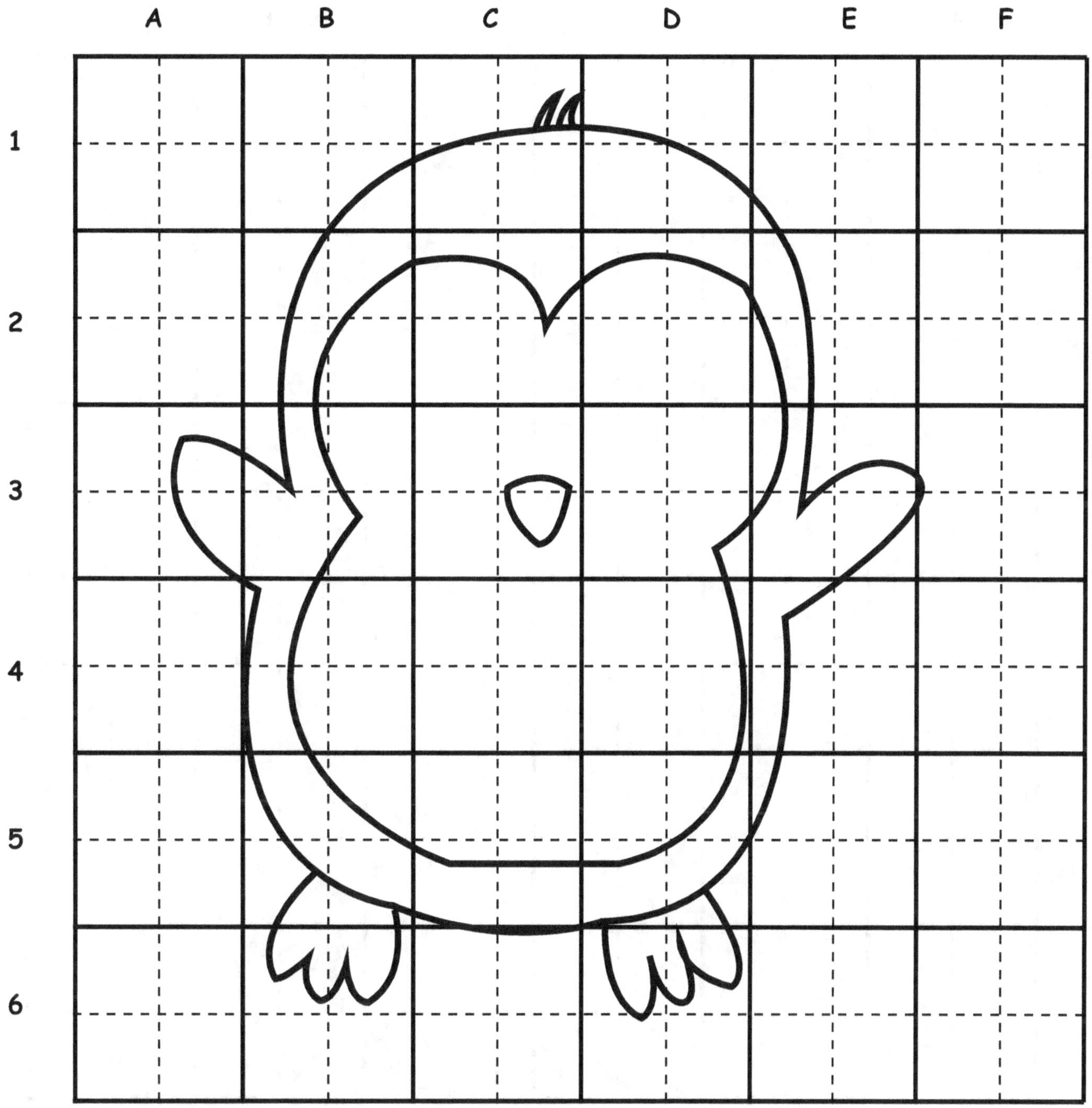

Practice Here With Gride

Add few hairs on the top of the penguin's head.

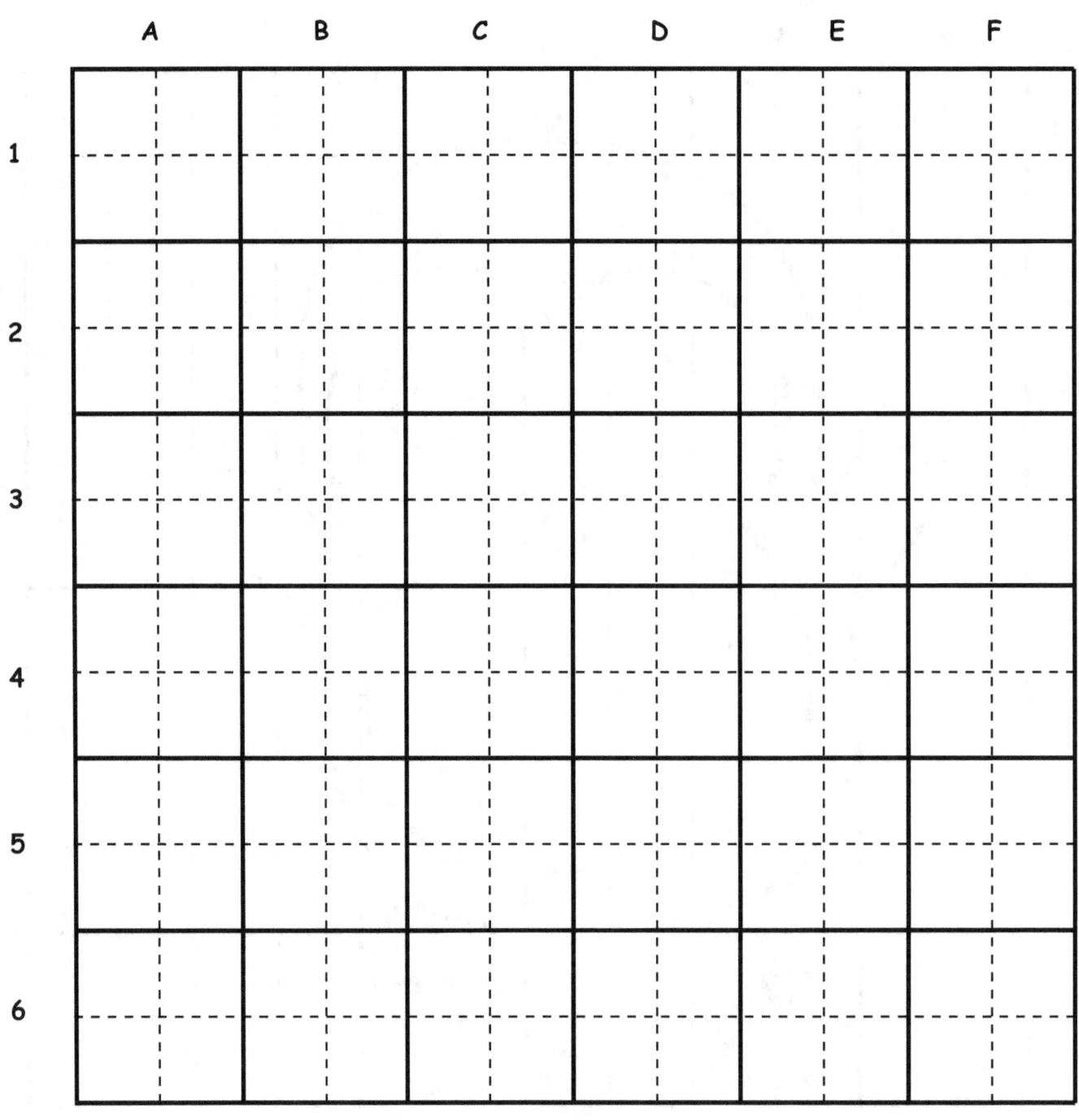

Penguin Art With Grid For Easy Way To Art

5 Draw lines of the Penguin's eyes.

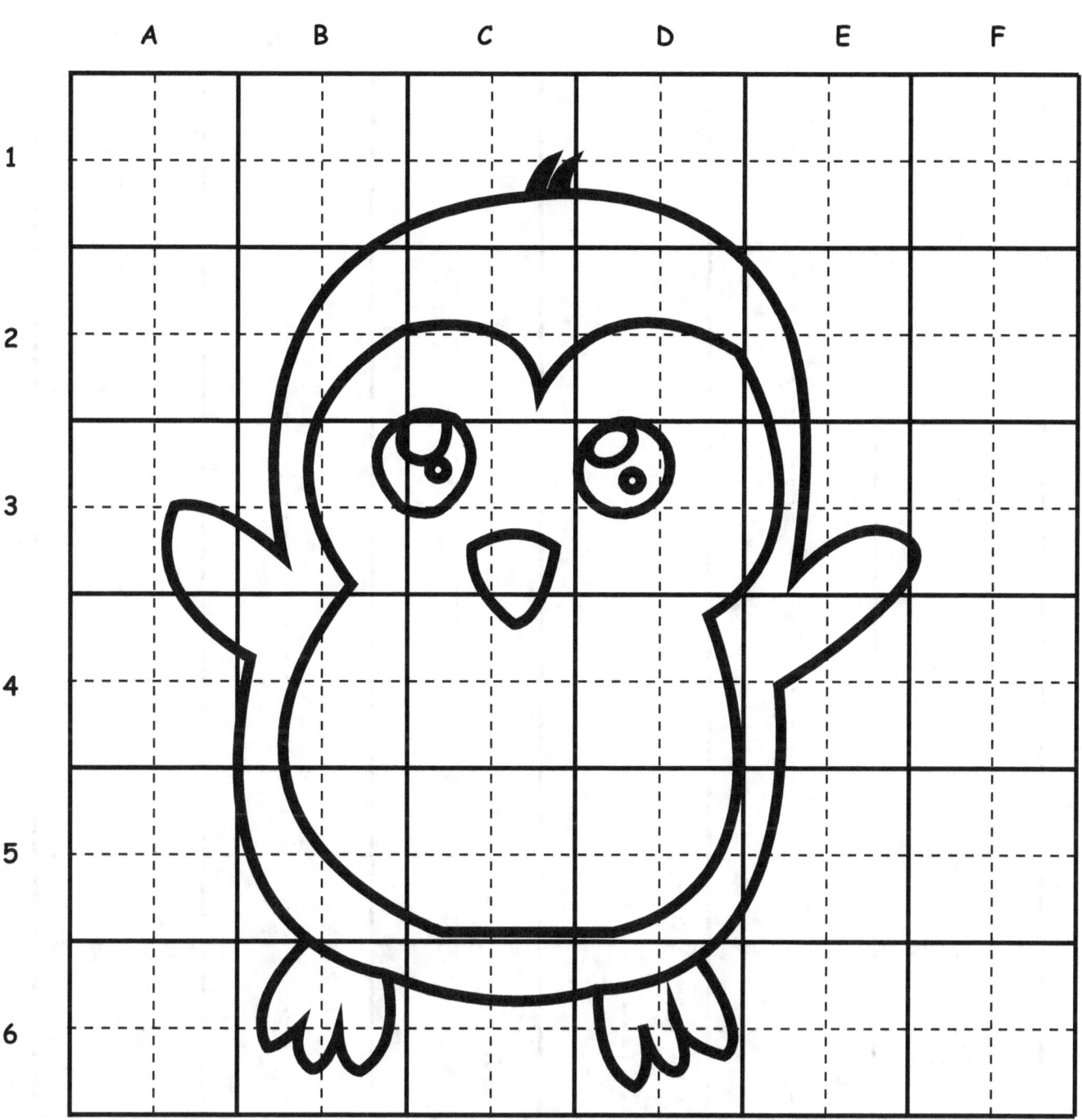

Practice Here With Gride

Draw lines of the Penguin's eyes.

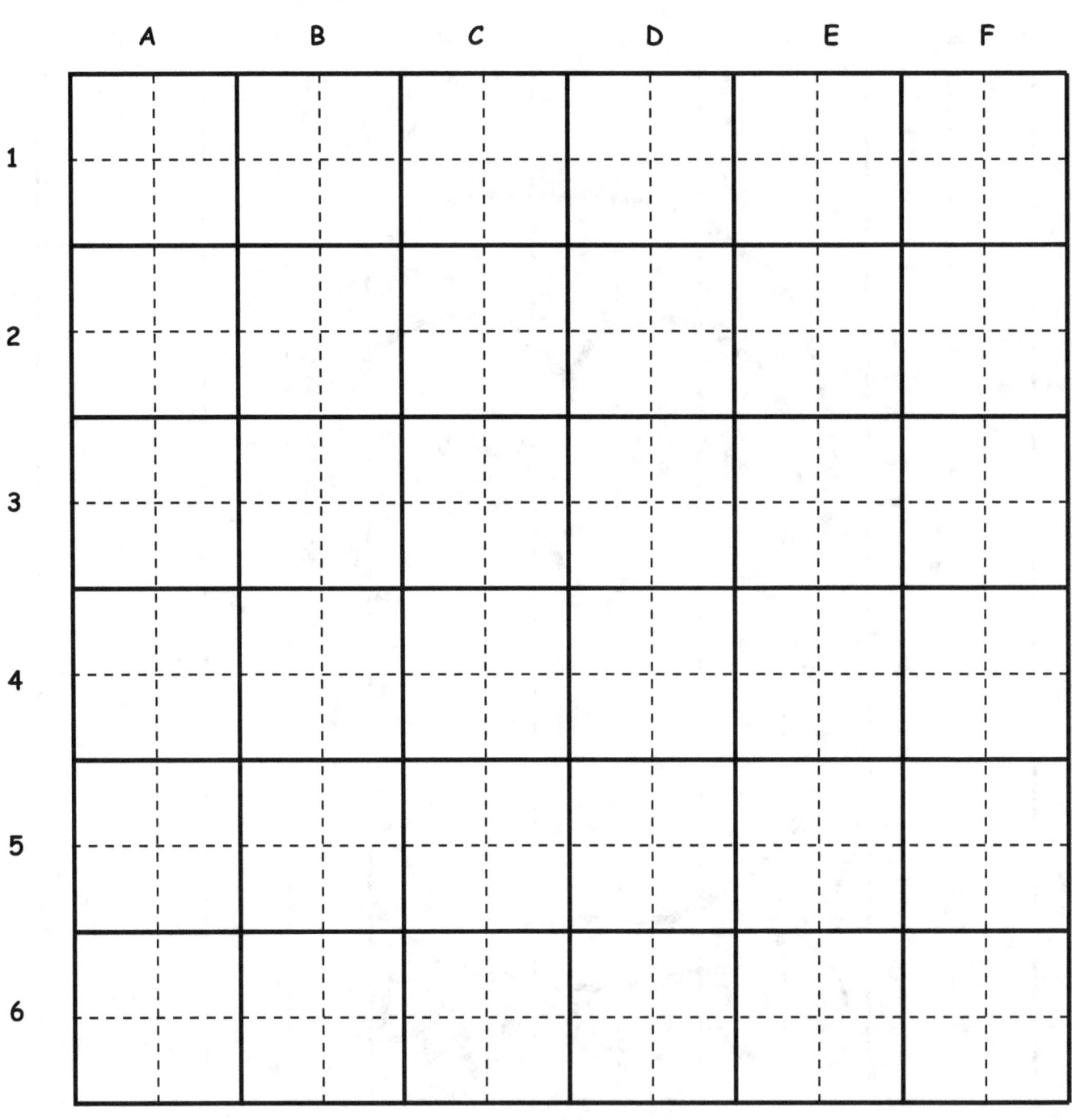

Your penguin is ready to color now!

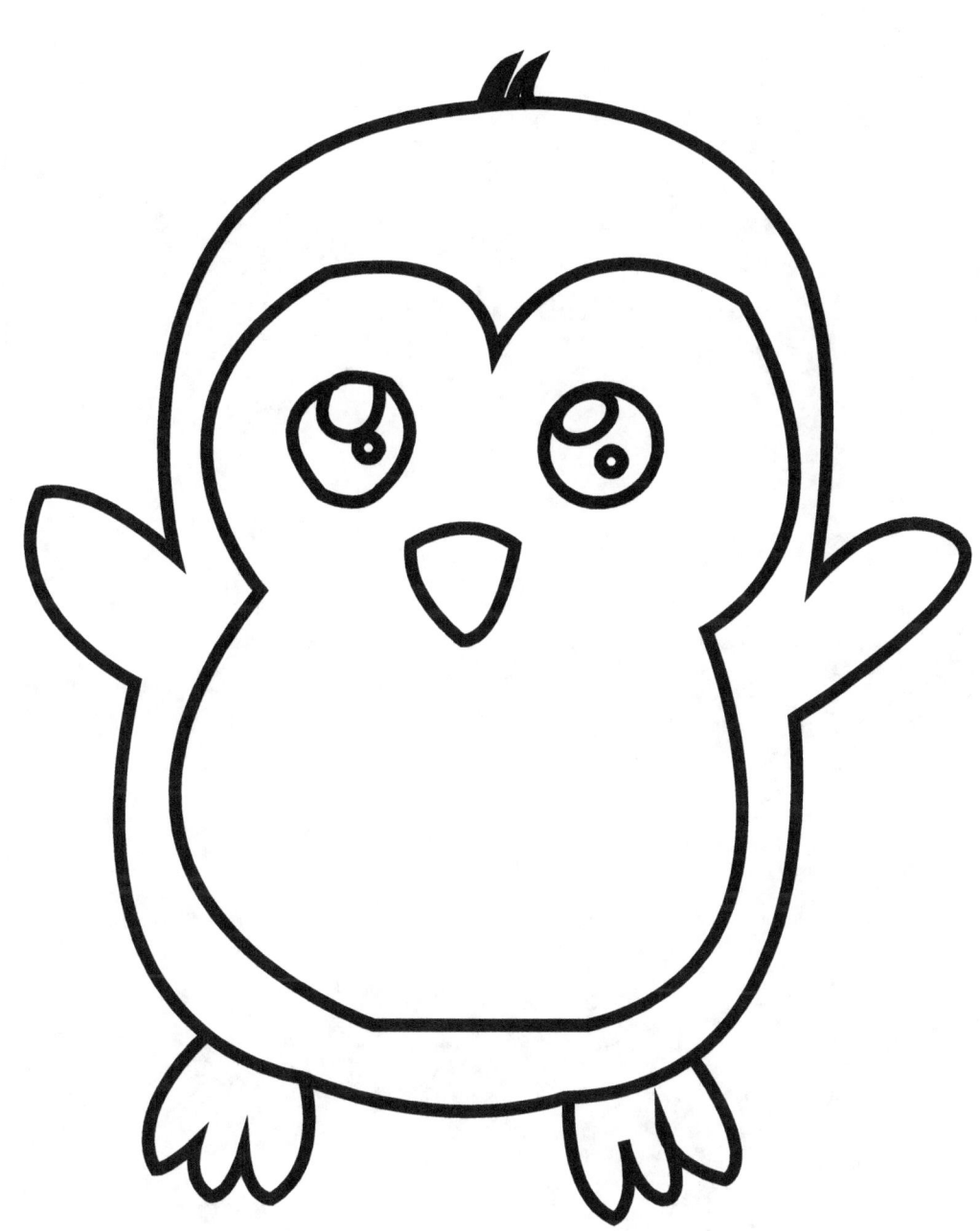

Practice Here Blind

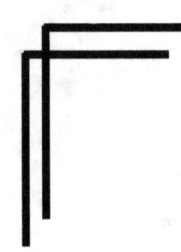

Video Tutorials

By
Global Baby Care

https://globalbabycare.com/
how-to-draw-penguin-for-kids-
book-review

Penguin Art With Grid For Easy Way To Art

Penguin 6

1 Start by drawing the head with hairs shape as shown

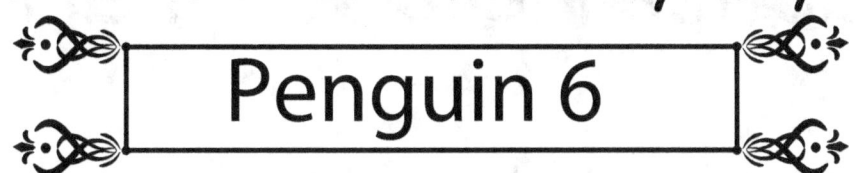

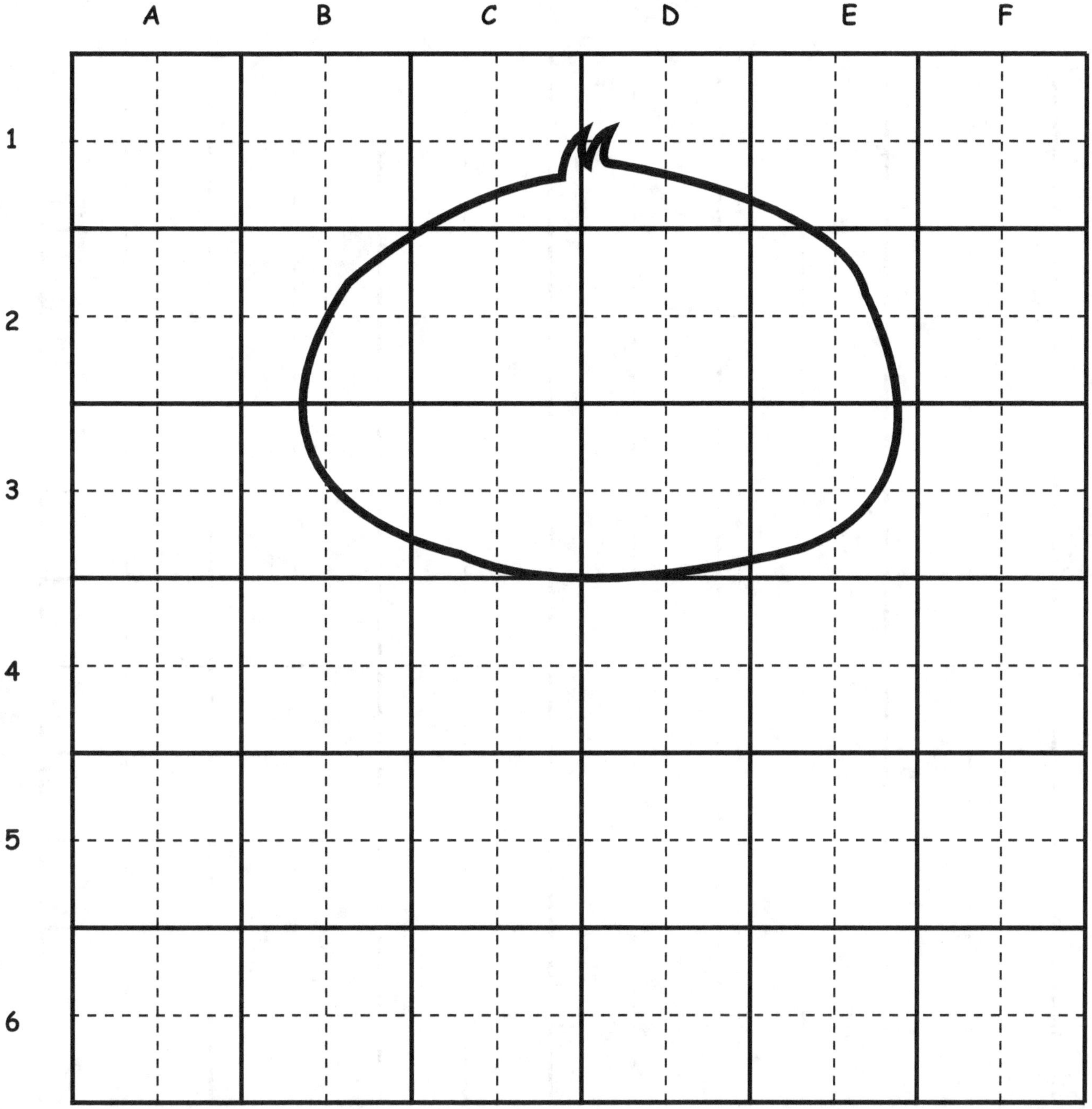

Practice Here With Gride

Start by drawing the head with hairs shape as shown

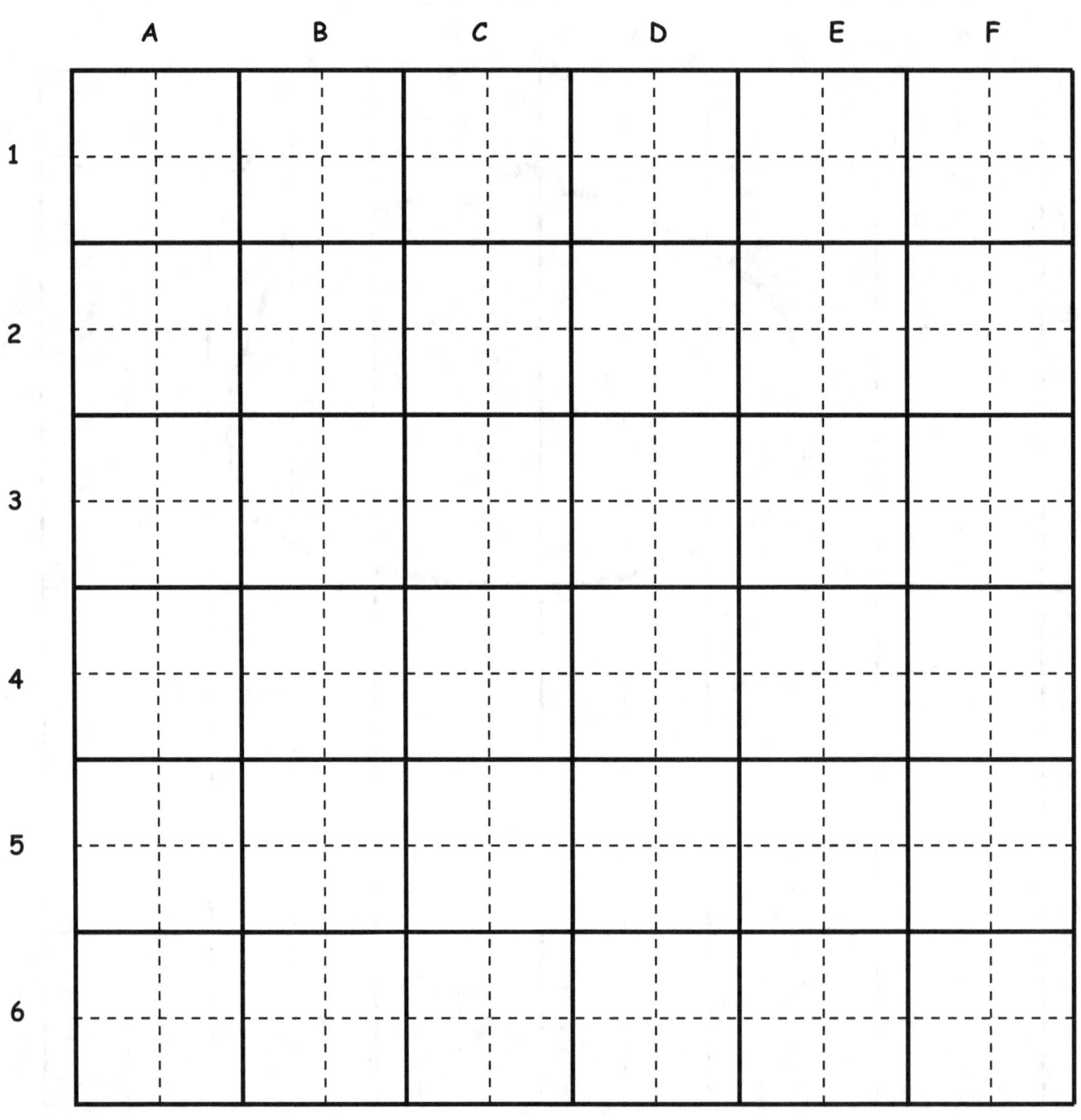

Penguin Art With Grid For Easy Way To Art

 Add body shape circle and an inner line in the head as shown.

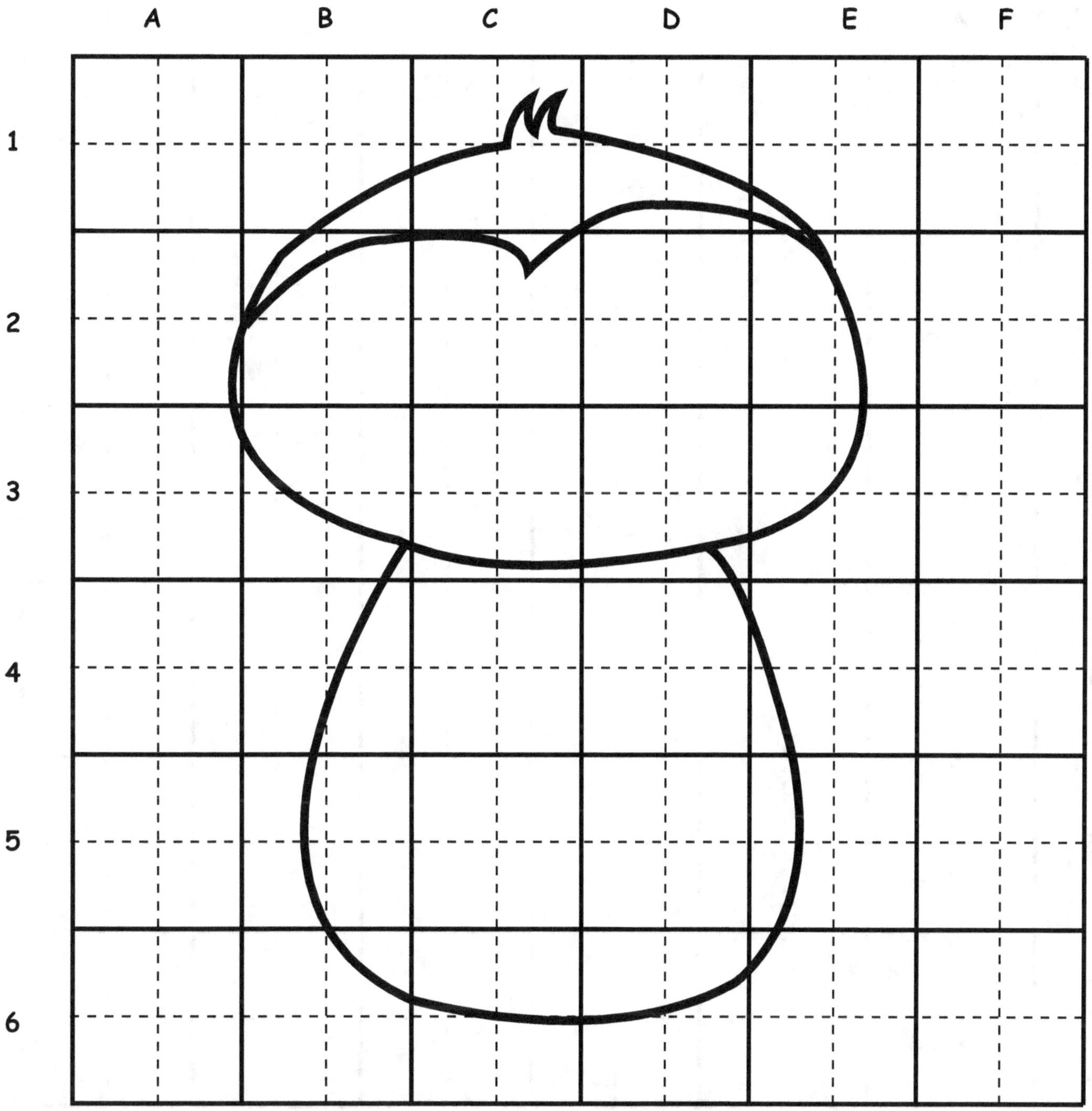

A   B   C   D   E   F

1

2

3

4

5

6

Practice Here With Gride

Add body shape circle and an inner line in the head as shown.

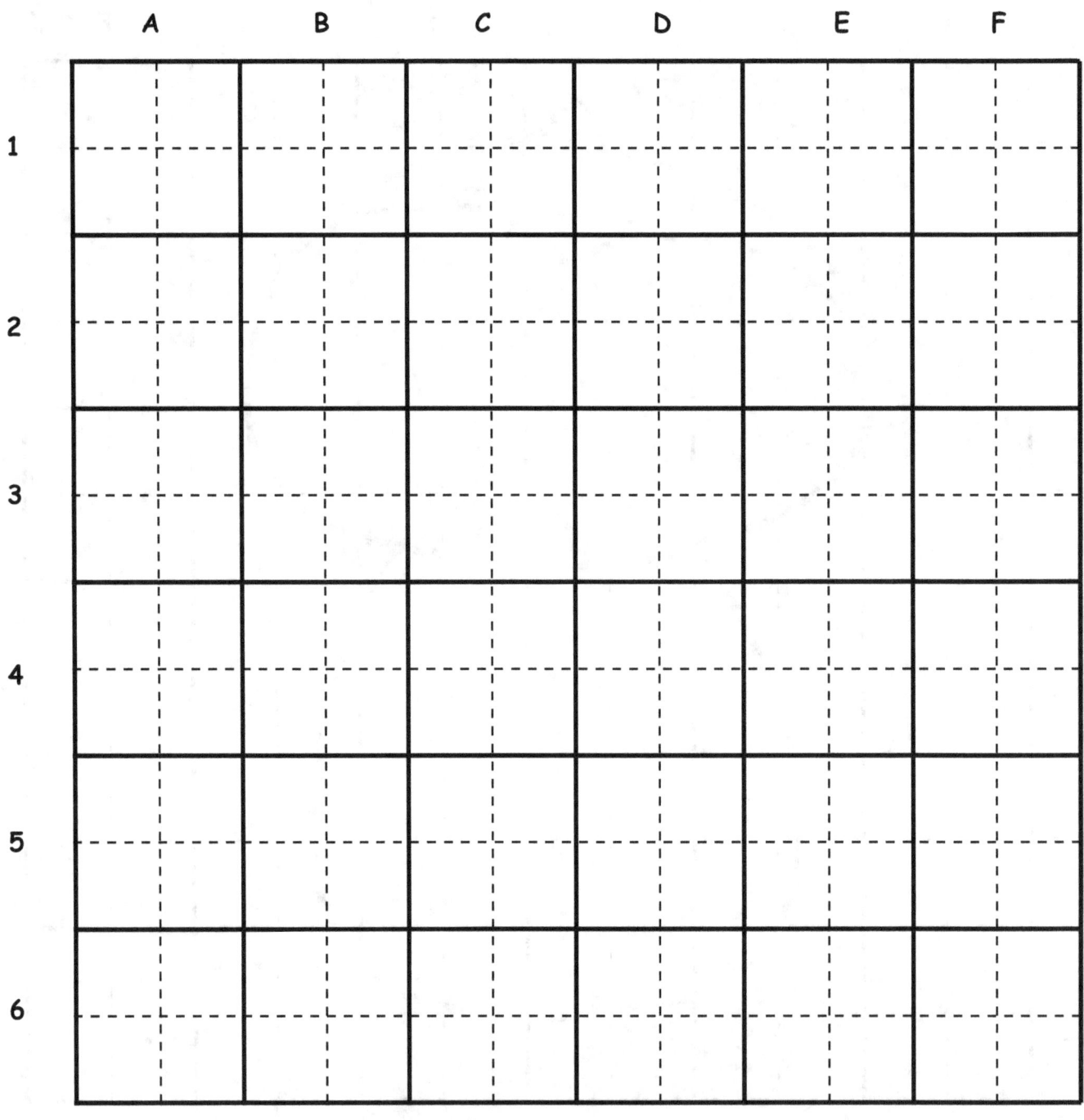

Penguin Art With Grid For Easy Way To Art

3 Draw lines of the Penguin's feather.

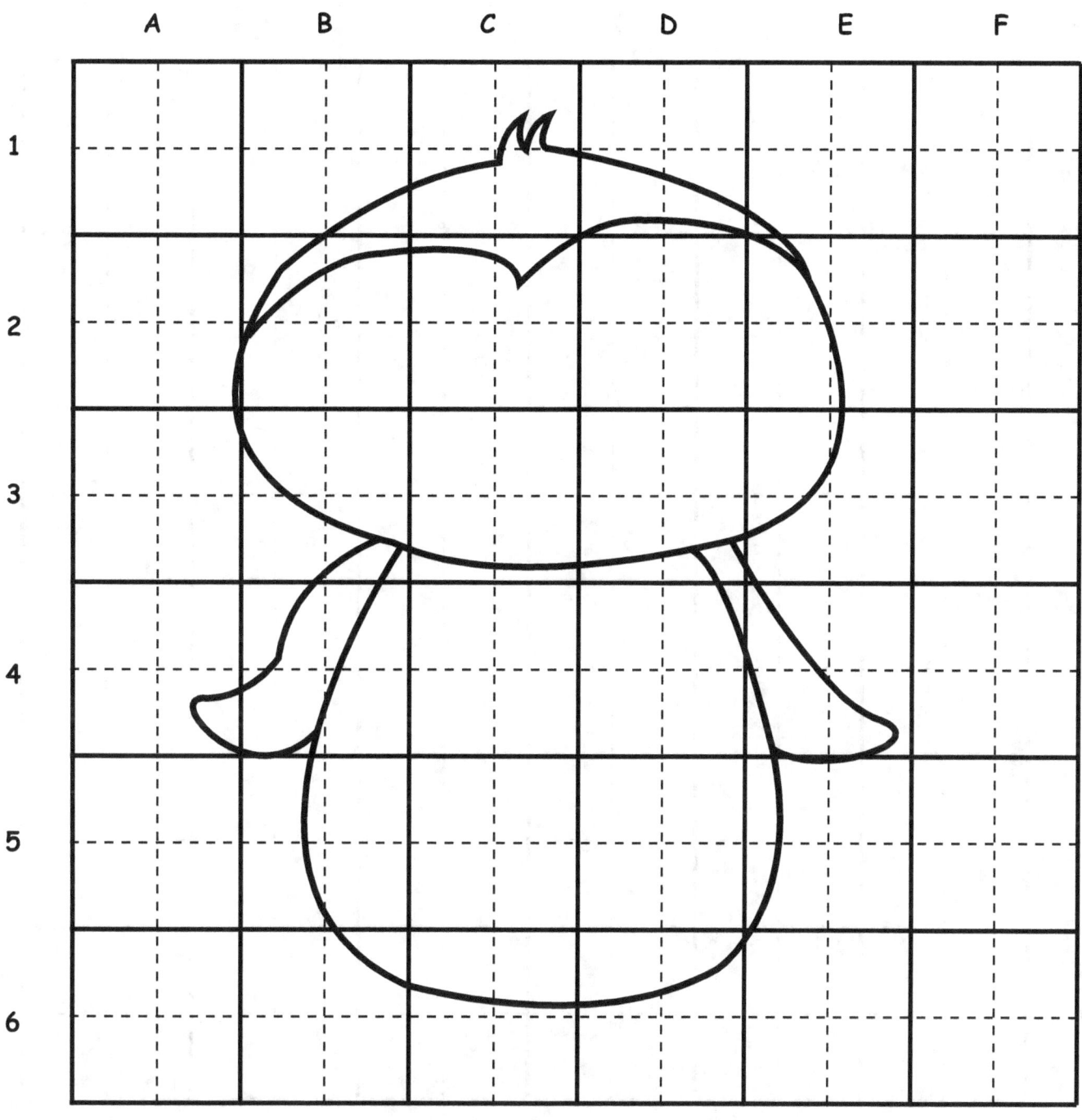

Practice Here With Gride

Draw lines of the Penguin's feather.

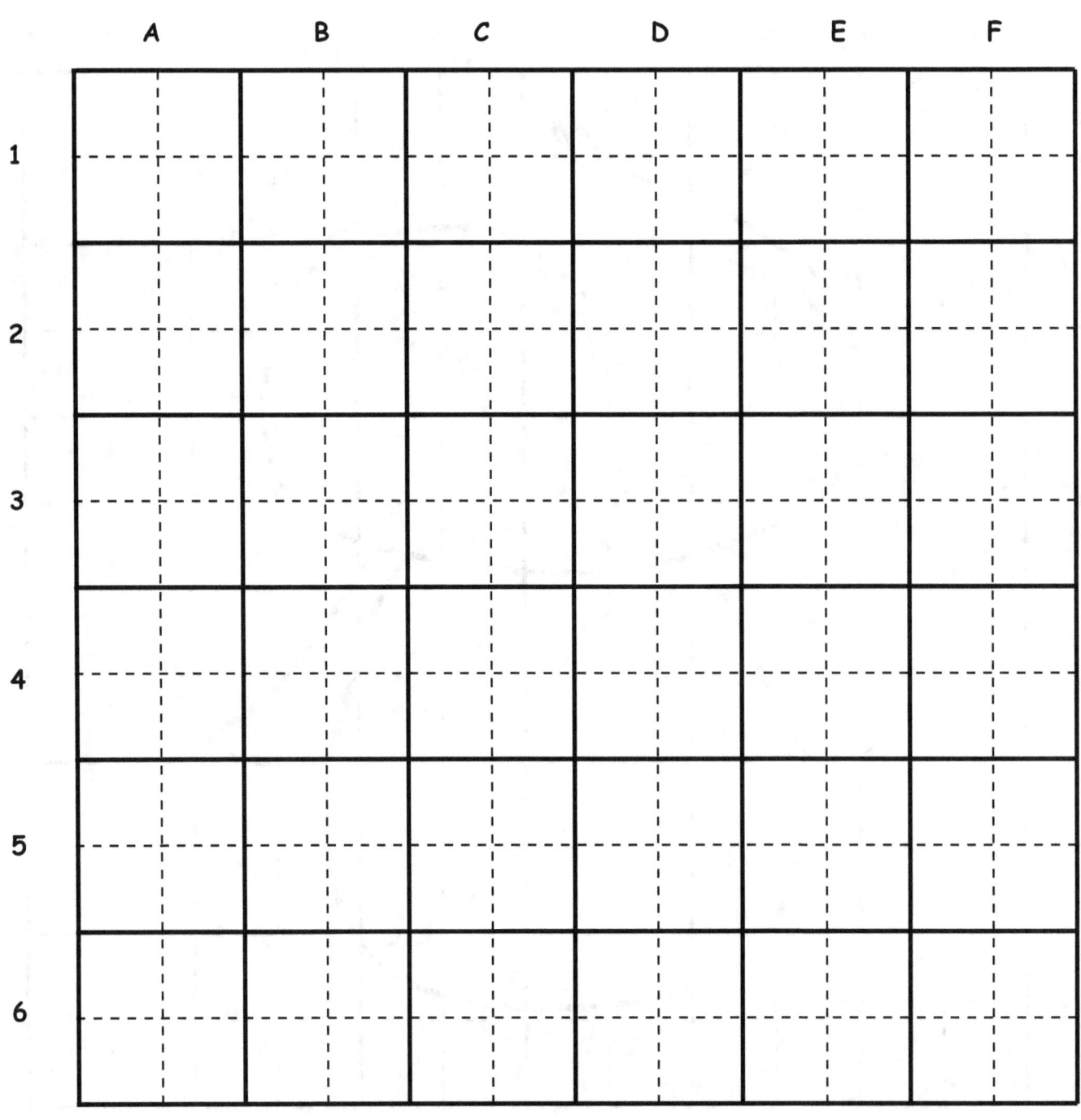

Penguin Art With Grid For Easy Way To Art

 Draw lines of the Penguin's feet and eyes with details.

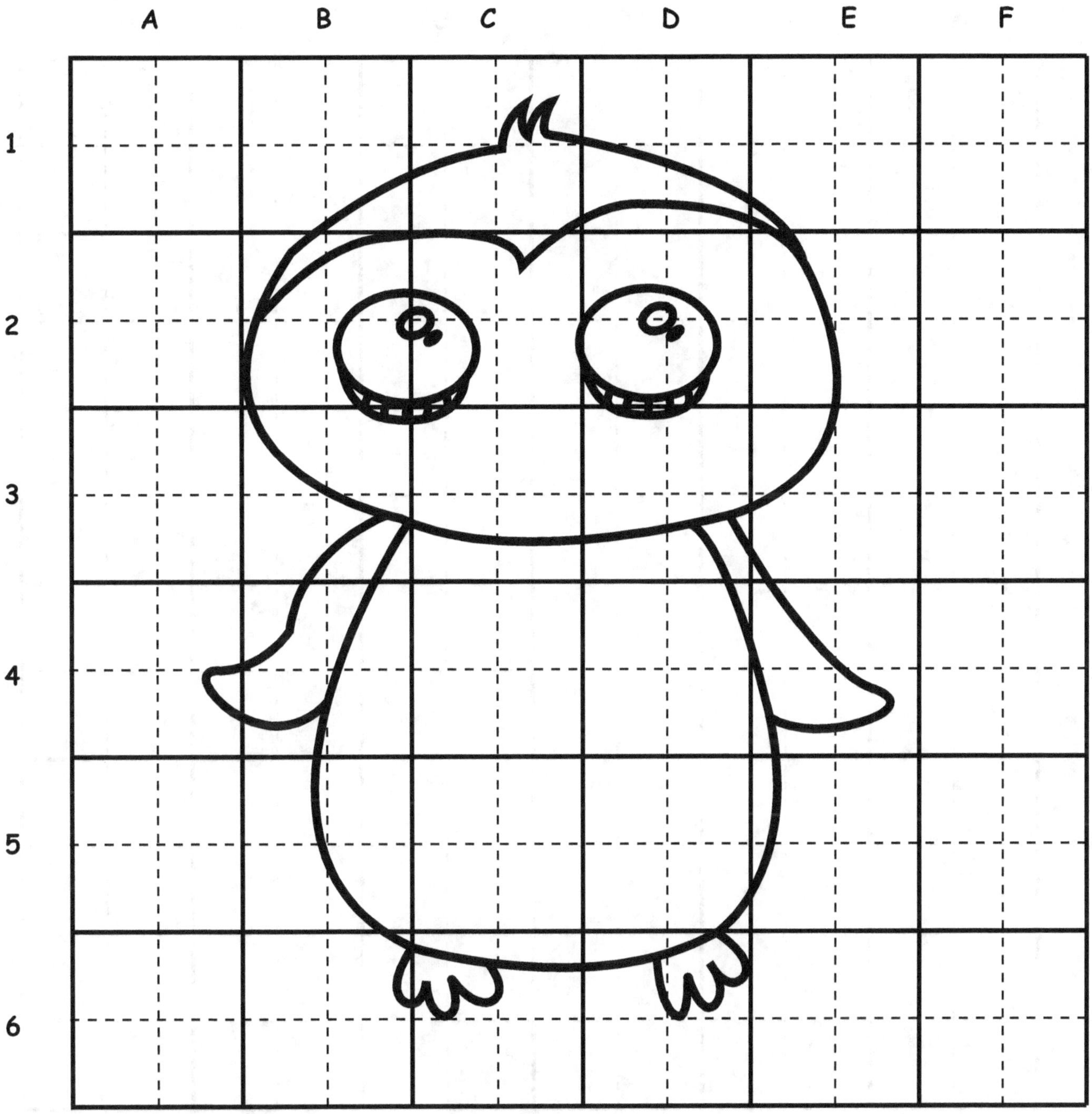

Practice Here With Gride

Draw lines of the Penguin's feet and eyes with details.

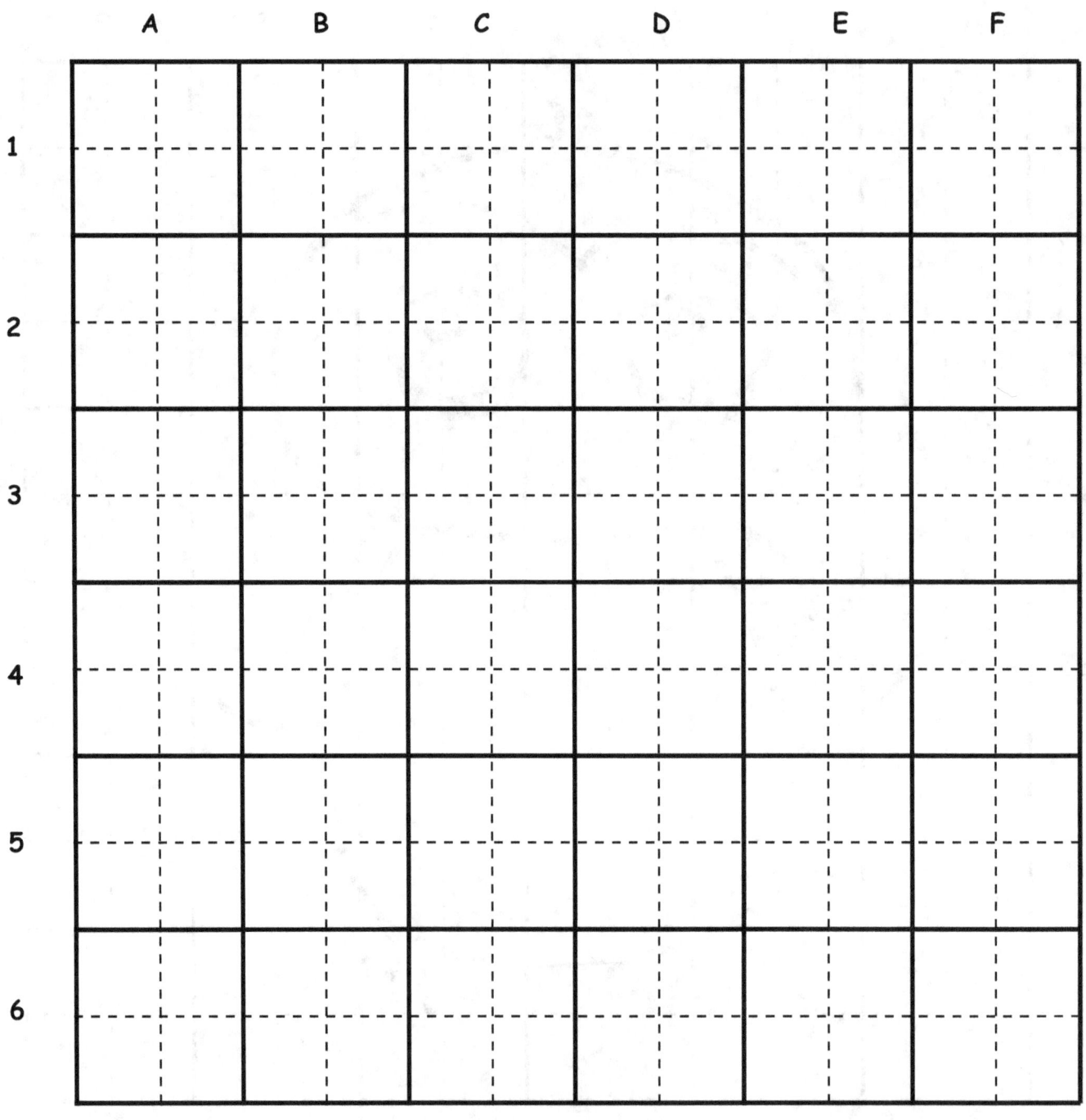

Penguin Art With Grid For Easy Way To Art

5 Draw lines of the Penguin's beak and an inner line in the body and a dot as naval point as shown.

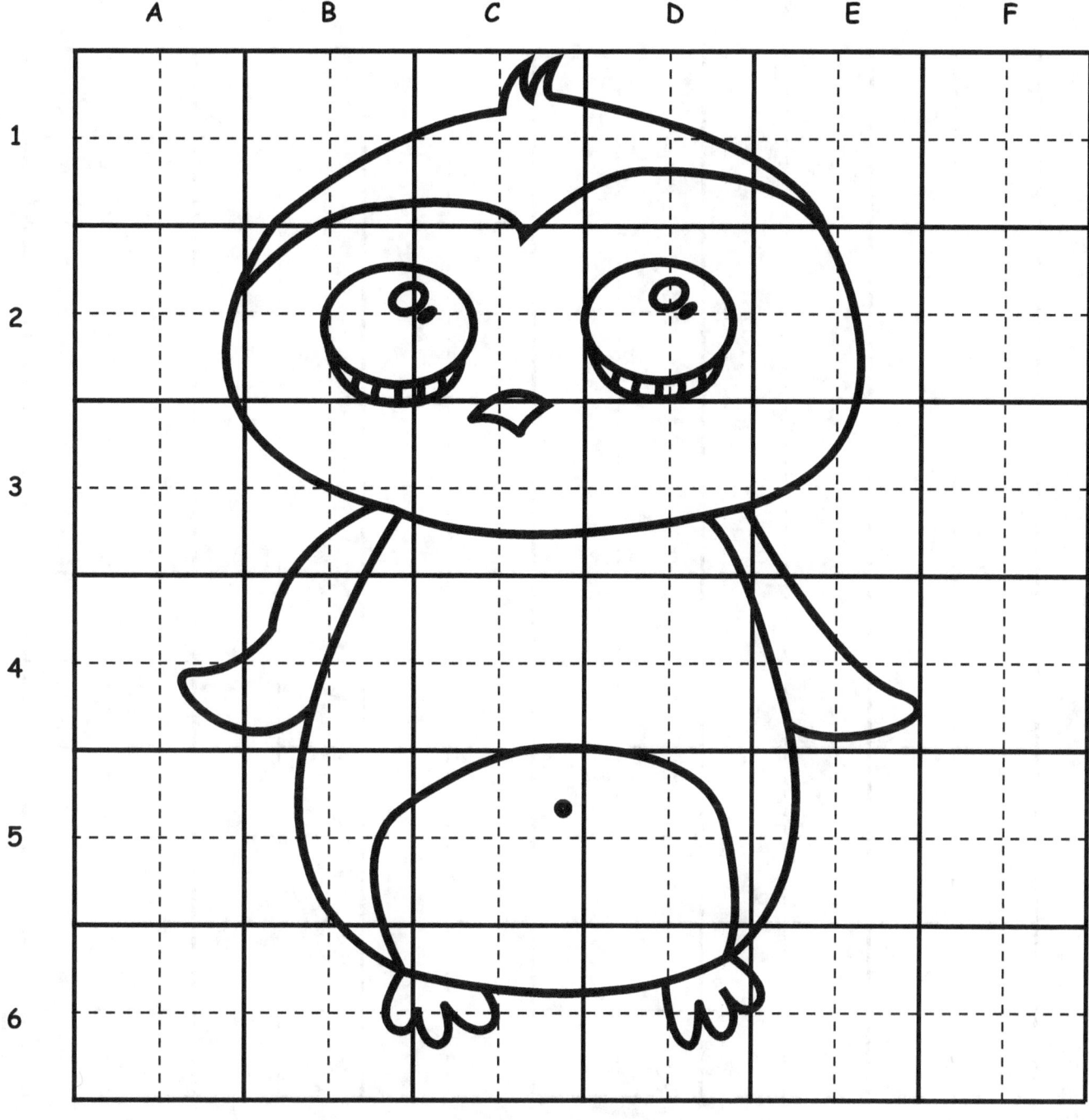

Practice Here With Gride

Draw lines of the Penguin's beak and an inner line in the body and a dot as naval point as shown.

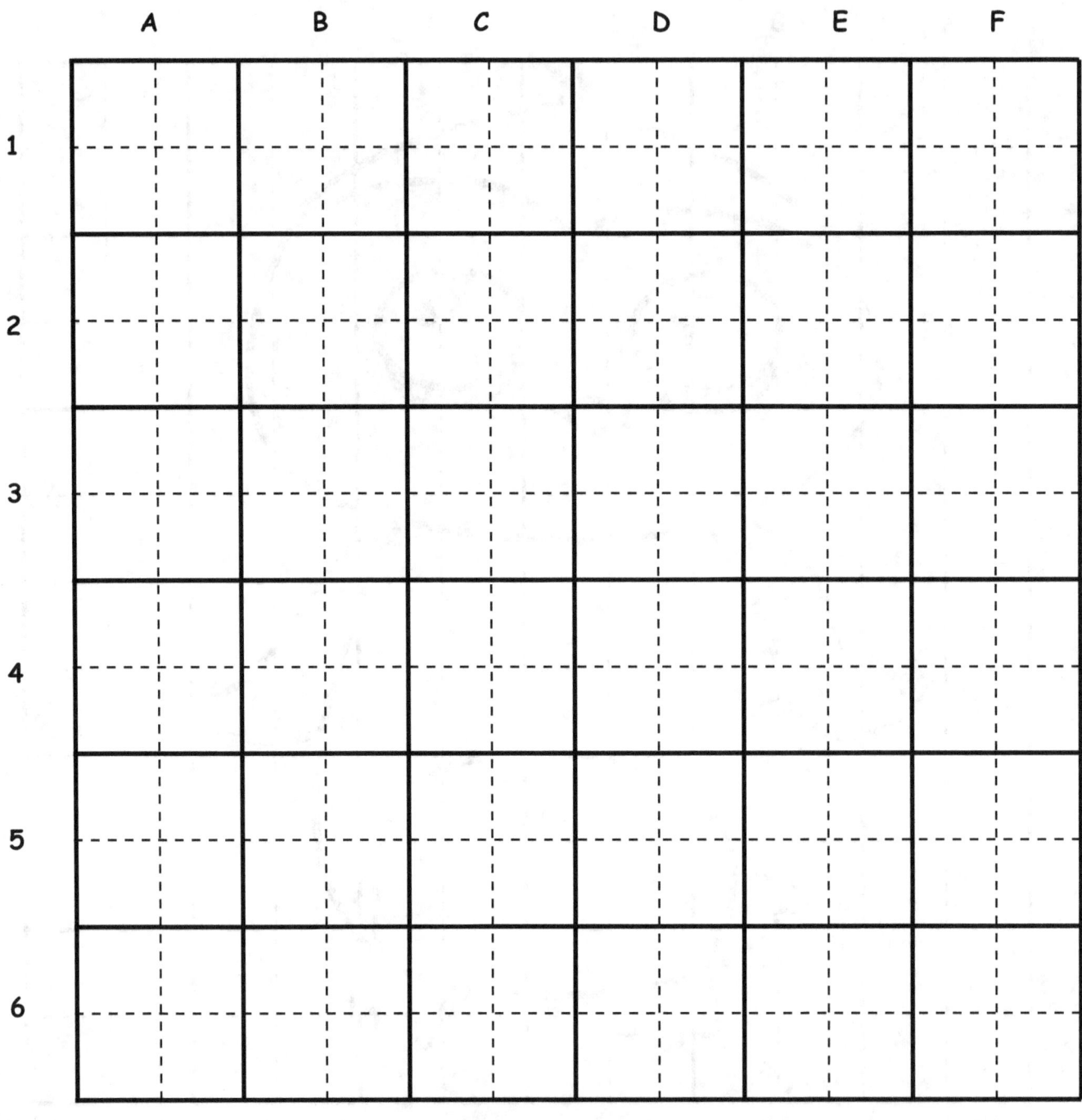

Your penguin is Done!

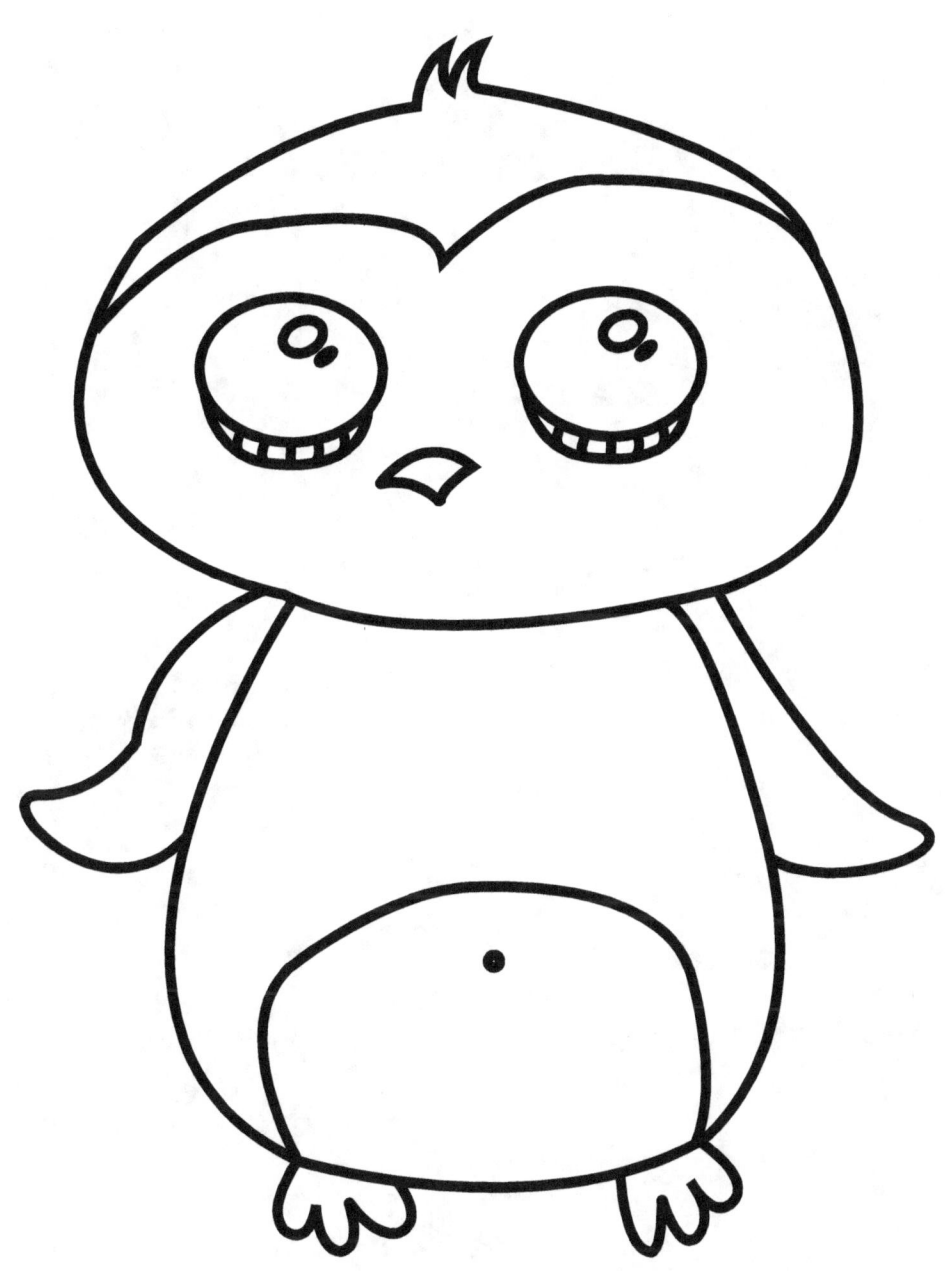

Practice Here Blind

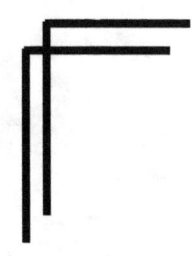

Penguin Art With Grid For Easy Way To Art

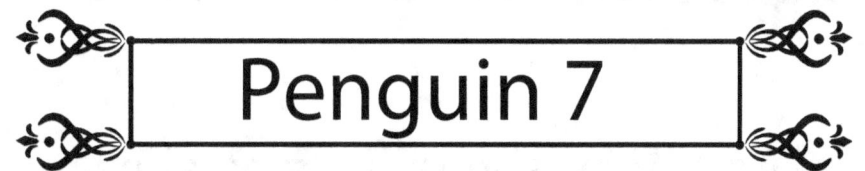

Penguin 7

1 Add body shape lines as shown.

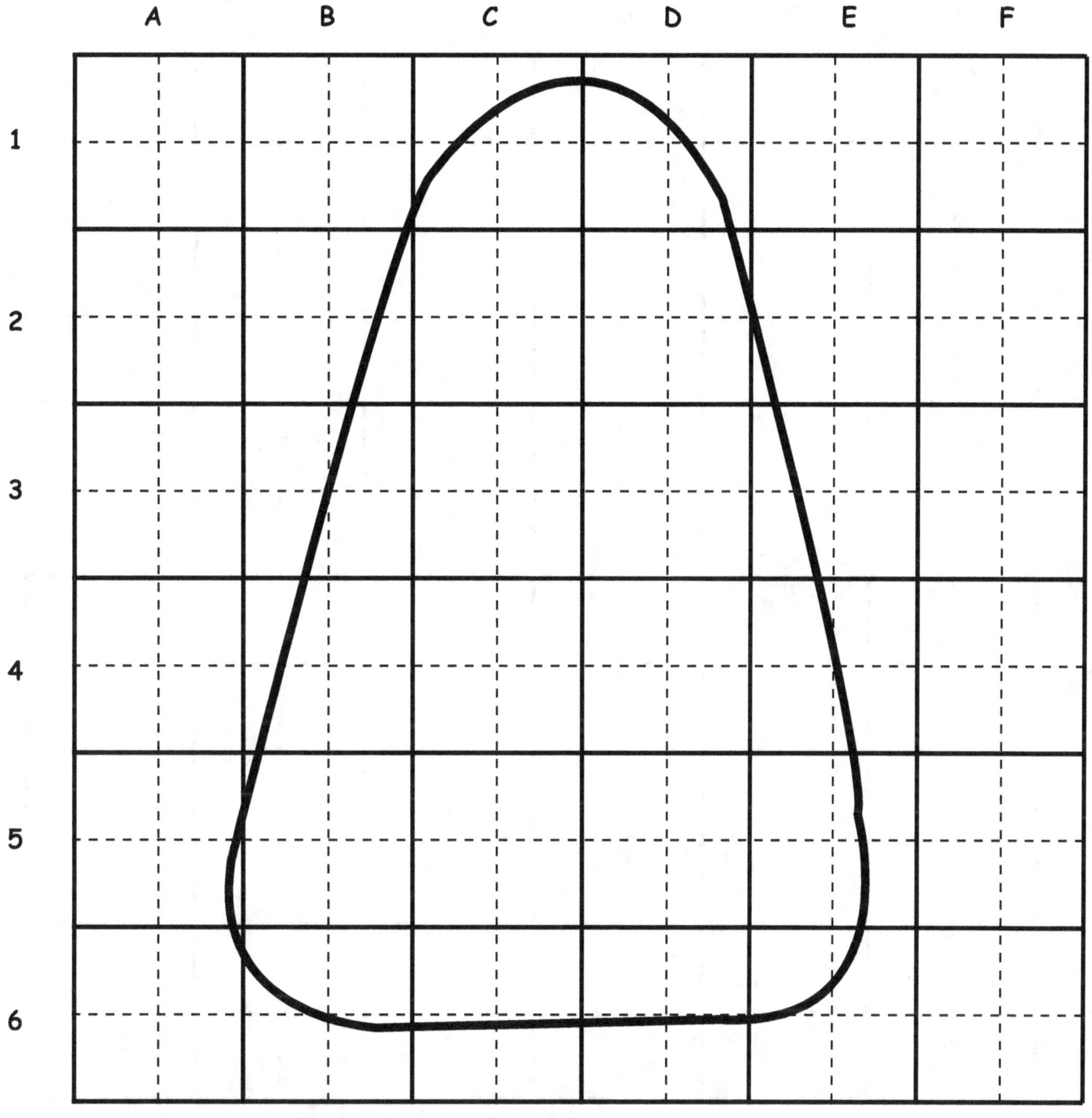

Practice Here With Gride

Add body shape lines as shown.

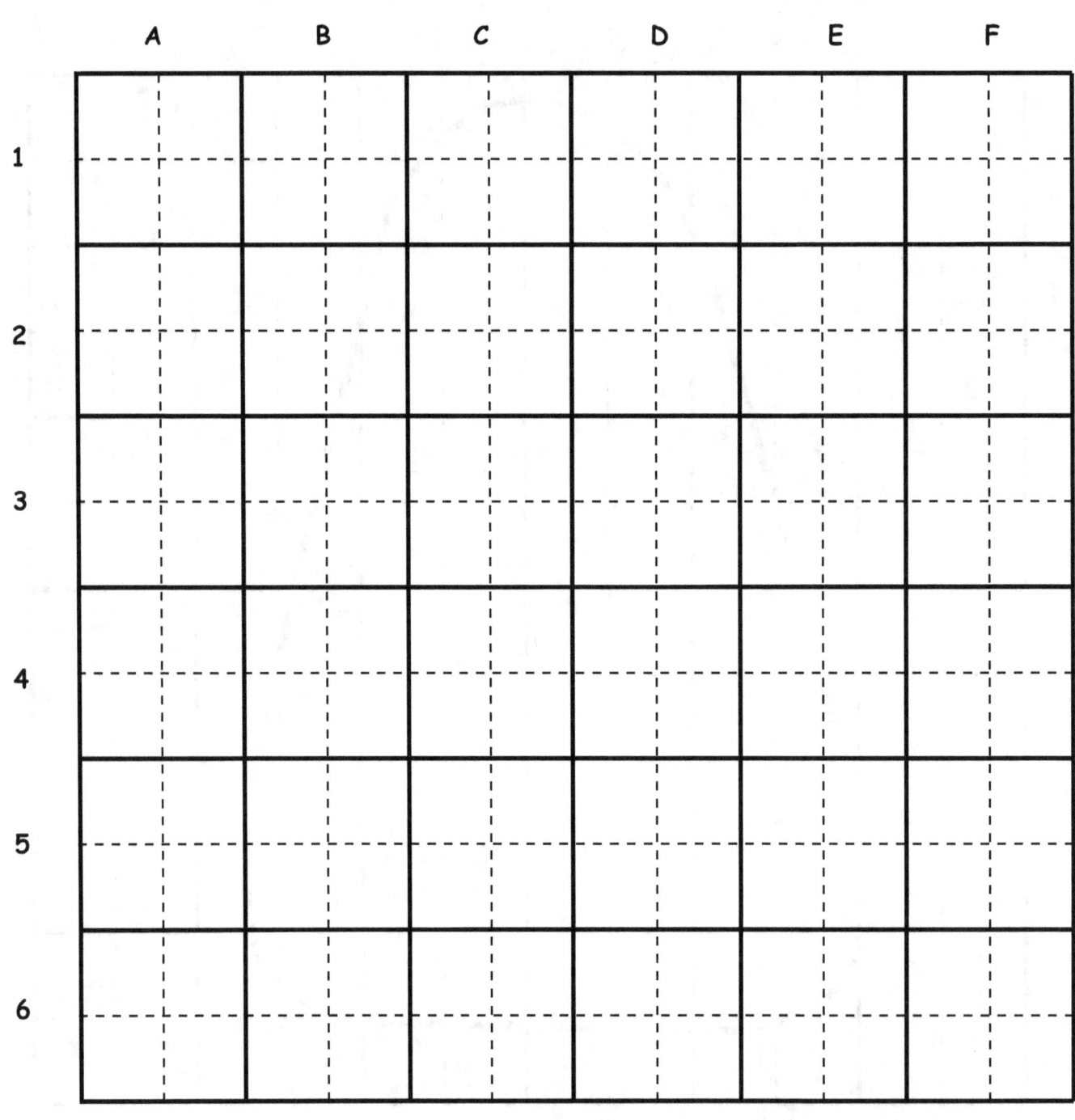

Penguin Art With Grid For Easy Way To Art

2 Draw lines of the Penguin's face details and feathers.

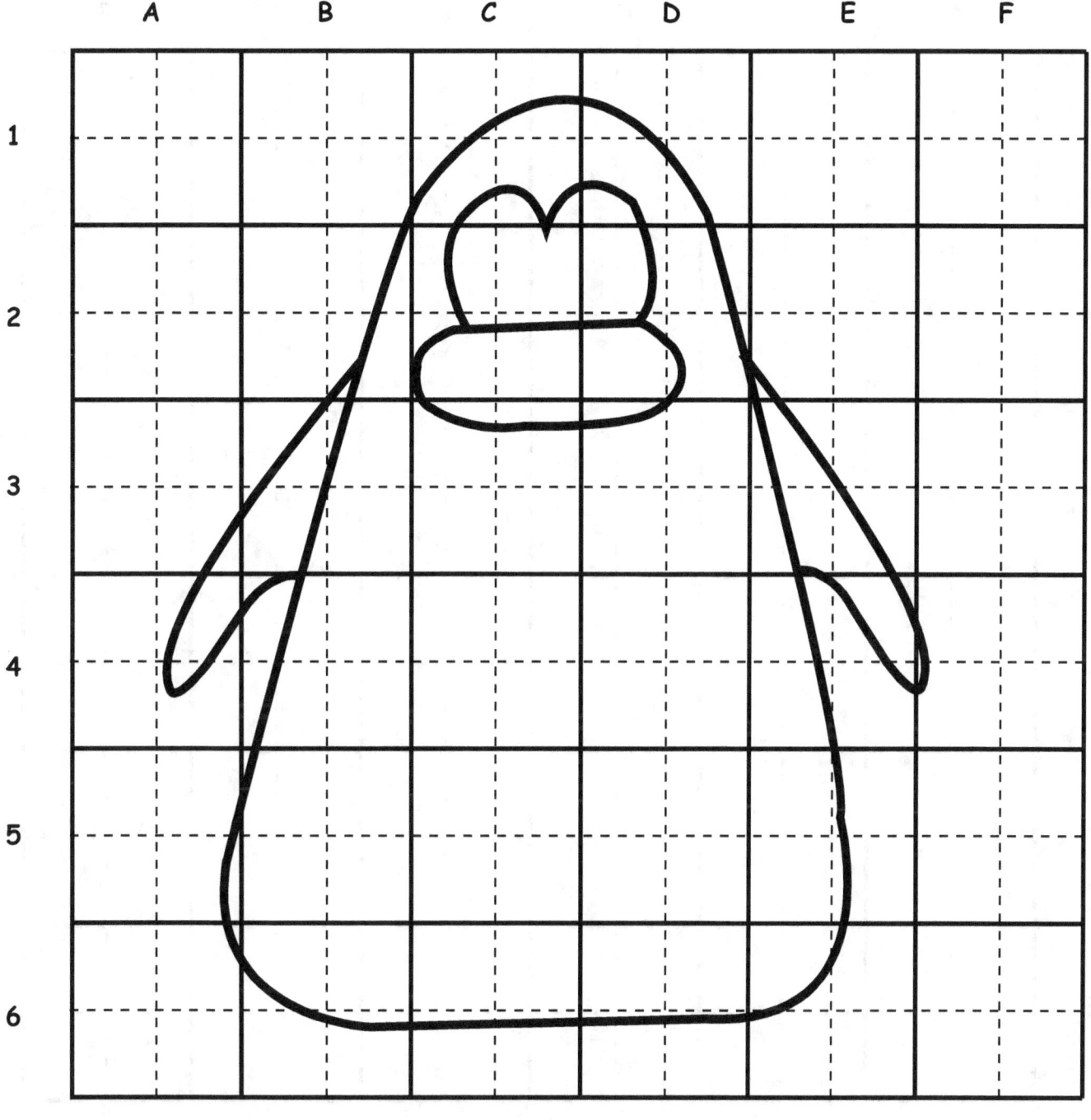

Practice Here With Gride

Draw lines of the Penguin's face details and feathers.

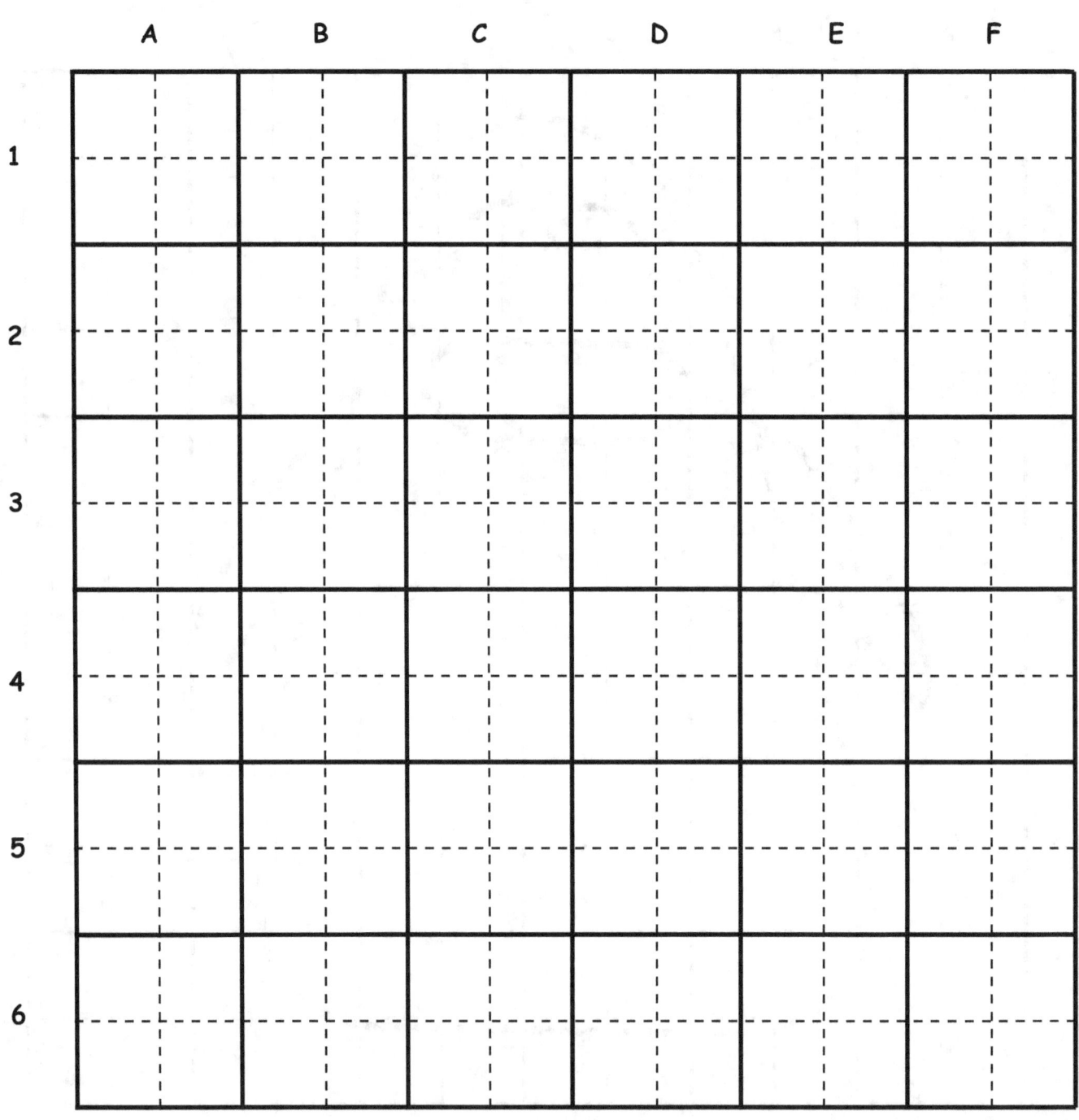

Penguin Art With Grid For Easy Way To Art

3 Add another body shape inner as shown.

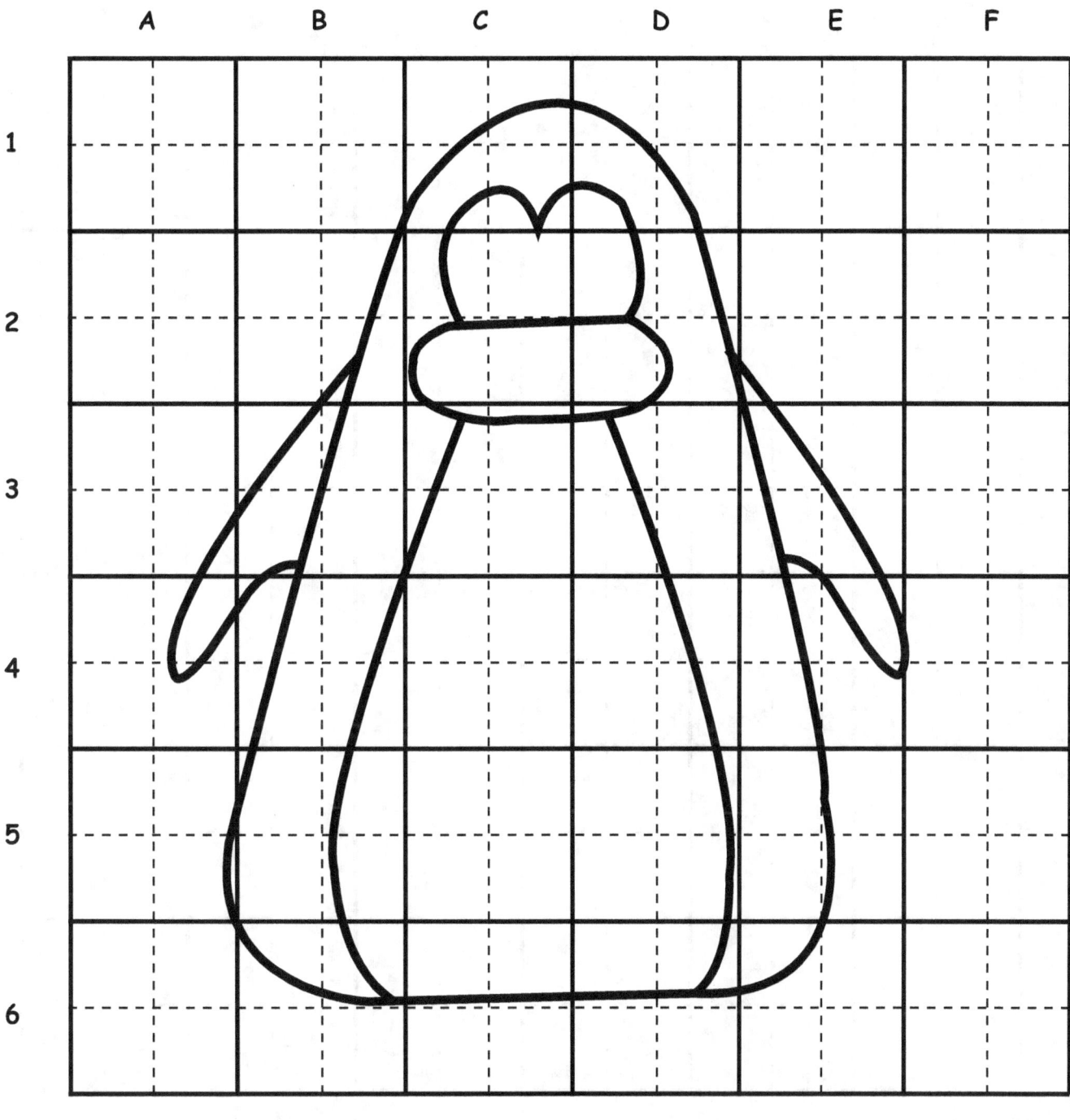

Practice Here With Gride

Add another body shape inner as shown.

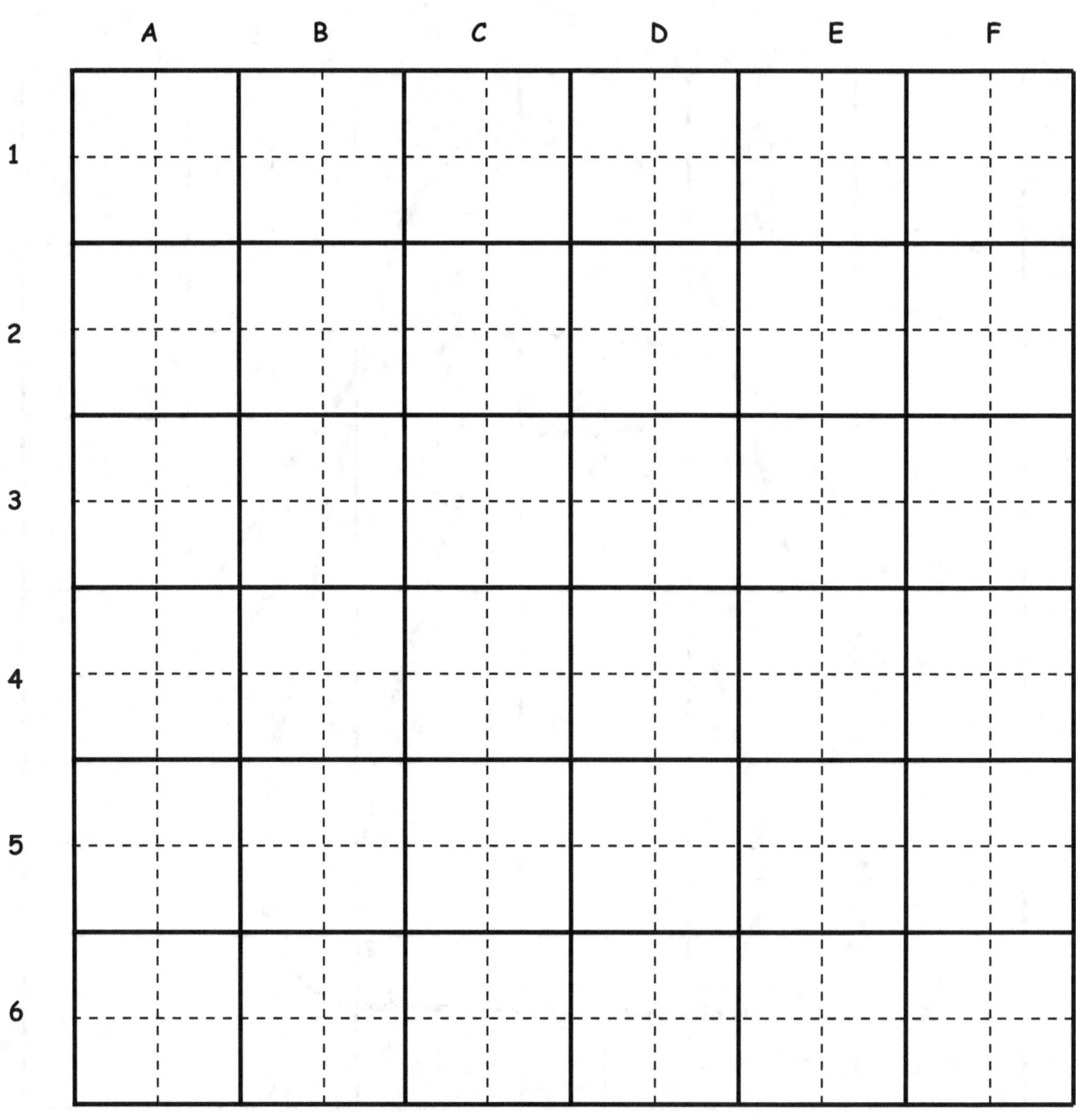

Penguin Art With Grid For Easy Way To Art

4 Draw lines of the Penguin's eyes and a smiling lip.

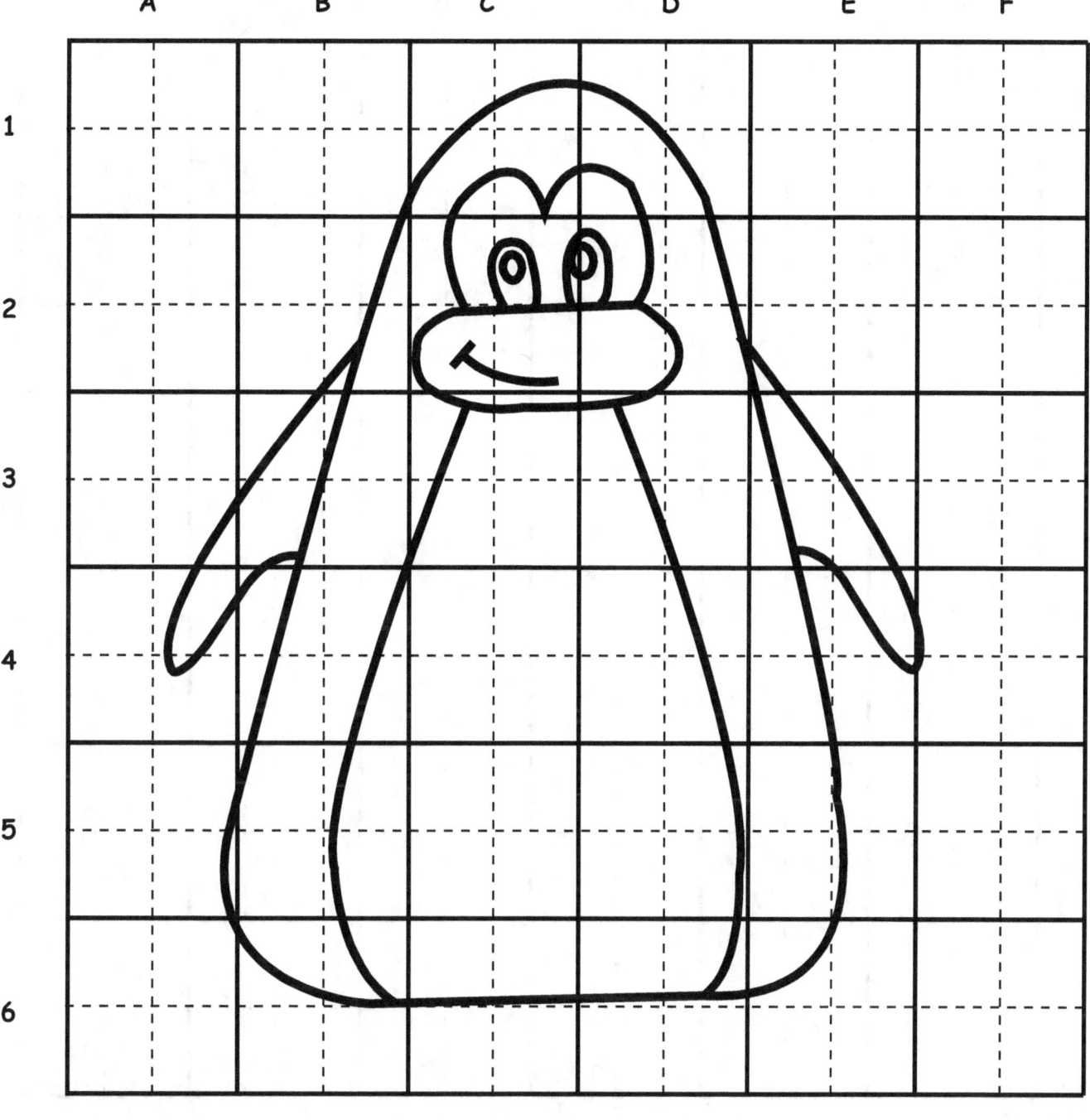

Practice Here With Gride

Draw lines of the Penguin's eyes and a smiling lip.

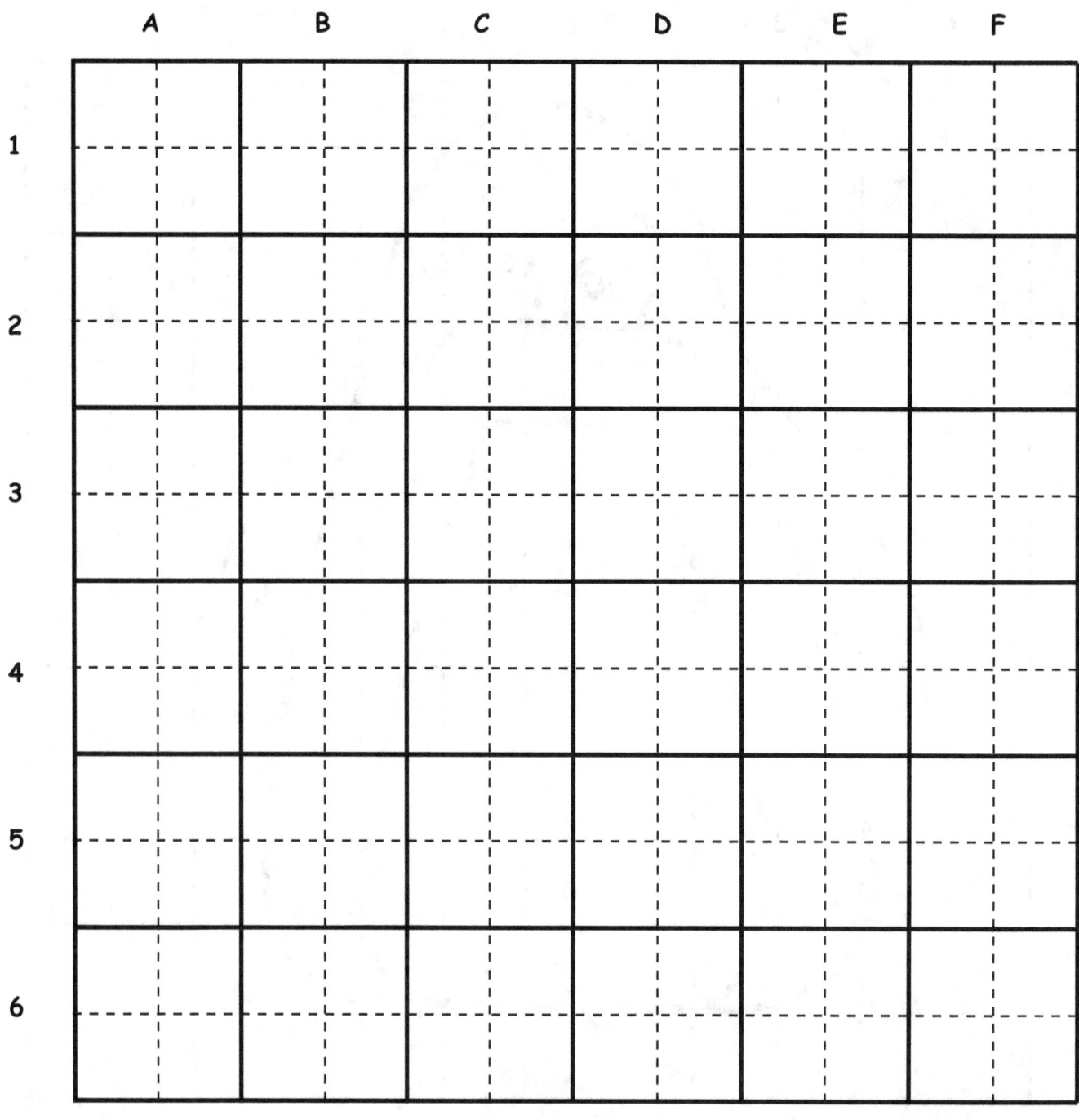

Penguin Art With Grid For Easy Way To Art

5 Draw lines of the Penguin's feet and erase all extra and unnecessary lines.

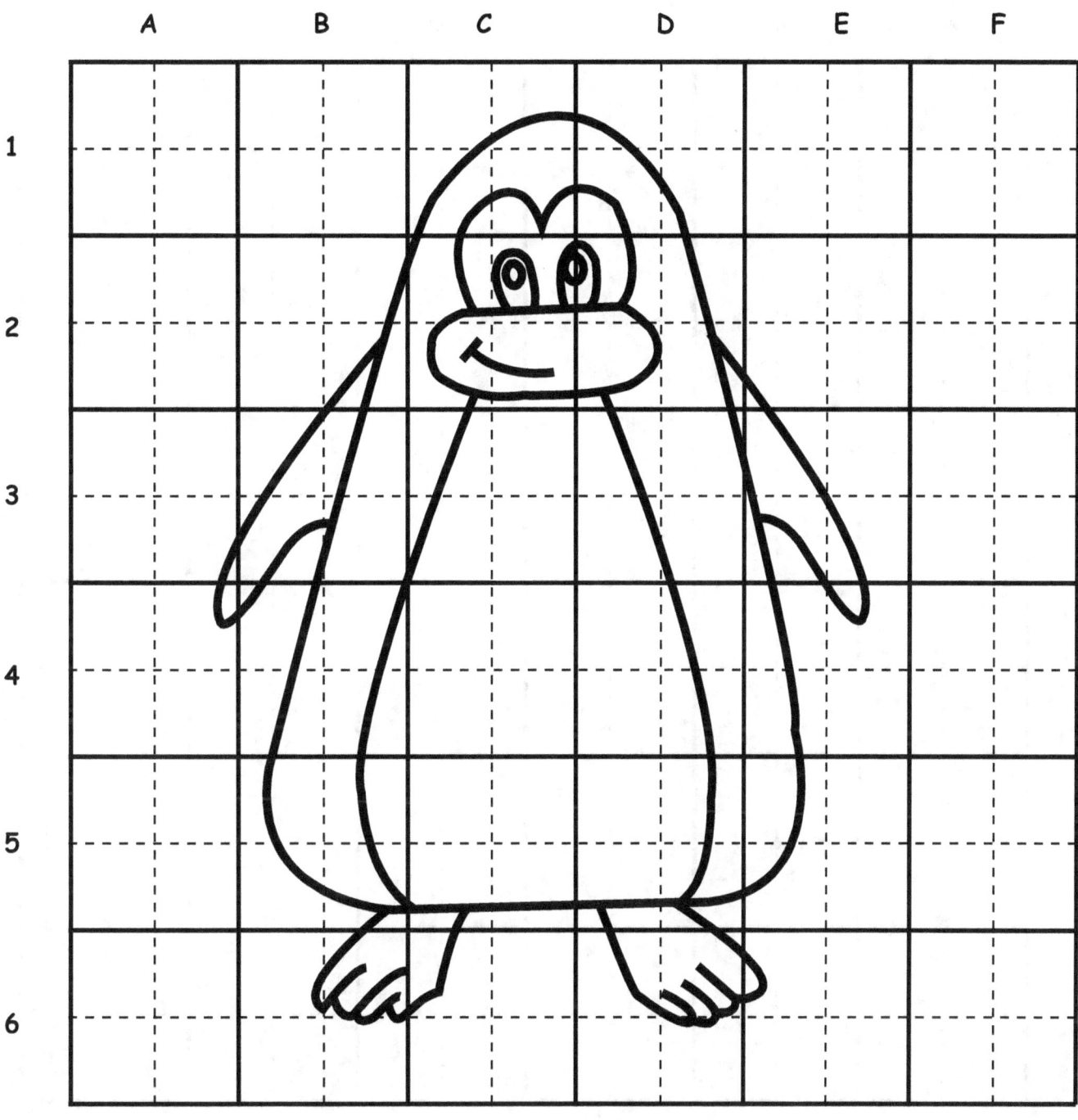

Practice Here With Gride

Draw lines of the Penguin's feet and erase all extra and unnecessary lines.

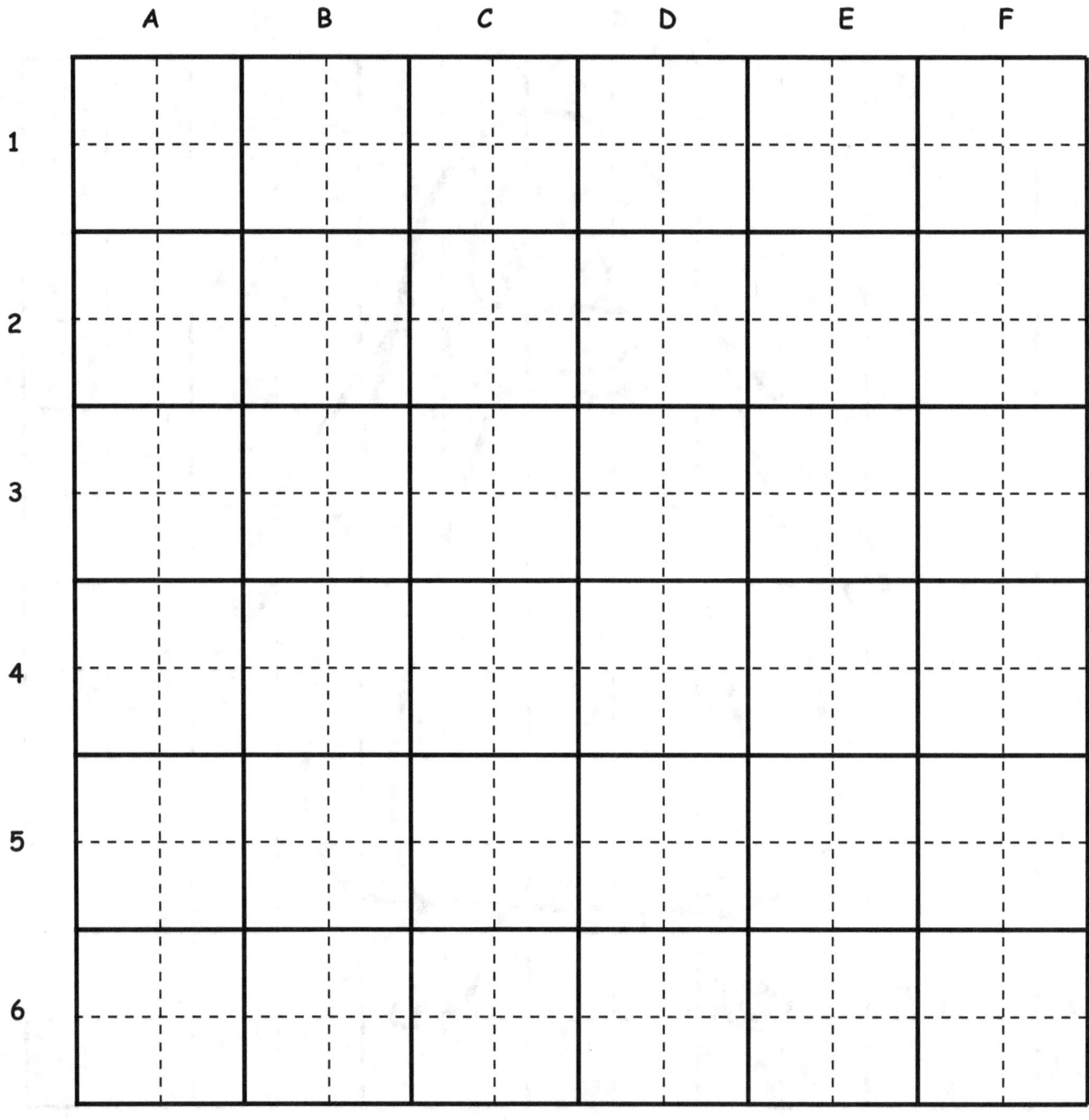

Your penguin drawing is finished!

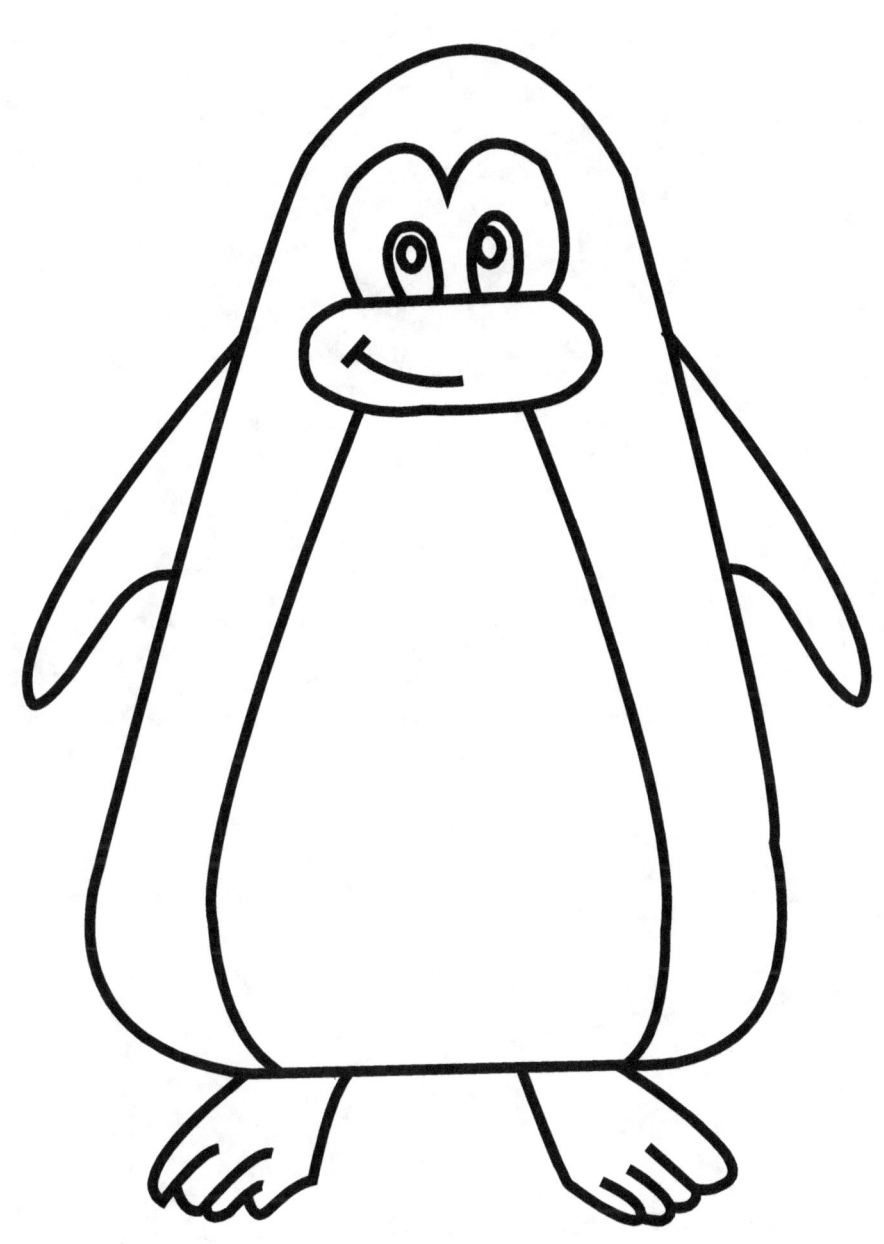

Practice Here Blind

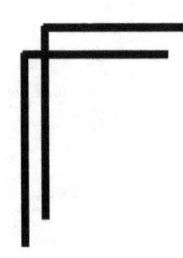

Penguin Art With Grid For Easy Way To Art

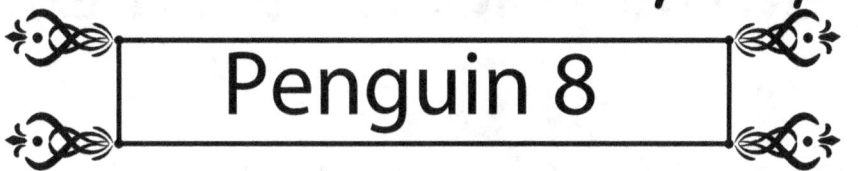

Penguin 8

1 Draw lines of the Penguin's Body shape and Beak.

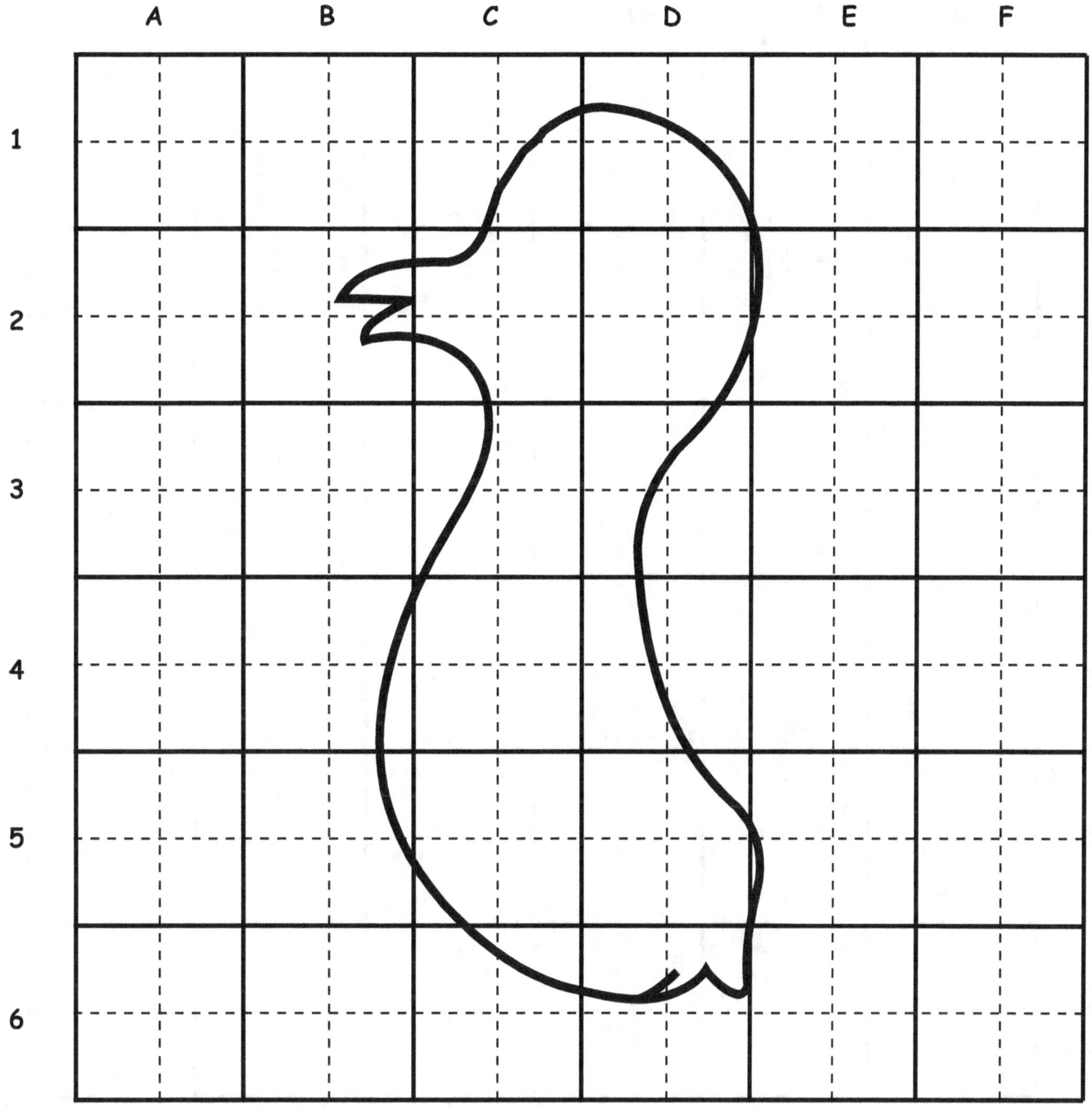

A   B   C   D   E   F

1

2

3

4

5

6

Practice Here With Gride

Draw lines of the Penguin's Body shape and Beak.

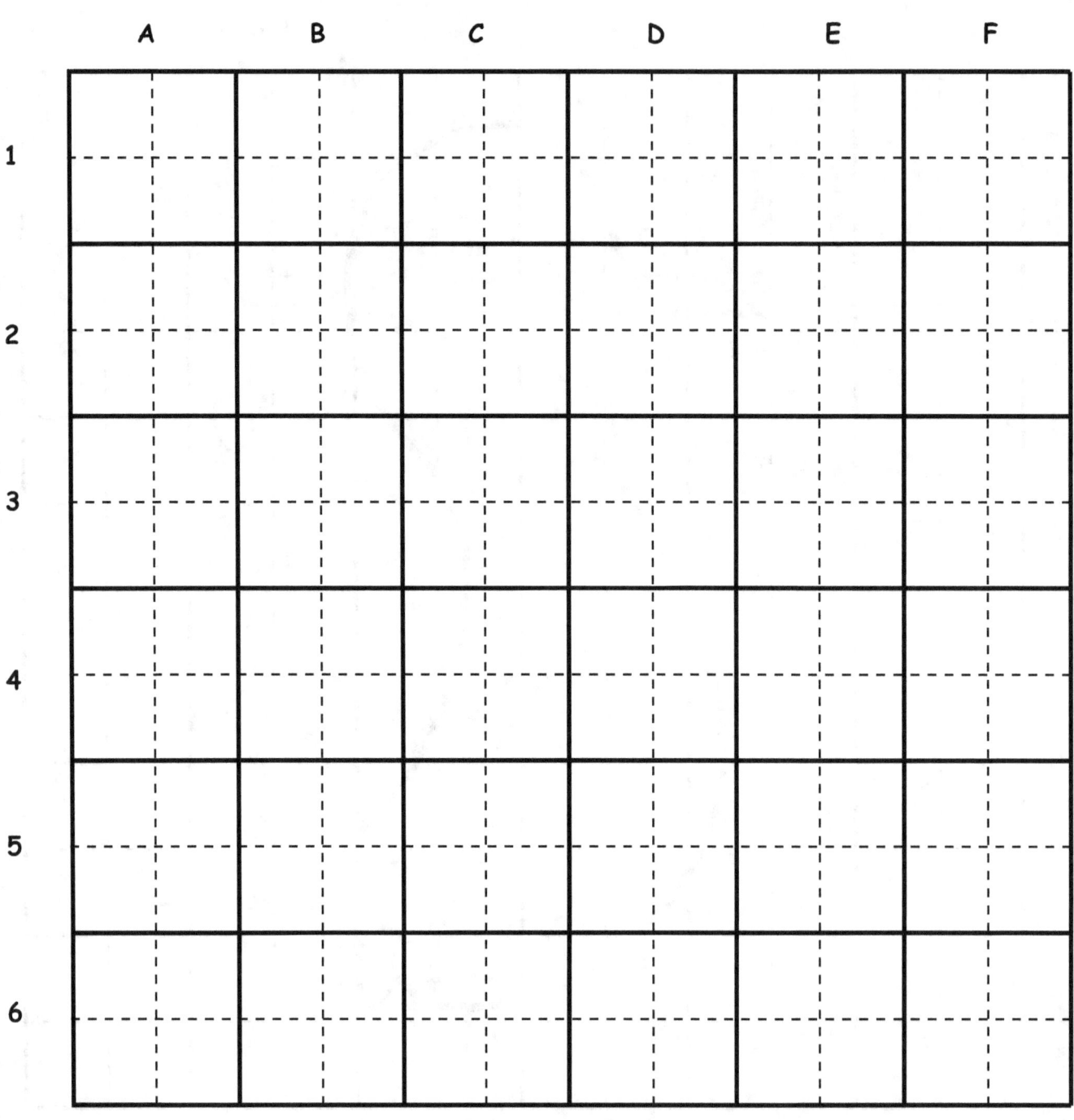

Penguin Art With Grid For Easy Way To Art

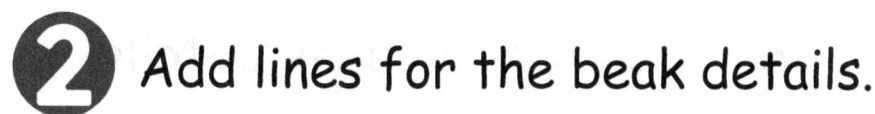 Add lines for the beak details.

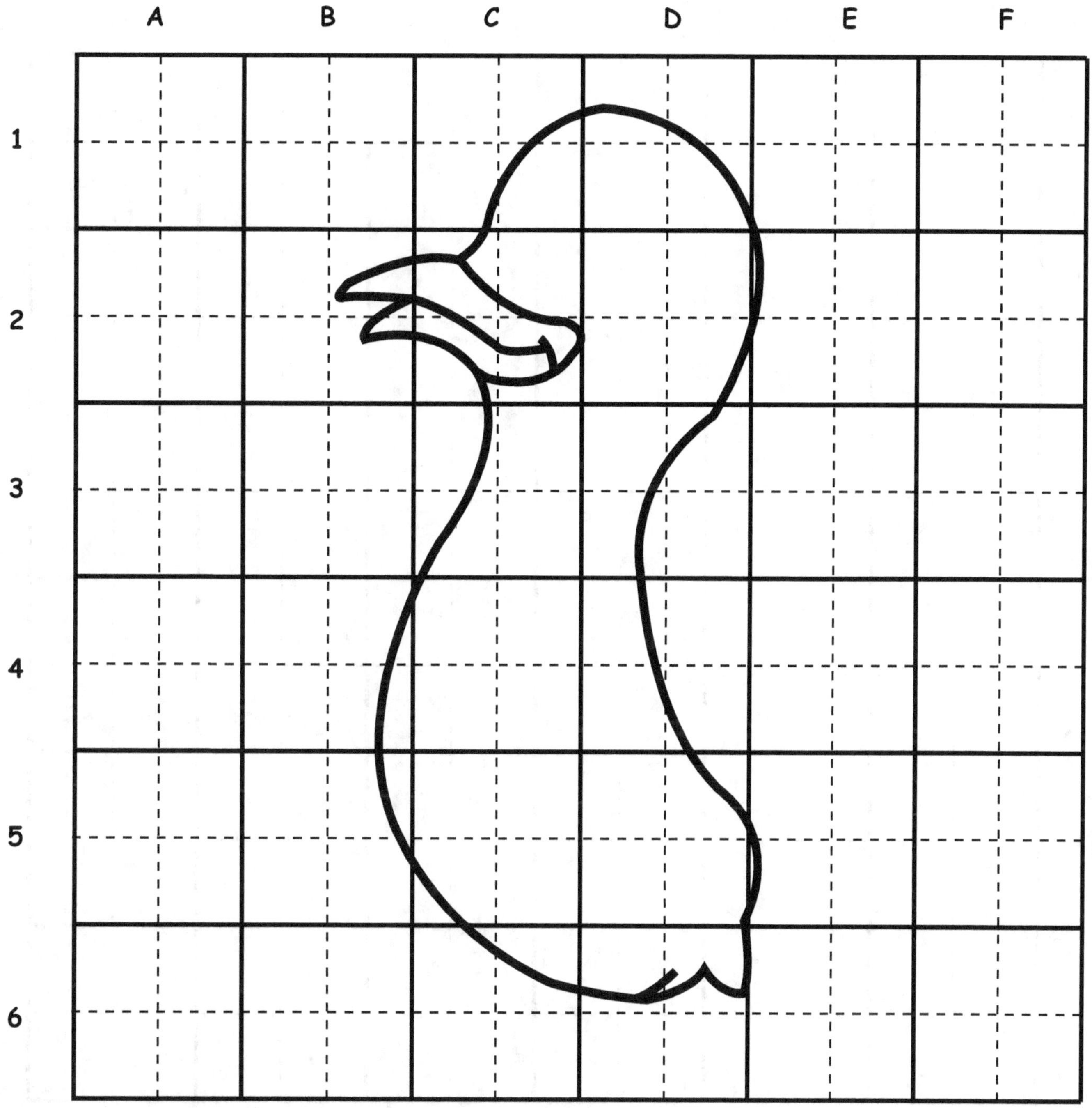

	A	B	C	D	E	F
1						
2						
3						
4						
5						
6						

Practice Here With Gride

Add lines for the beak details.

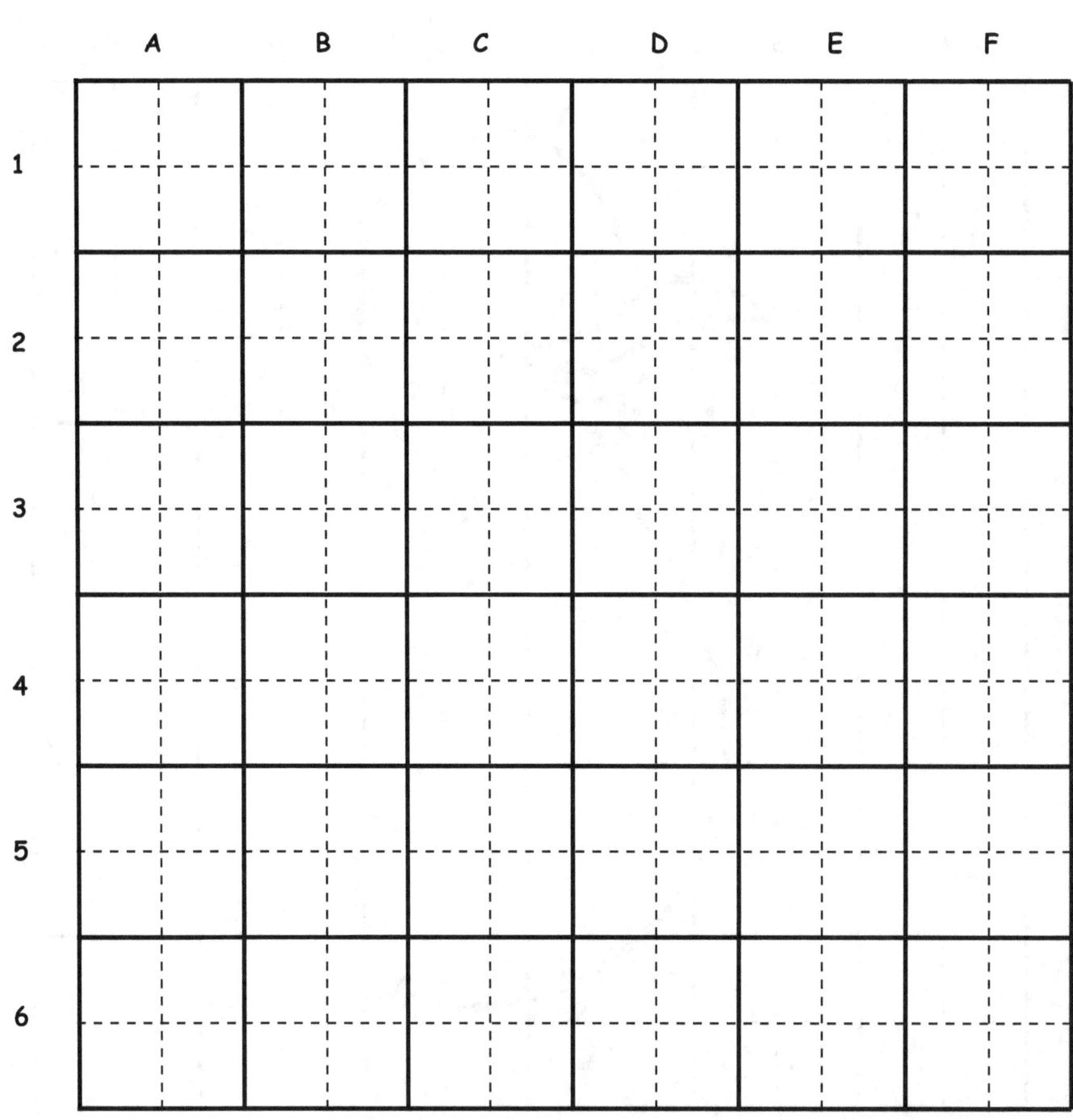

Penguin Art With Grid For Easy Way To Art

3 Draw lines of the Penguin's eye with details.

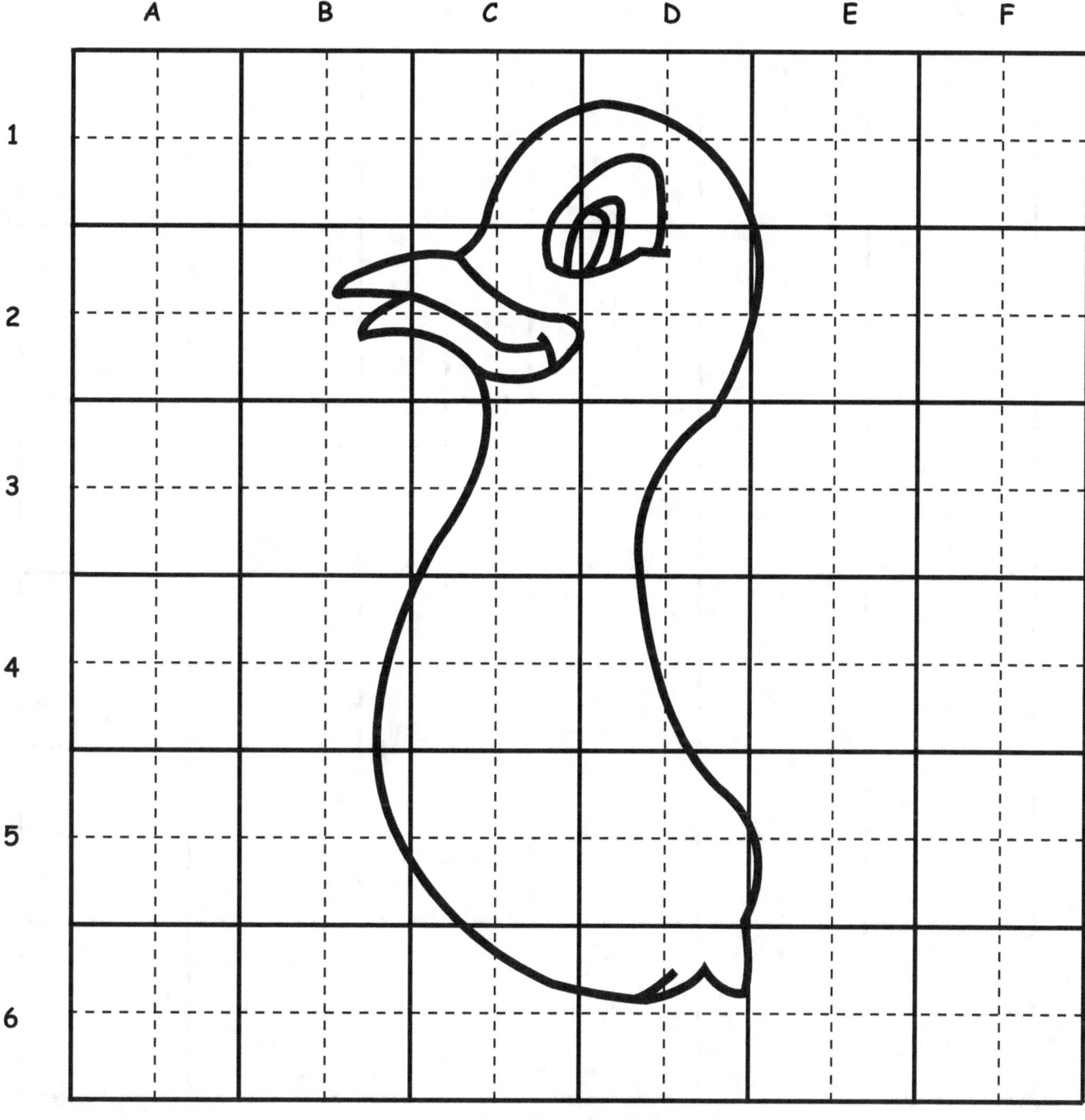

Practice Here With Gride

Draw lines of the Penguin's eye with details.

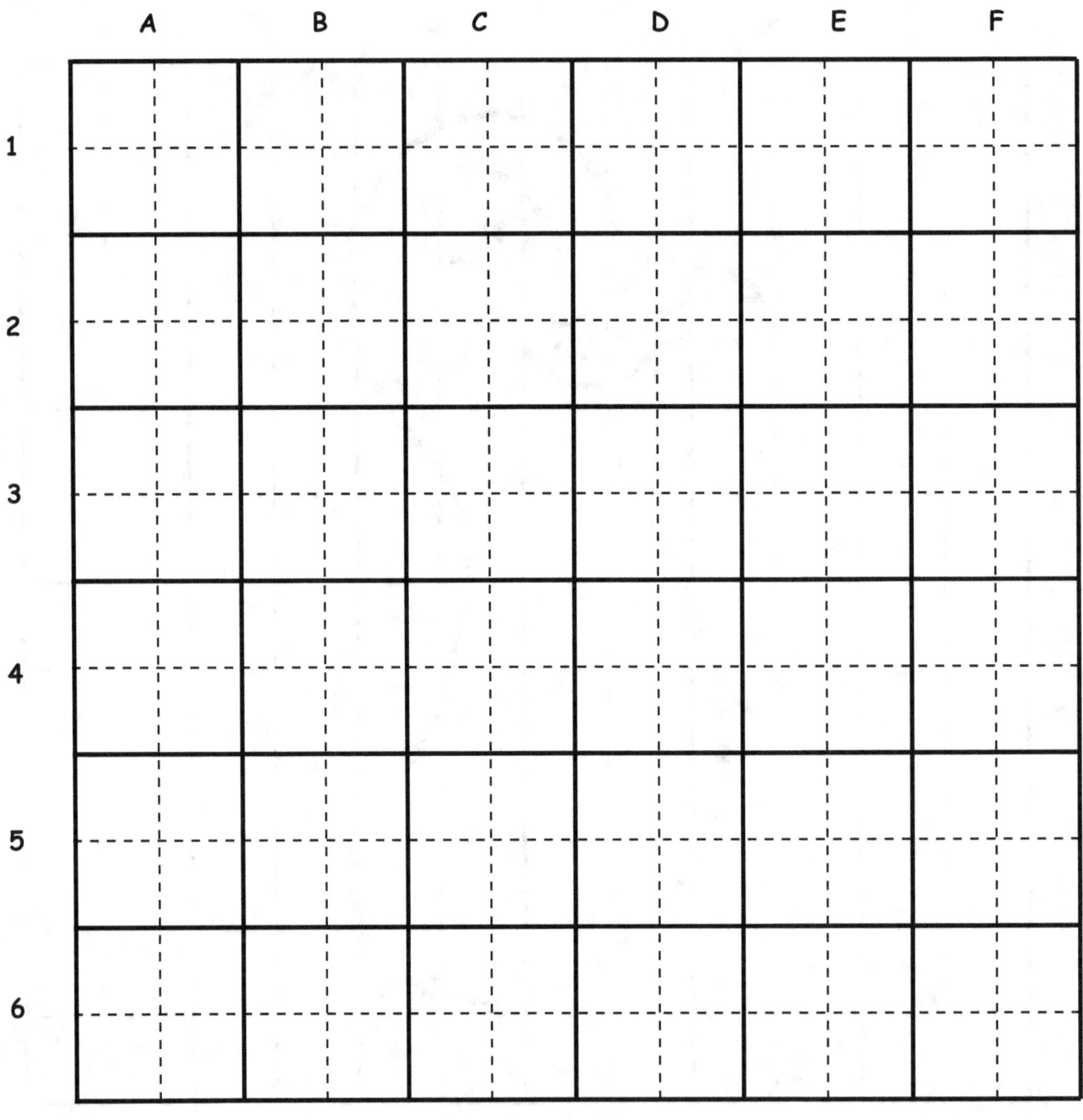

Penguin Art With Grid For Easy Way To Art

4 Draw lines of the Penguin's feather and other body details.

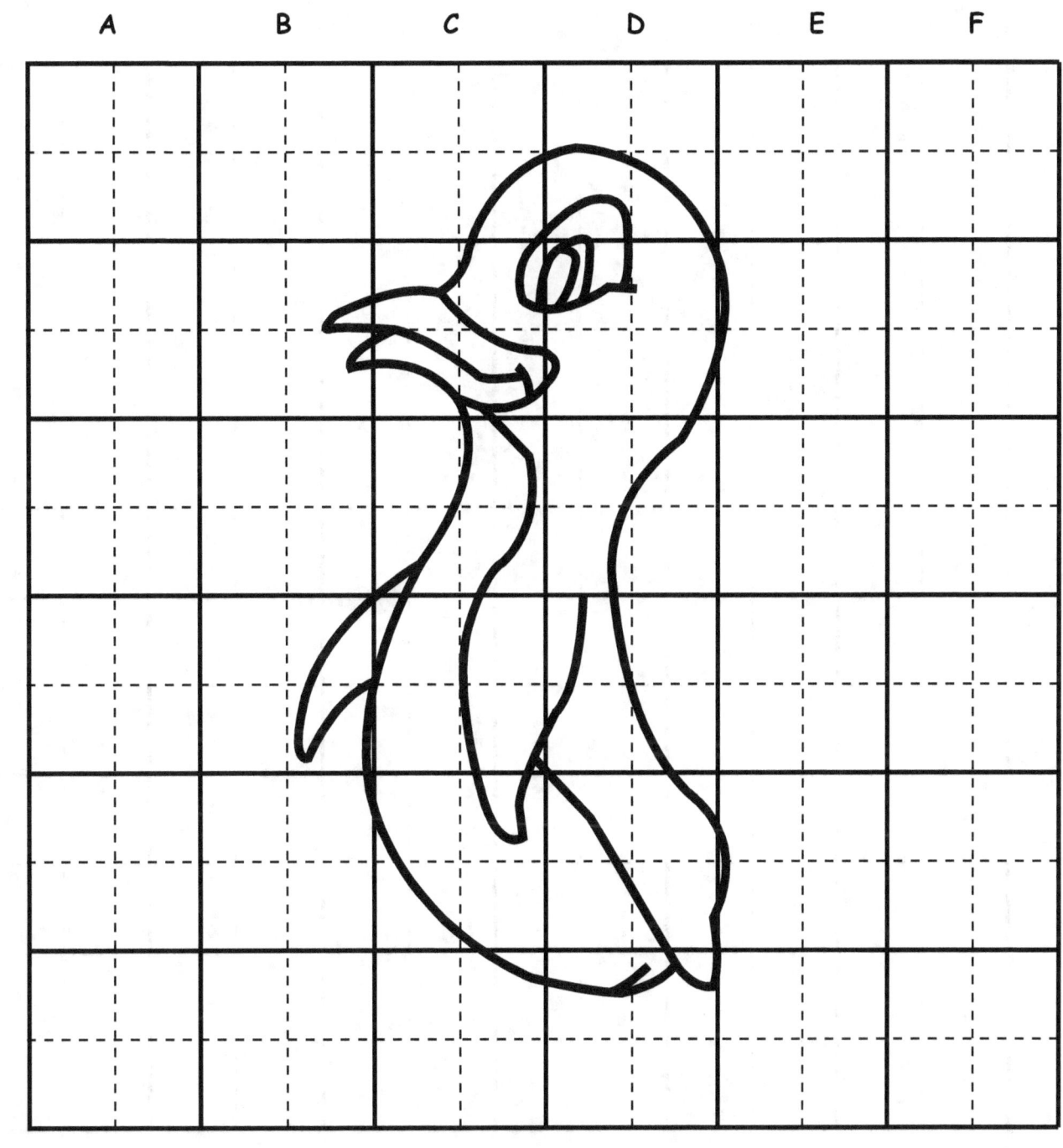

Practice Here With Gride

Draw lines of the Penguin's feather and other body details.

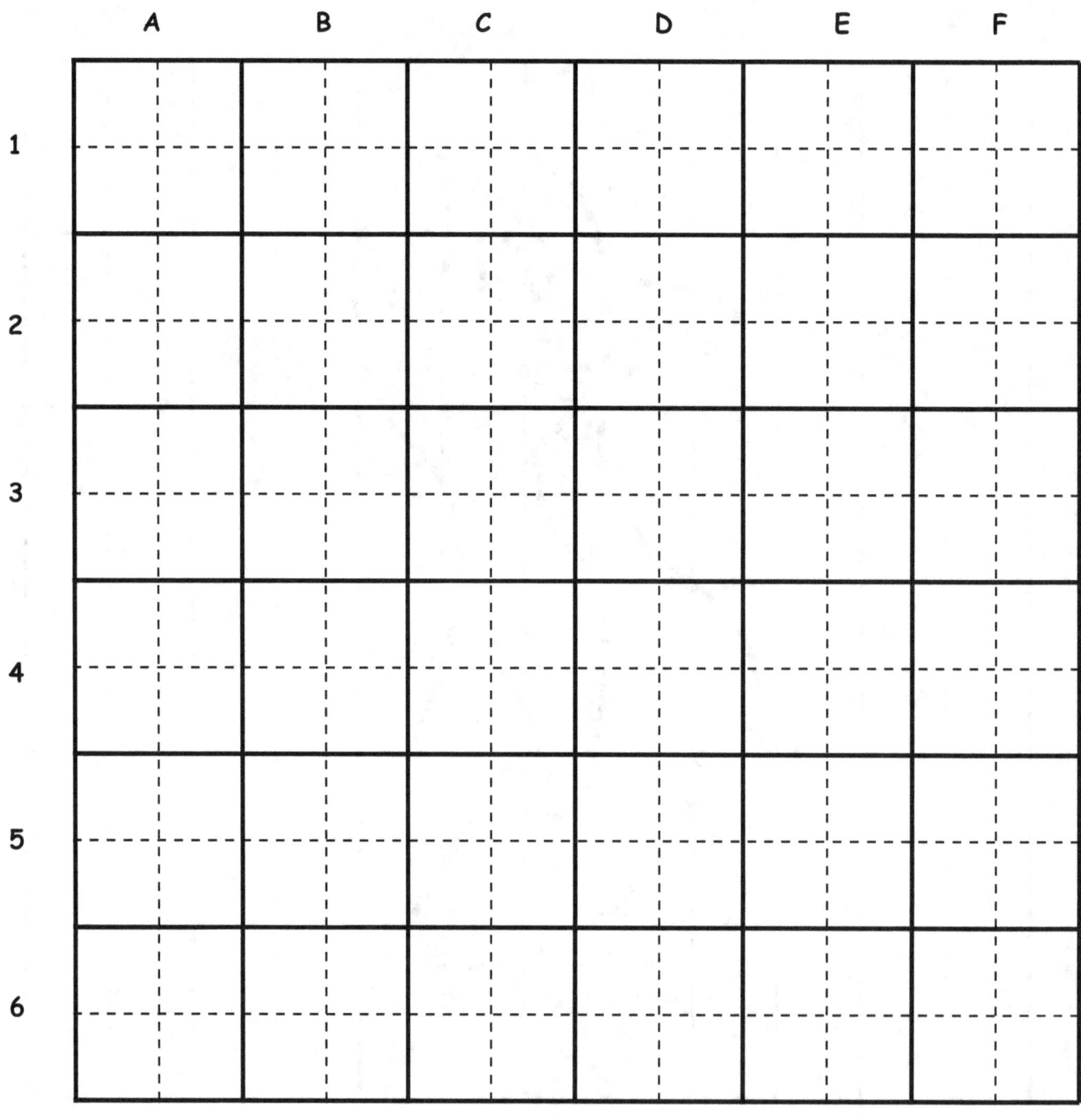

Penguin Art With Grid For Easy Way To Art

5 Draw lines for the Penguin's feet and erase all extra and unnecessary lines.

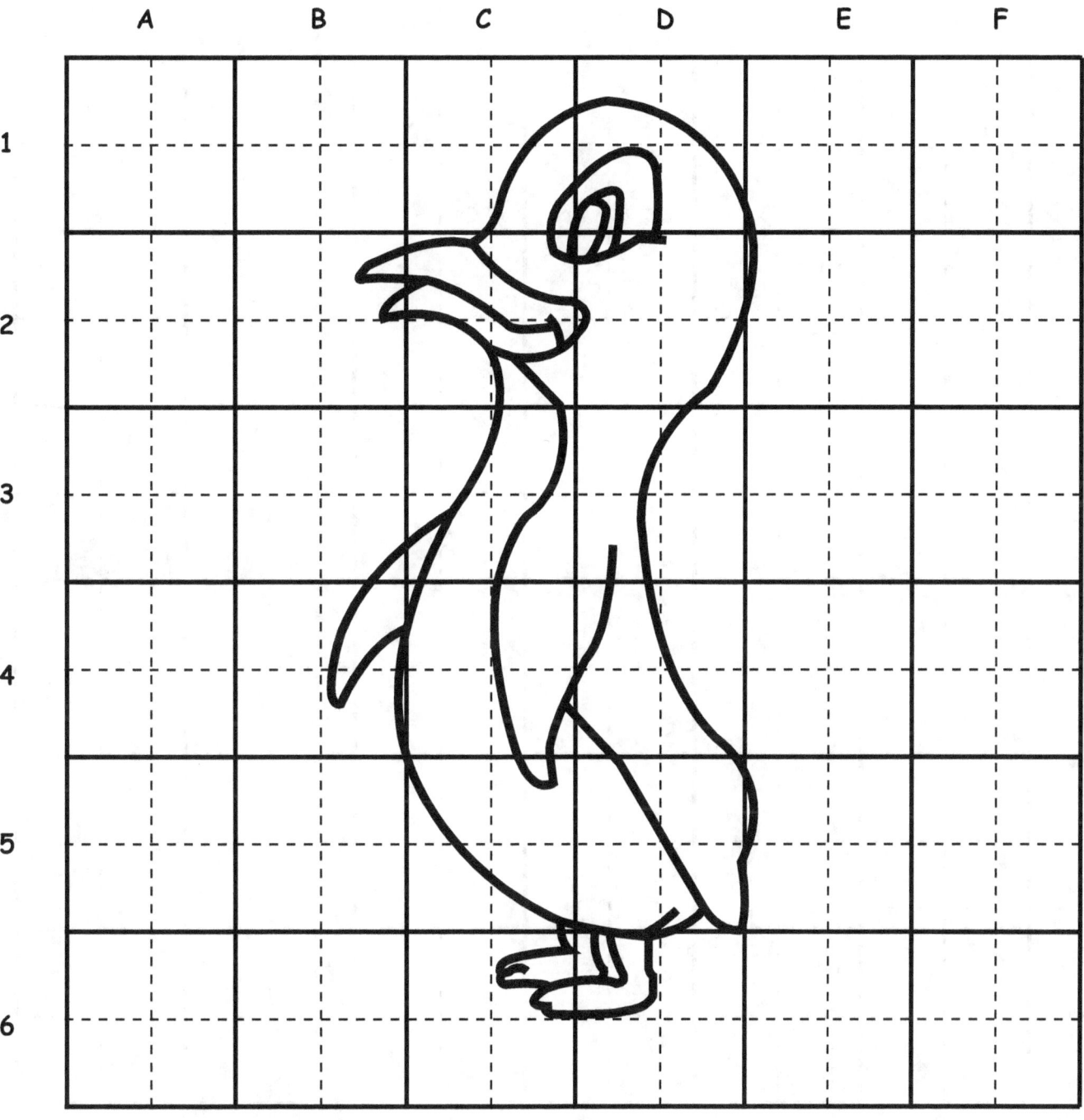

Practice Here With Gride

Draw lines for the Penguin's feet and erase all extra and unnecessary lines.

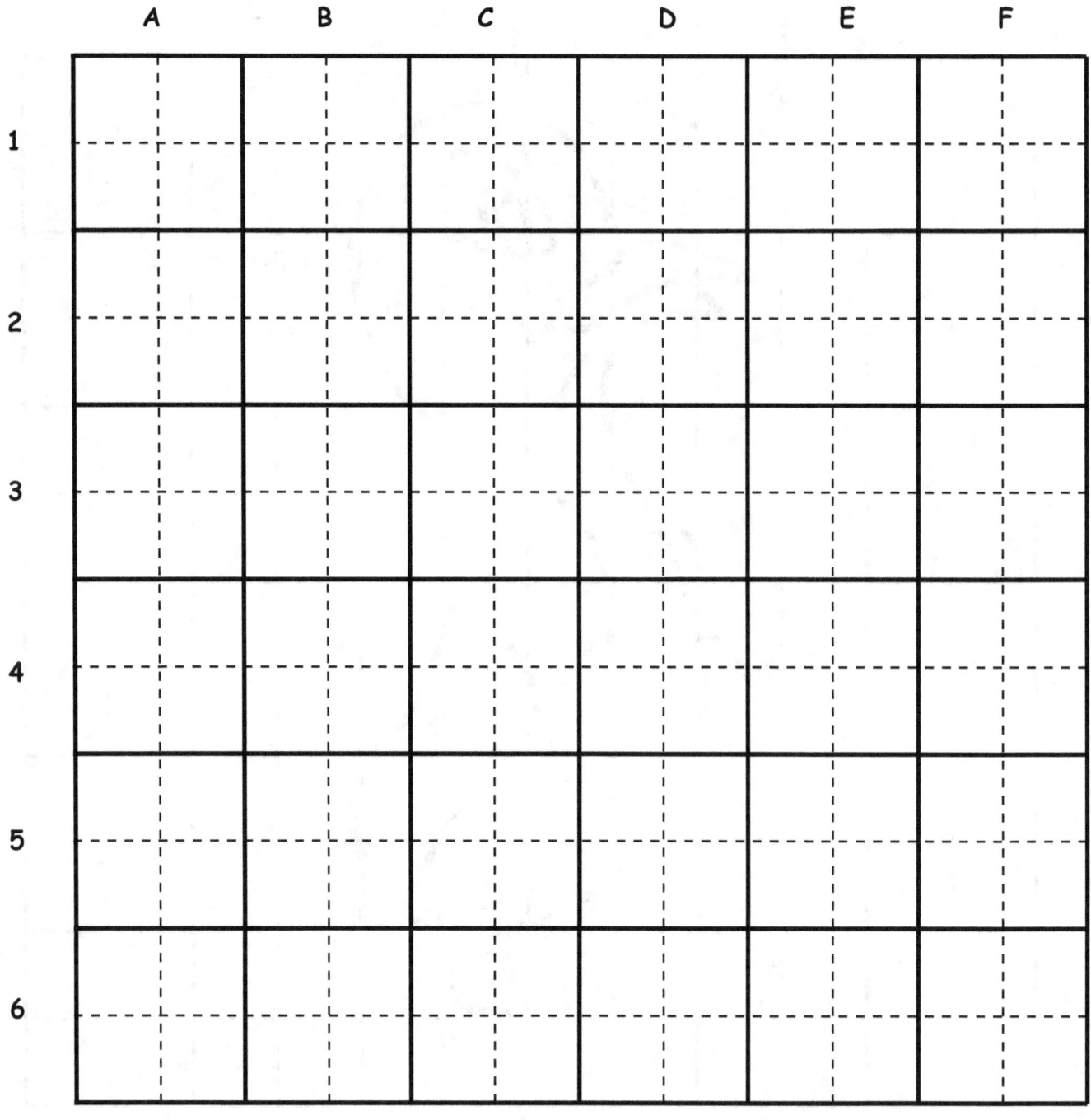

There is your ready Penguin.

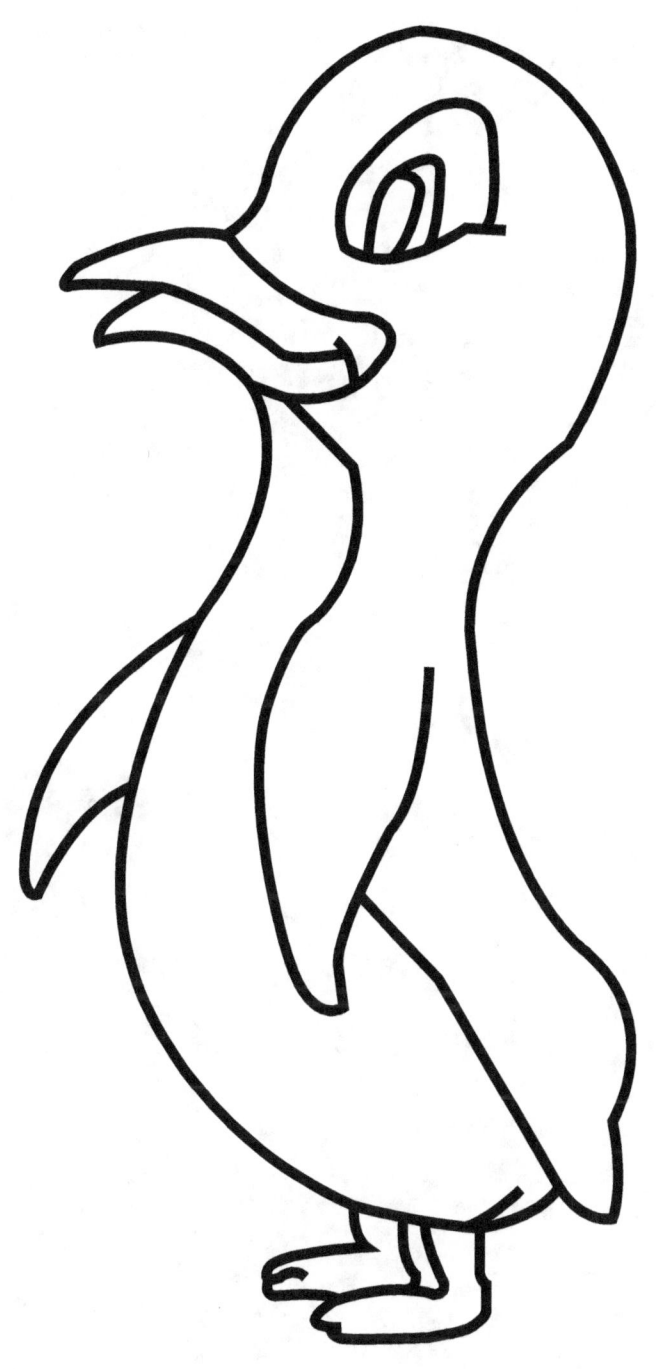

Practice Here Blind

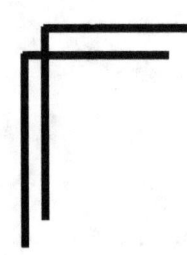

Penguin Art With Grid For Easy Way To Art

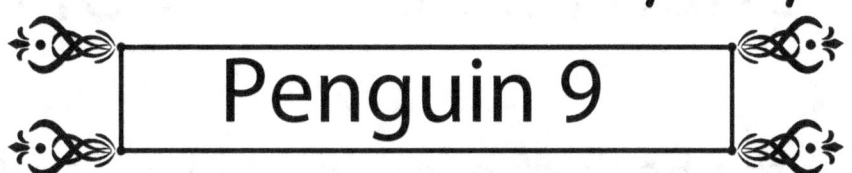

Penguin 9

1 Draw the beak of penguin and half outline of body.

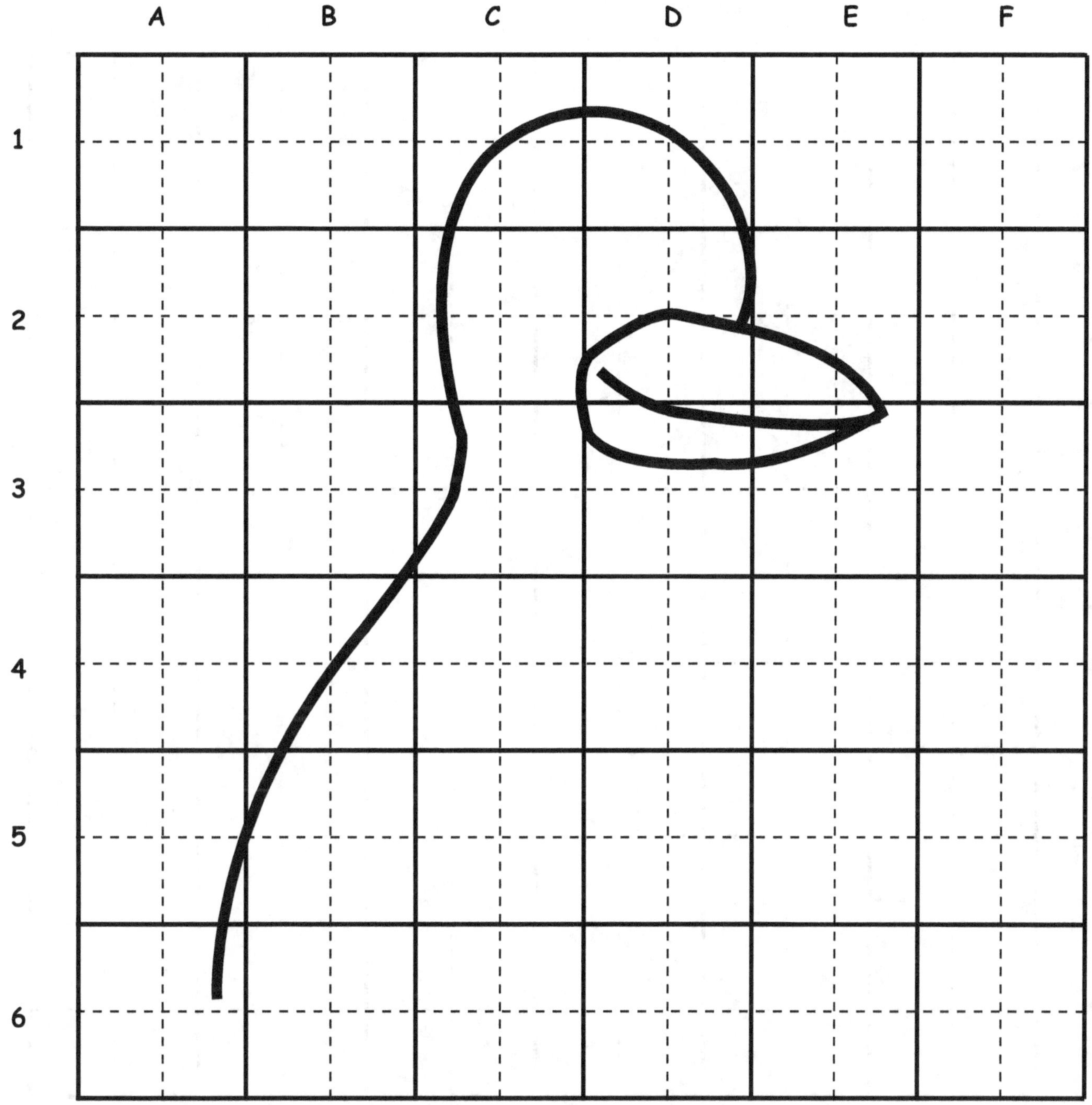

Practice Here With Gride

Draw the beak of penguin and half outline of body.

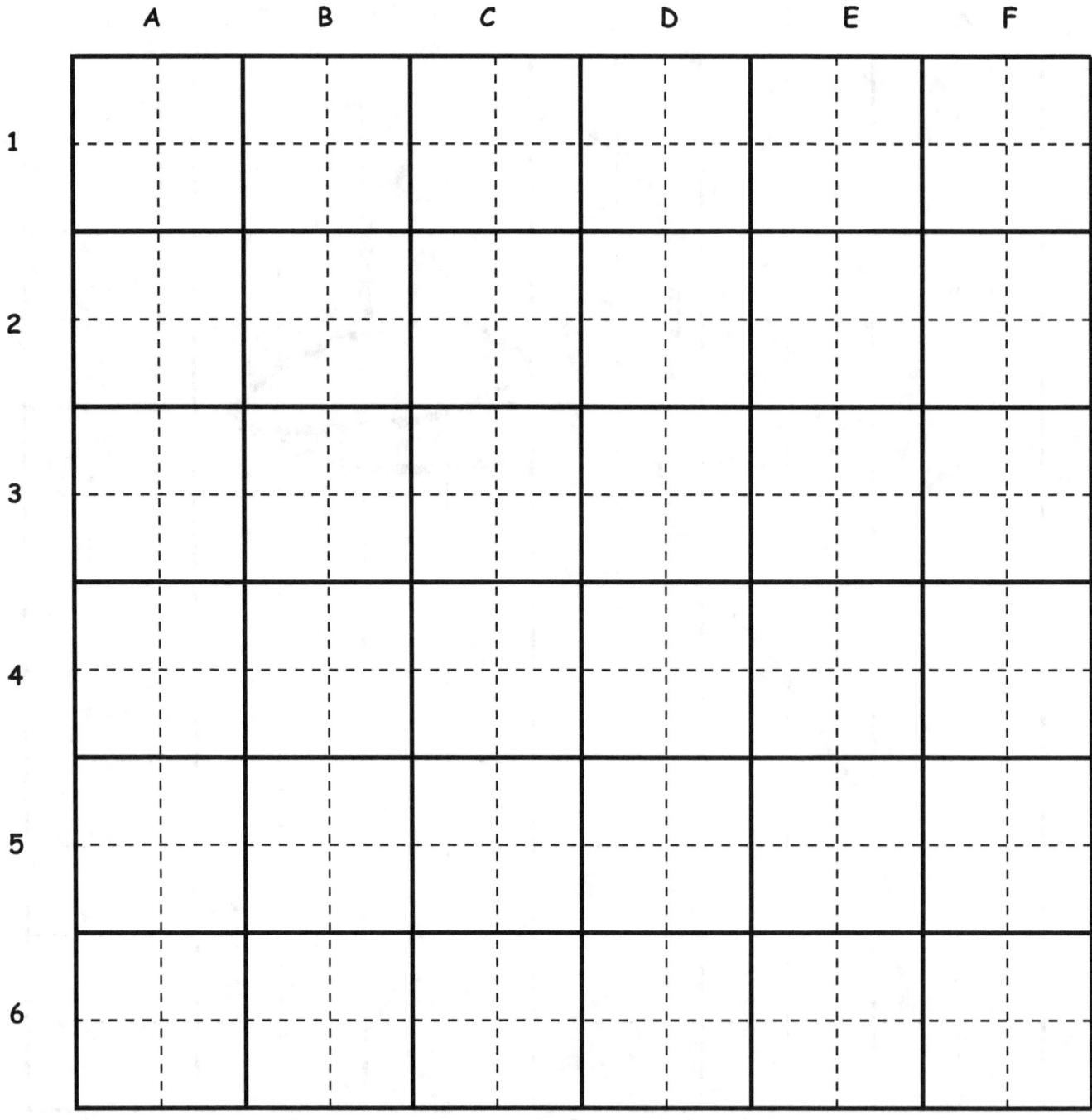

Penguin Art With Grid For Easy Way To Art

 Draw the lines for full body shape as shown with one feather.

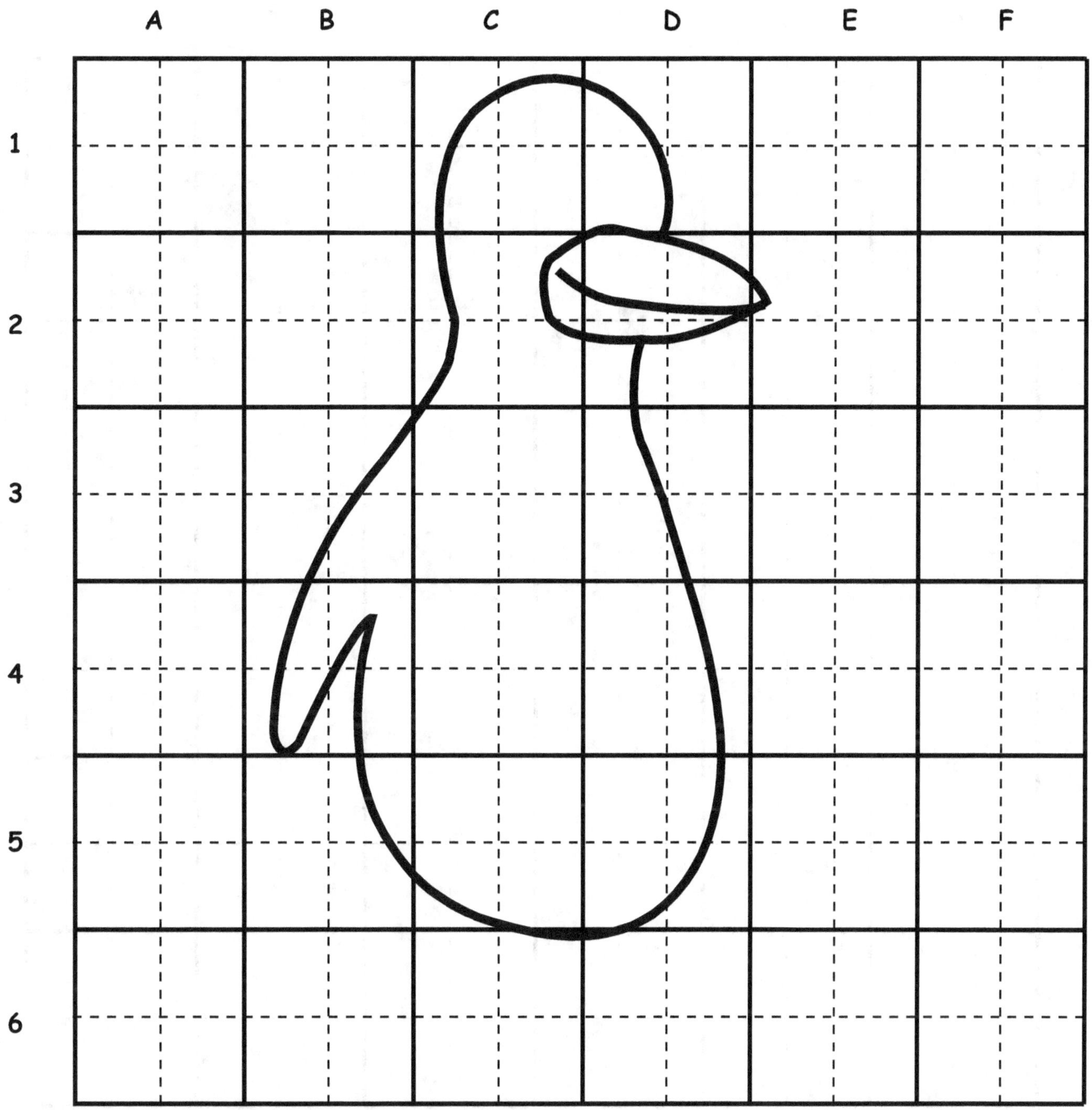

105

Practice Here With Gride

Draw the lines for full body shape as shown
with one feather.

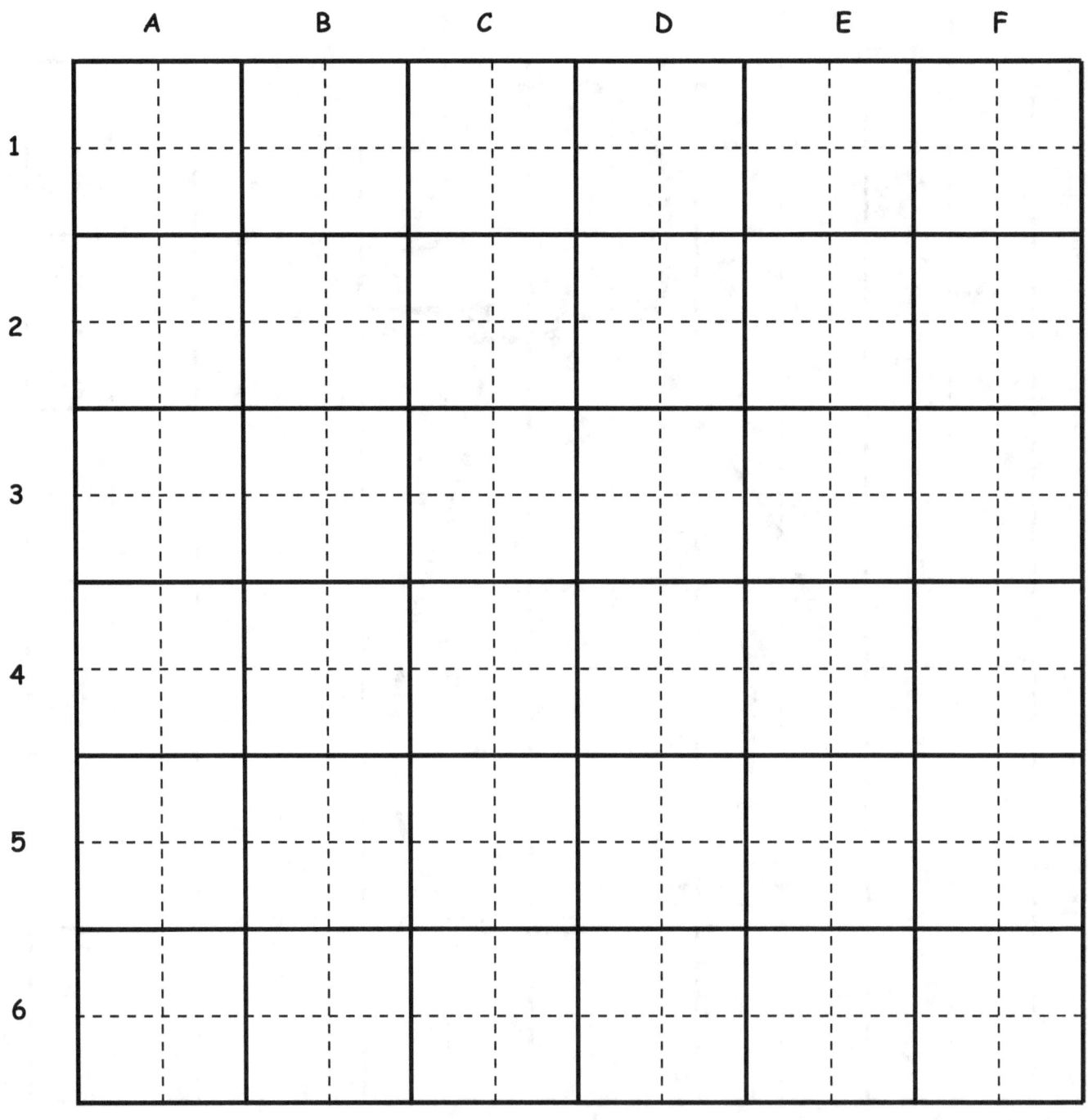

Penguin Art With Grid For Easy Way To Art

3 Draw another feather with body shape.

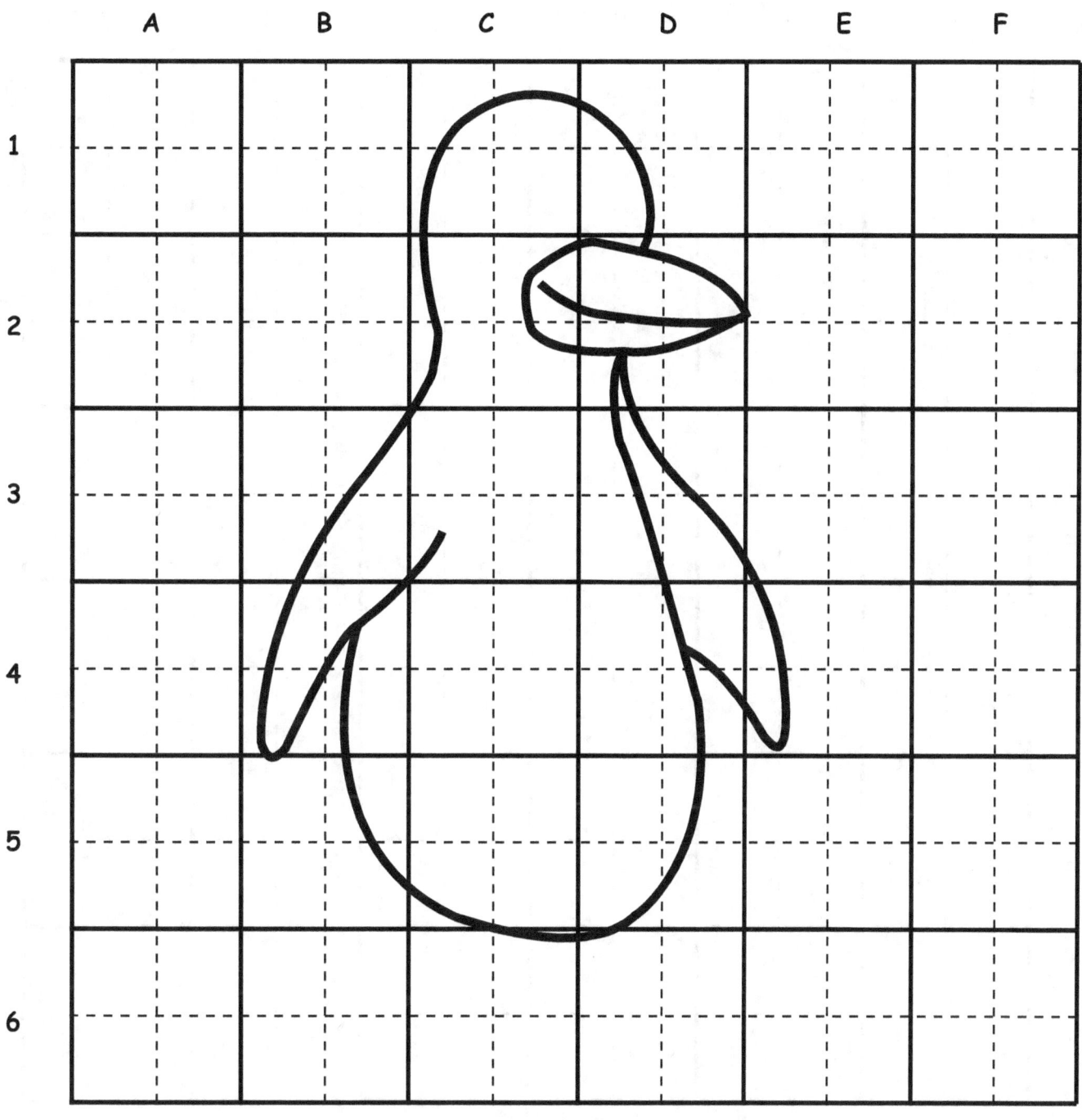

Practice Here With Gride

Draw another feather with body shape.

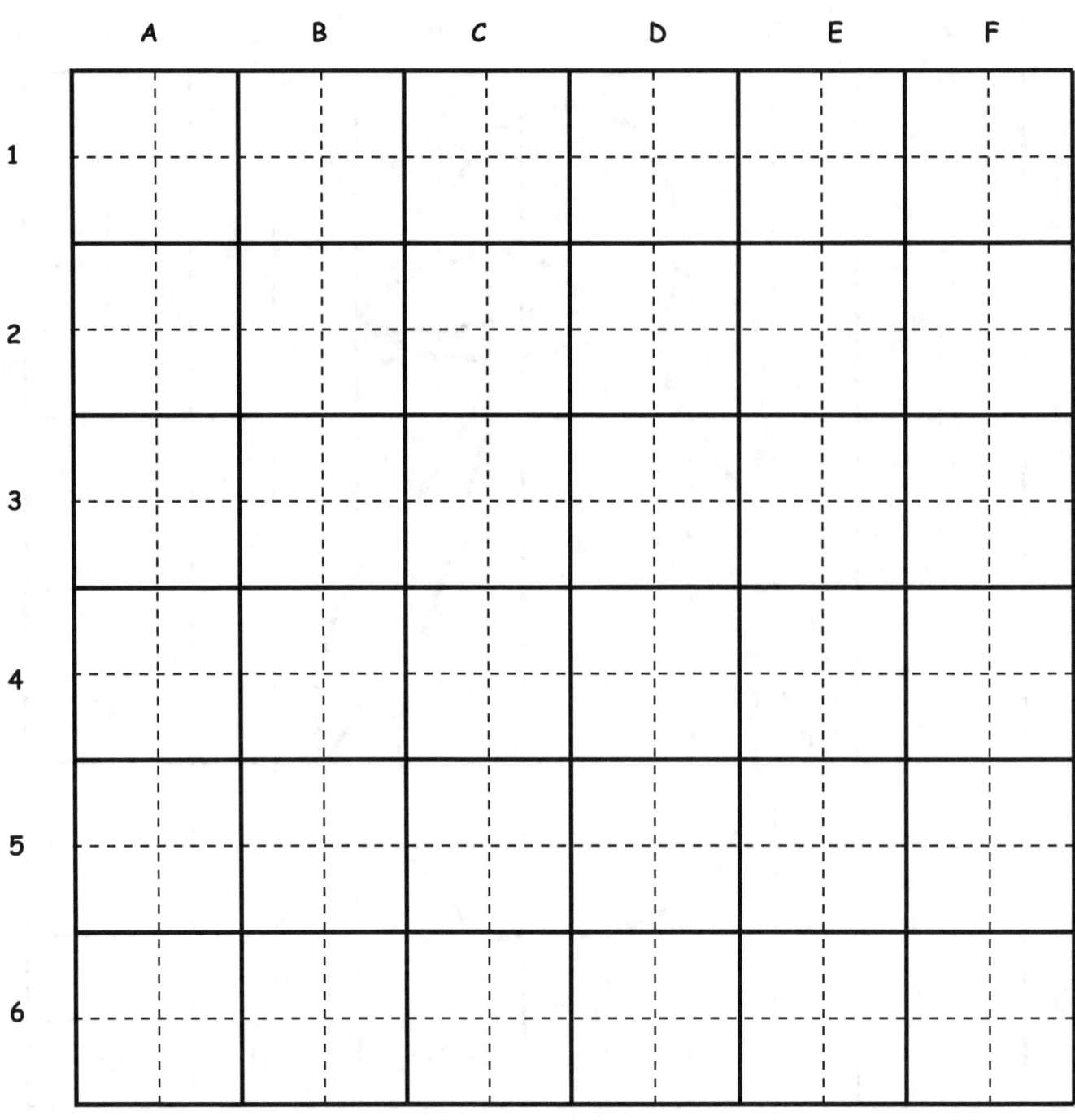

Penguien Art With Grid For Easy Way To Art

 Draw lines for the Penguin's feet and inner lines in belly as shown.

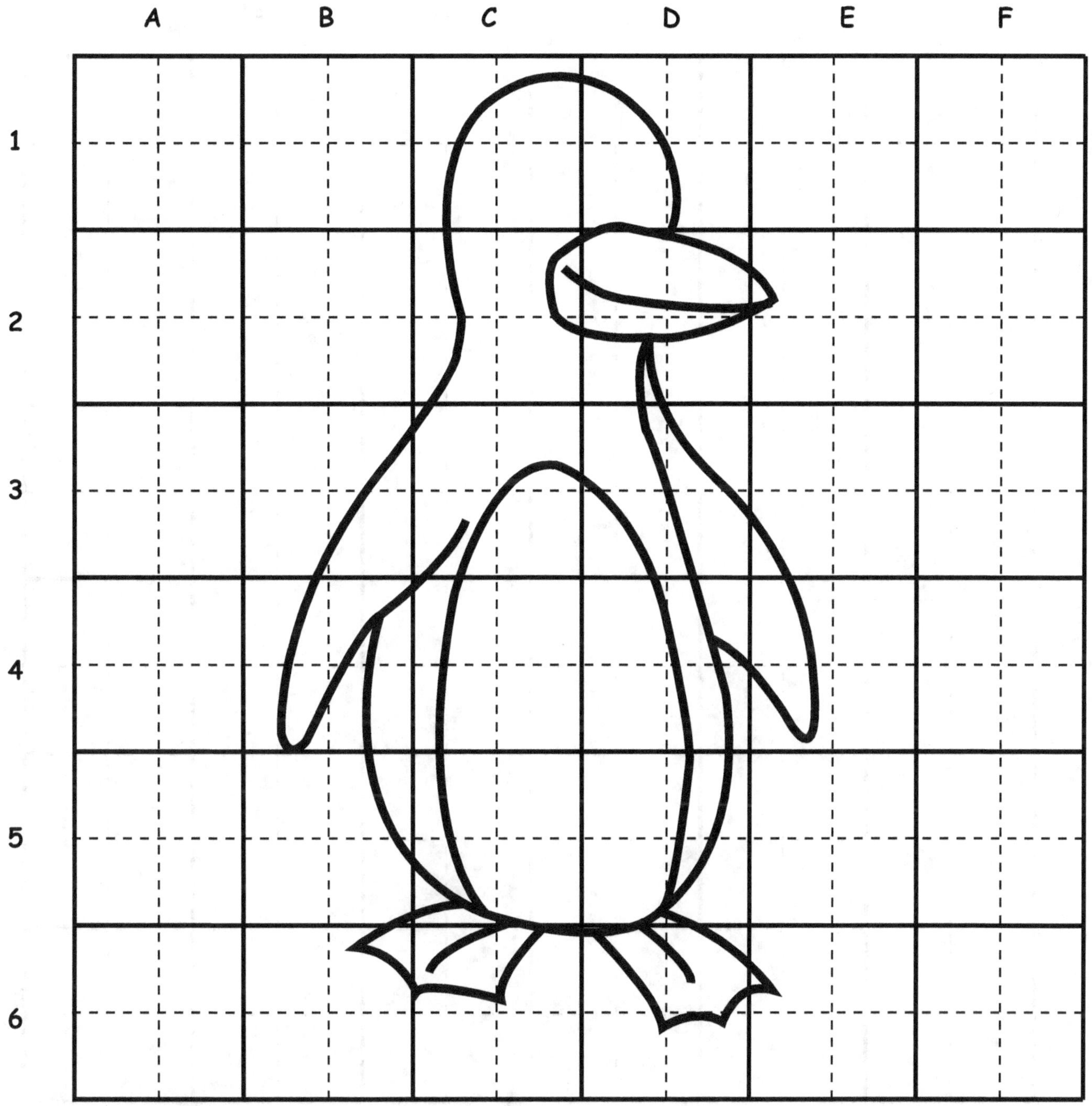

Practice Here With Gride

Draw lines for the Penguin's feet and inner lines in belly as shown.

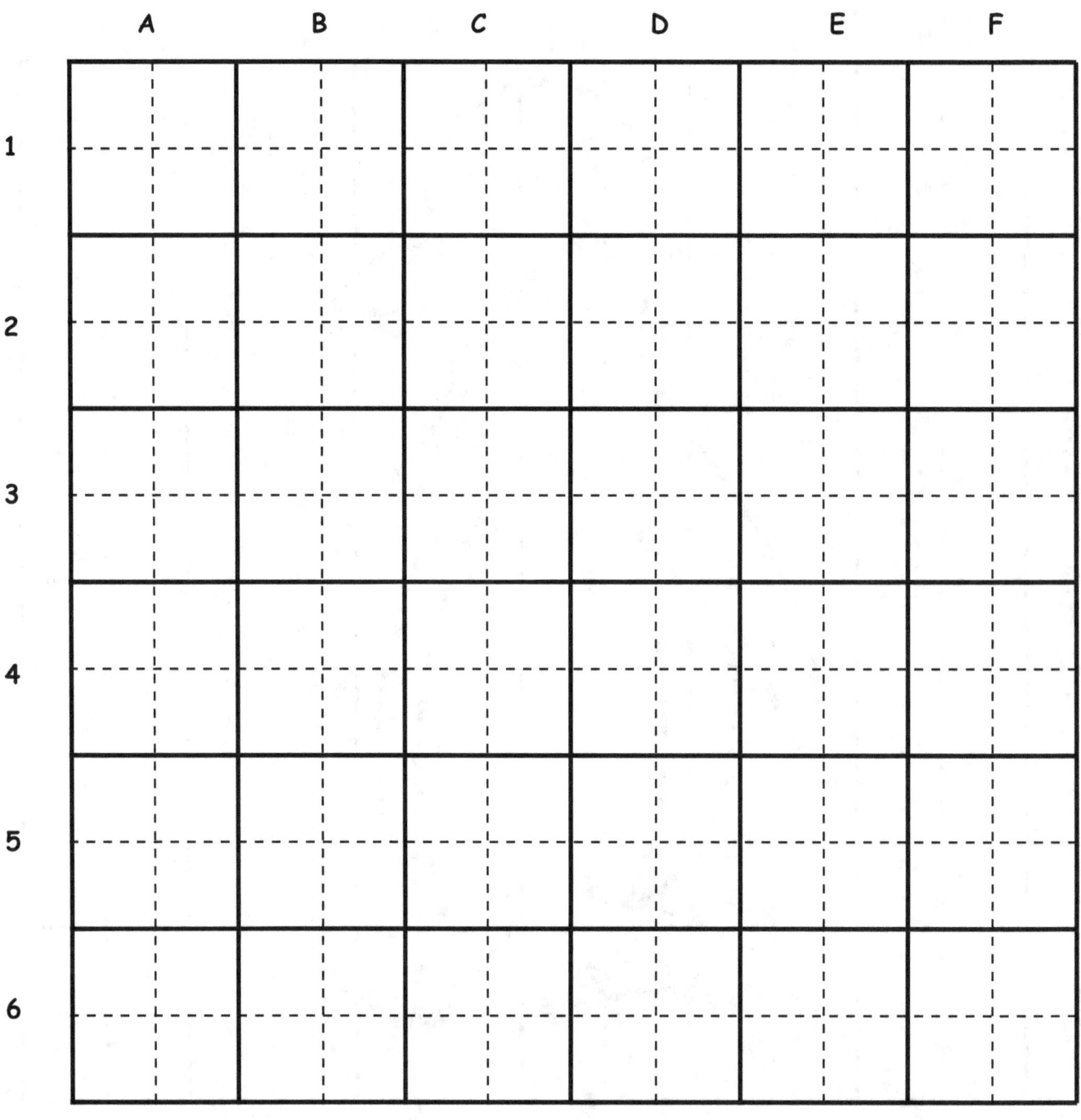

Penguin Art With Grid For Easy Way To Art

5 Draw lines of the Penguin's eye, eyebrows and few hairs on the head top.

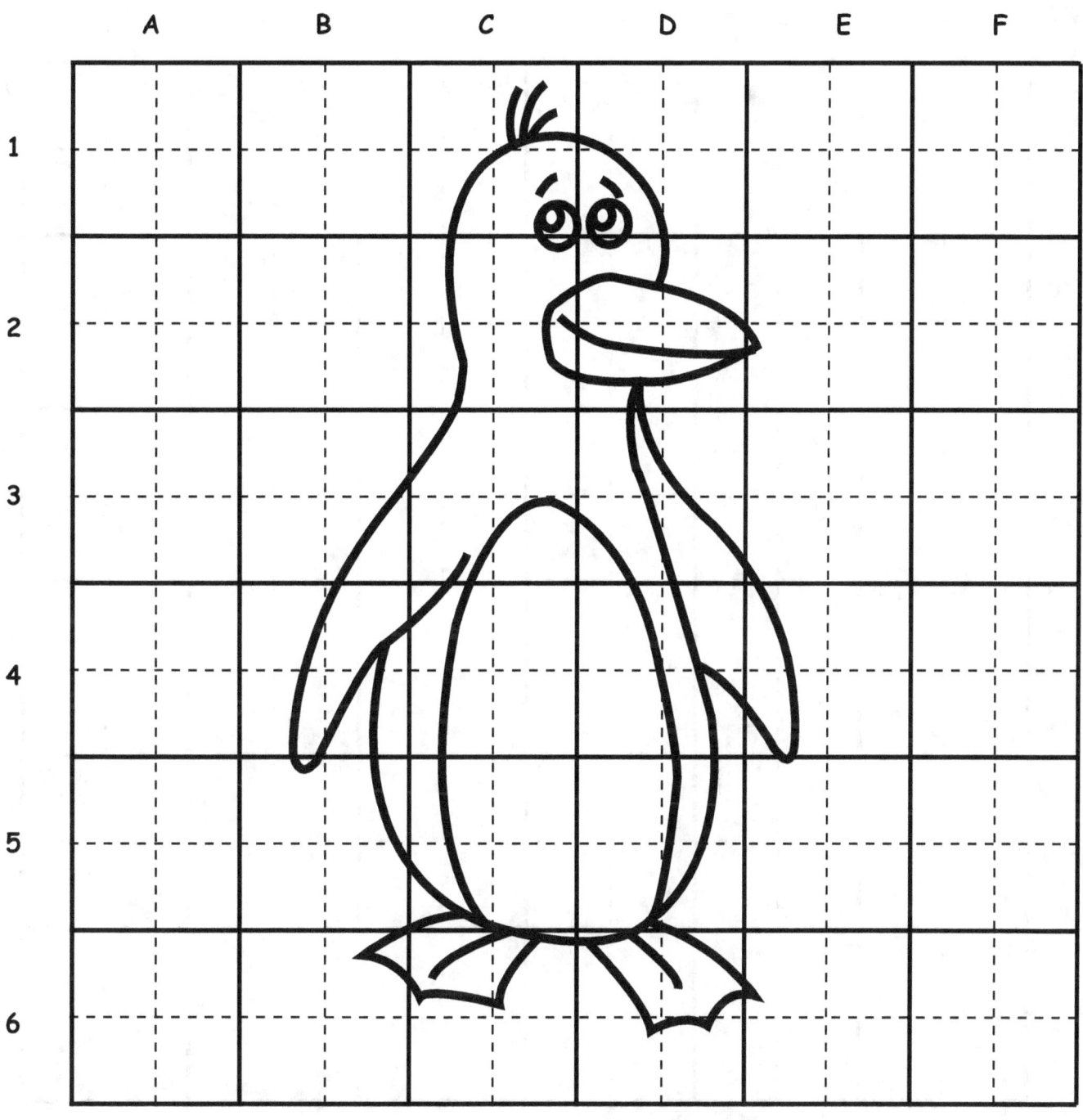

Practice Here With Gride

Draw lines of the Penguin's eye, eyebrows and few hairs on the head top.

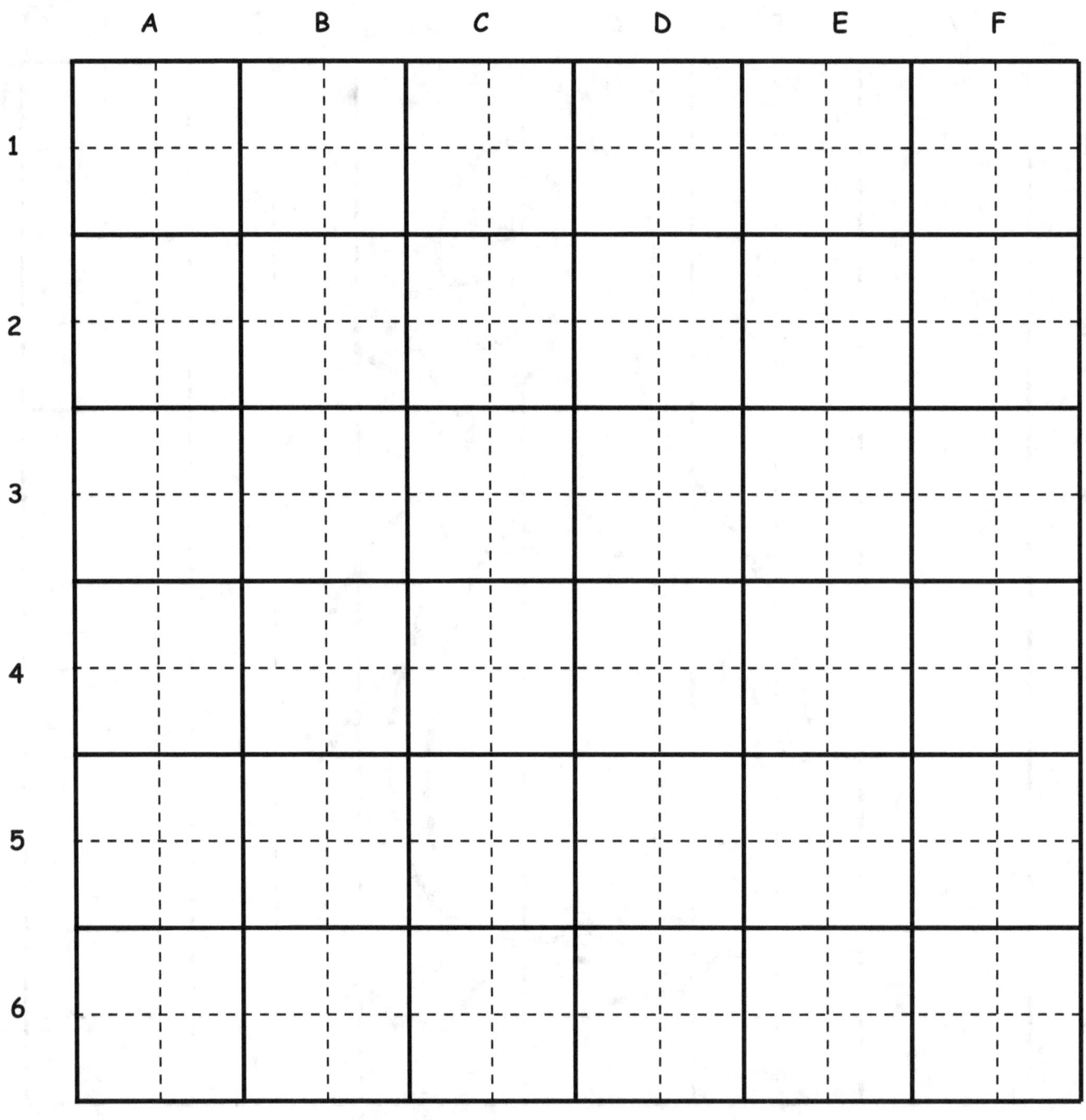

There is your completed Penguin.

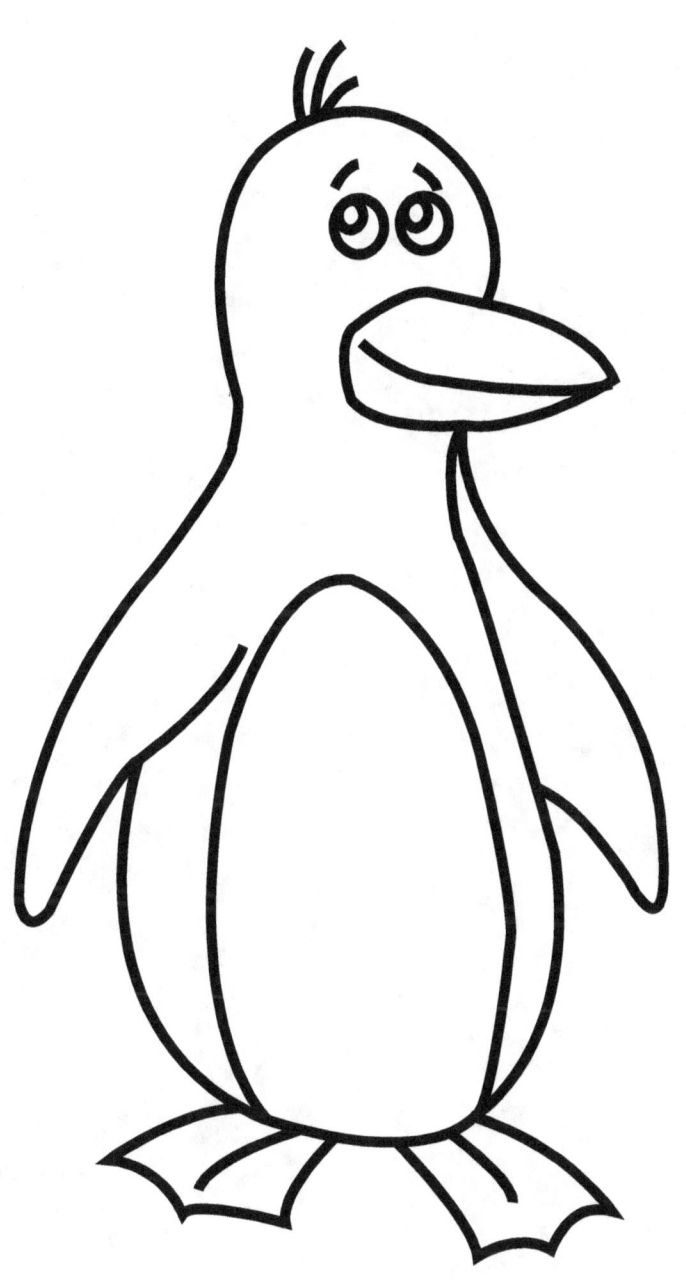

Practice Here Blind

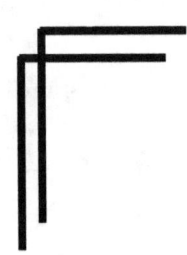

Penguin Art With Grid For Easy Way To Art

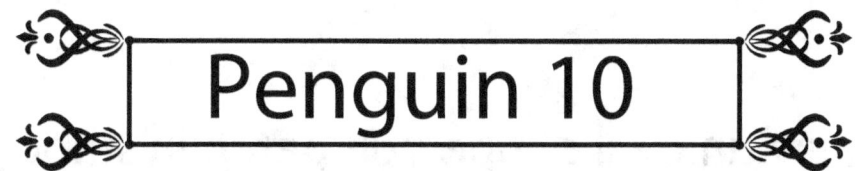

Penguin 10

1 Draw an oval shape for penguin's body.

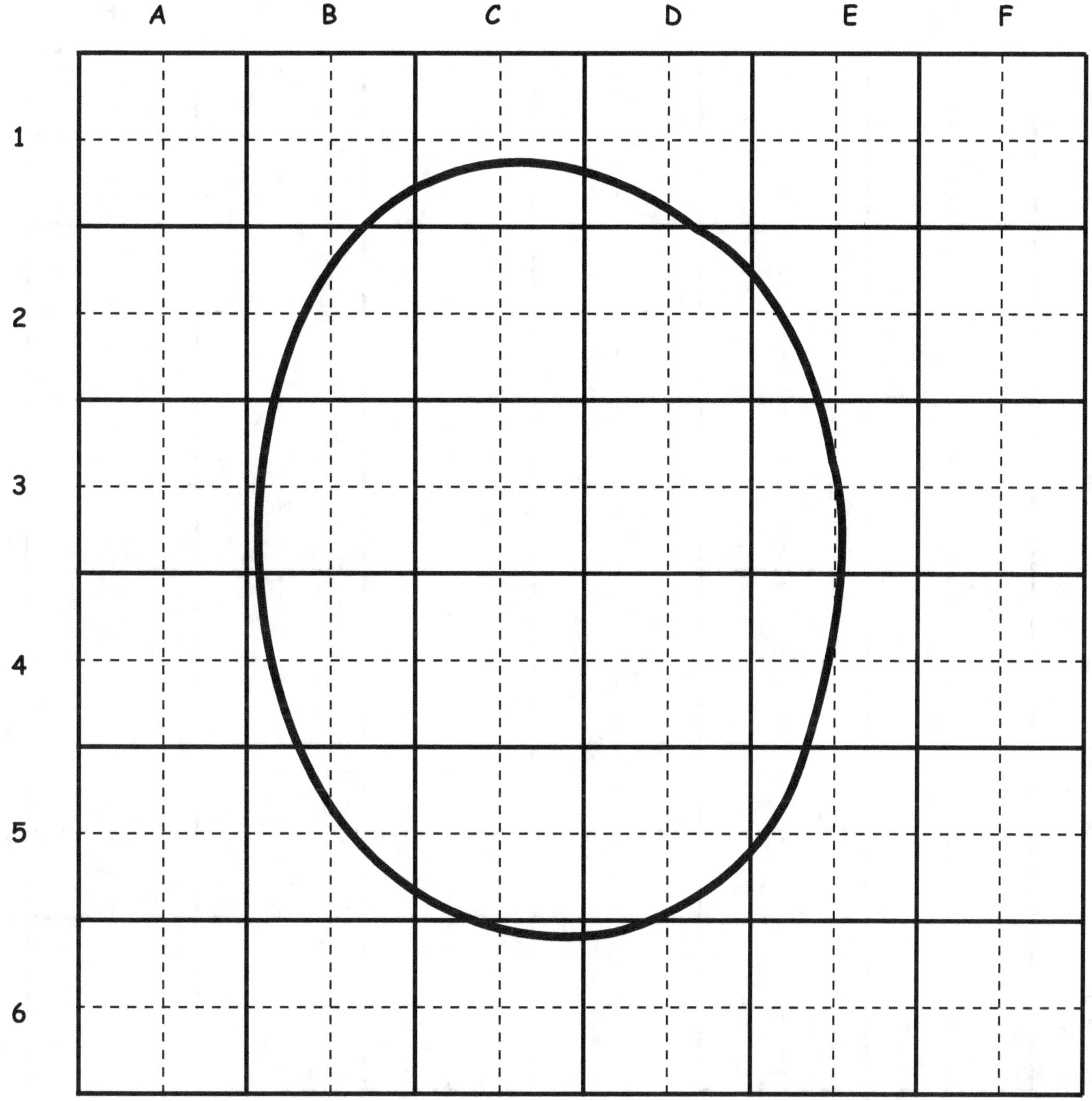

Practice Here With Gride

Draw an oval shape for penguin's body.

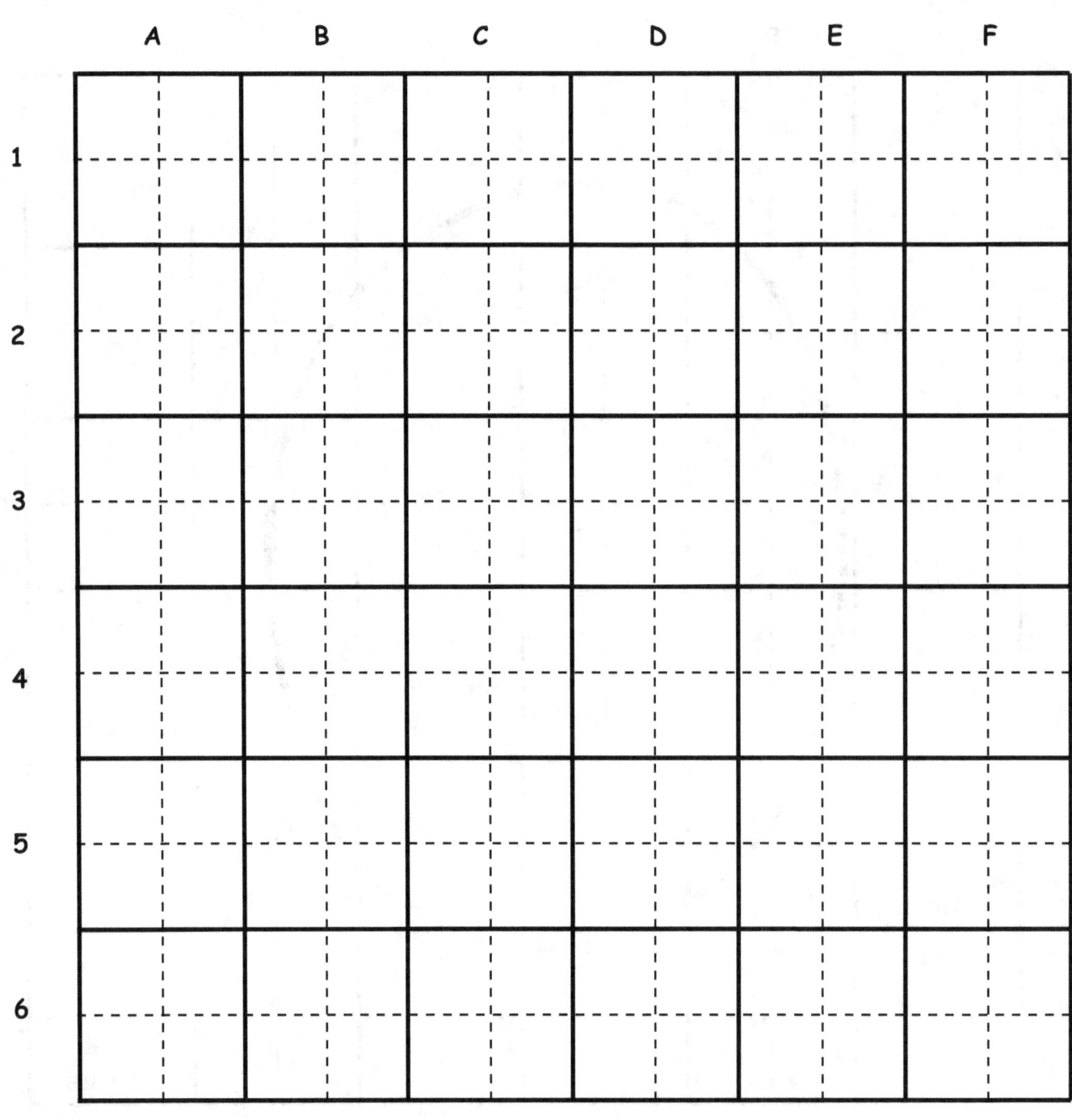

Penguin Art With Grid For Easy Way To Art

2 Draw lines for the Penguin's Feather.

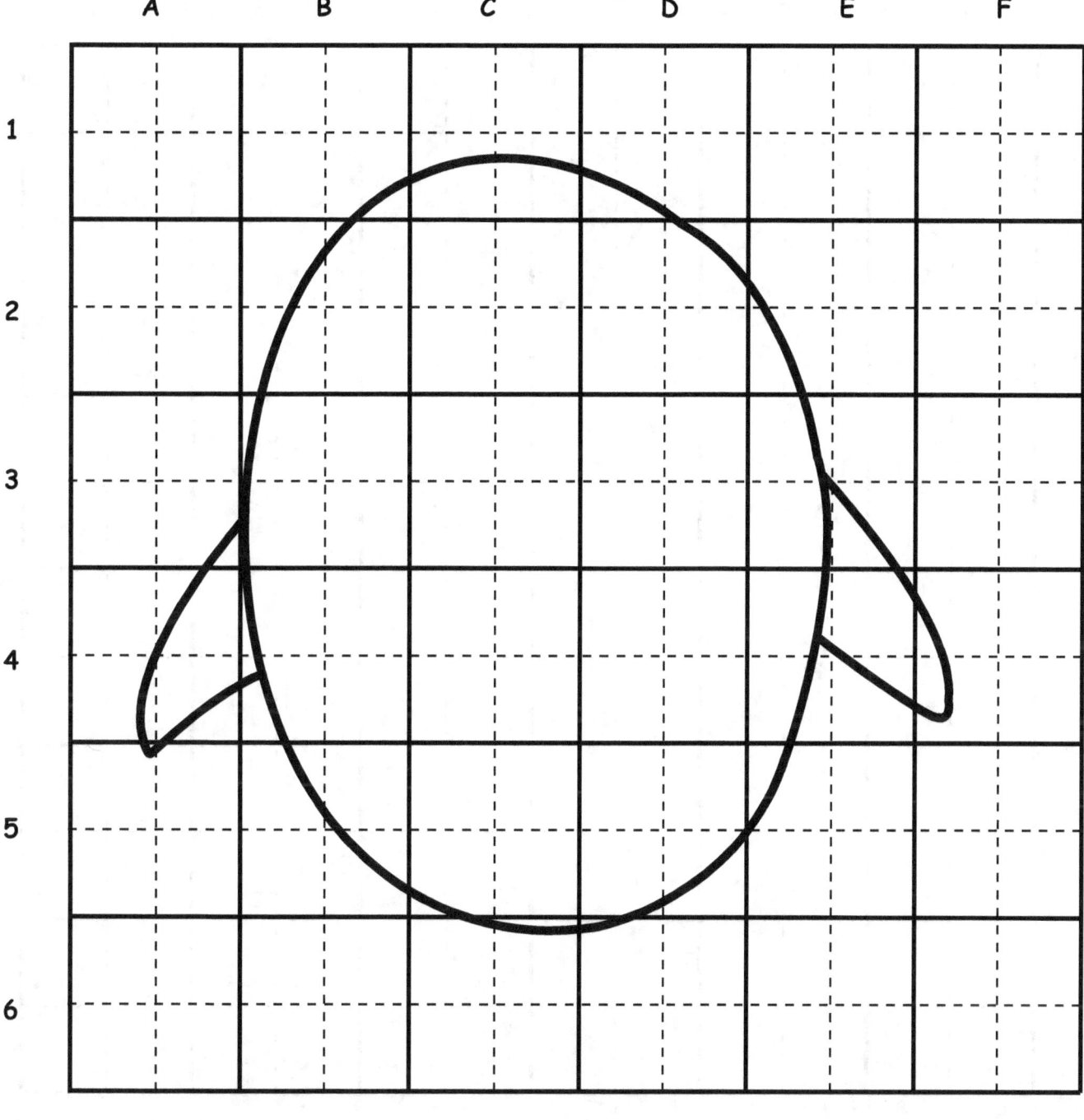

Practice Here With Gride

Draw lines for the Penguin's Feather.

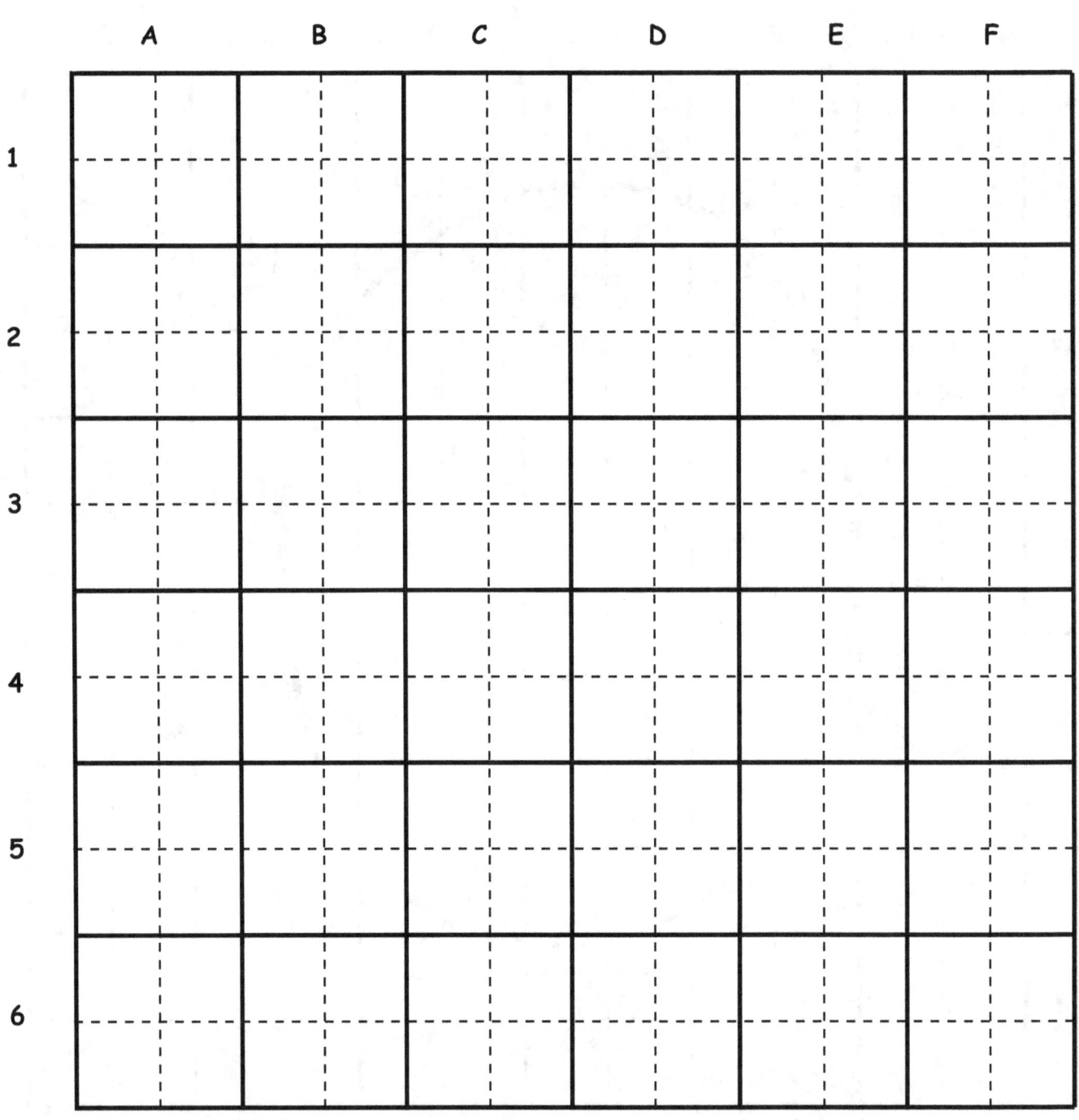

Penguin Art With Grid For Easy Way To Art

3 Draw lines of the Penguin's eyes.

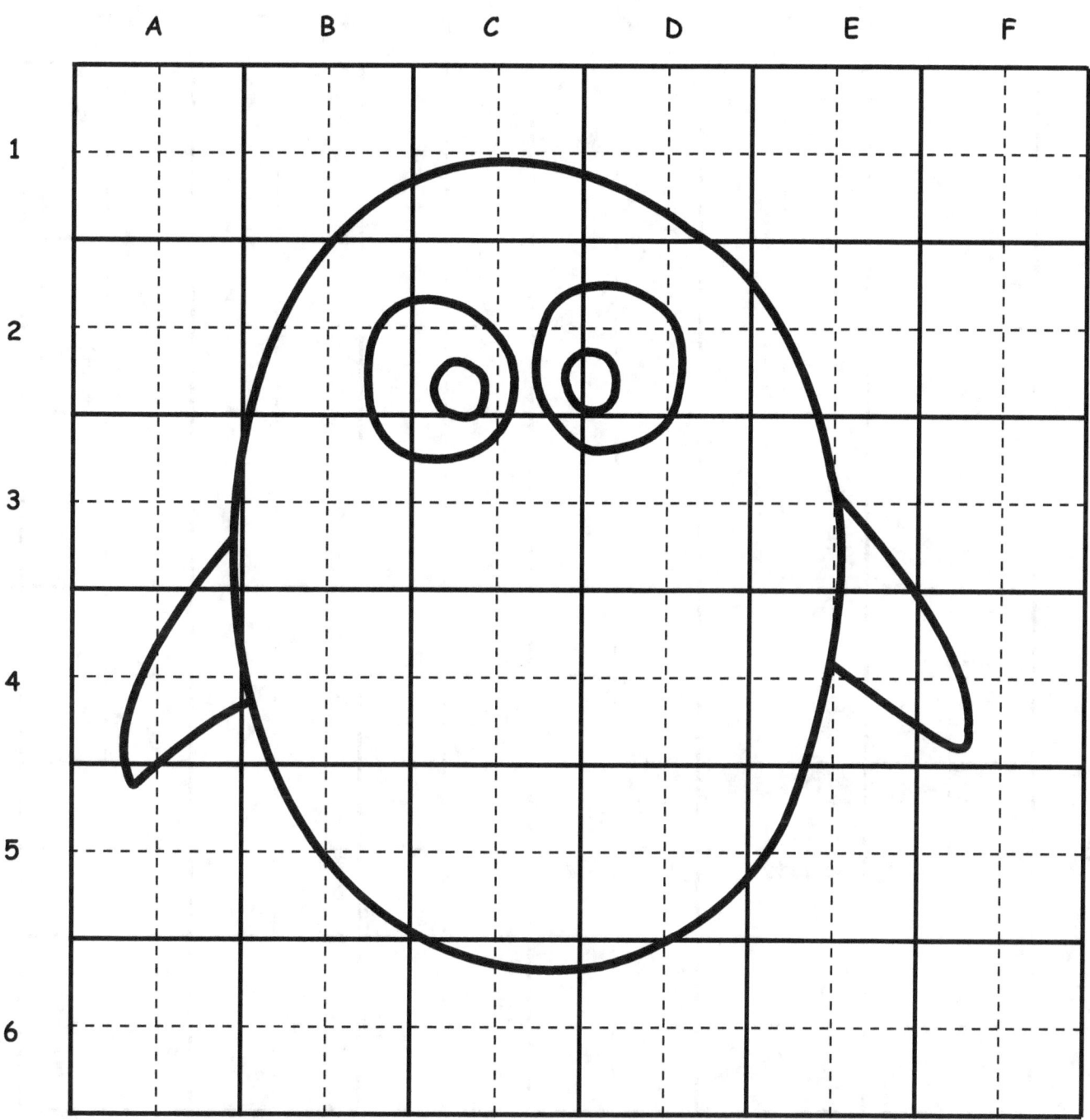

Practice Here With Gride

Draw lines of the Penguin's eyes.

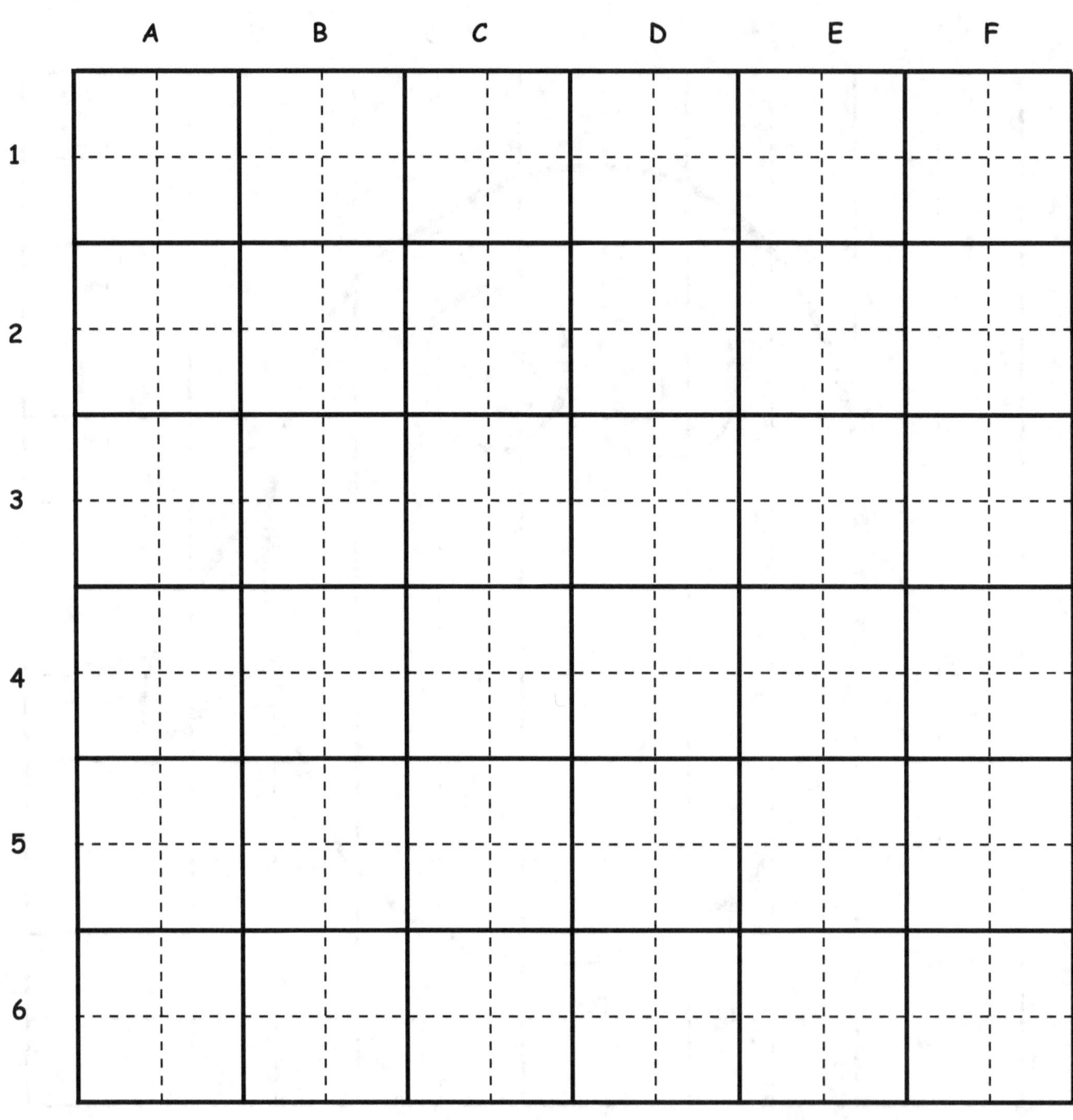

Penguin Art With Grid For Easy Way To Art

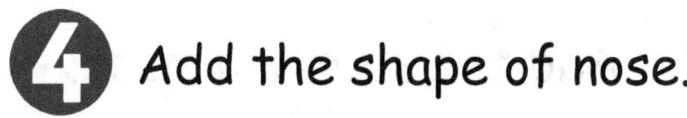 Add the shape of nose.

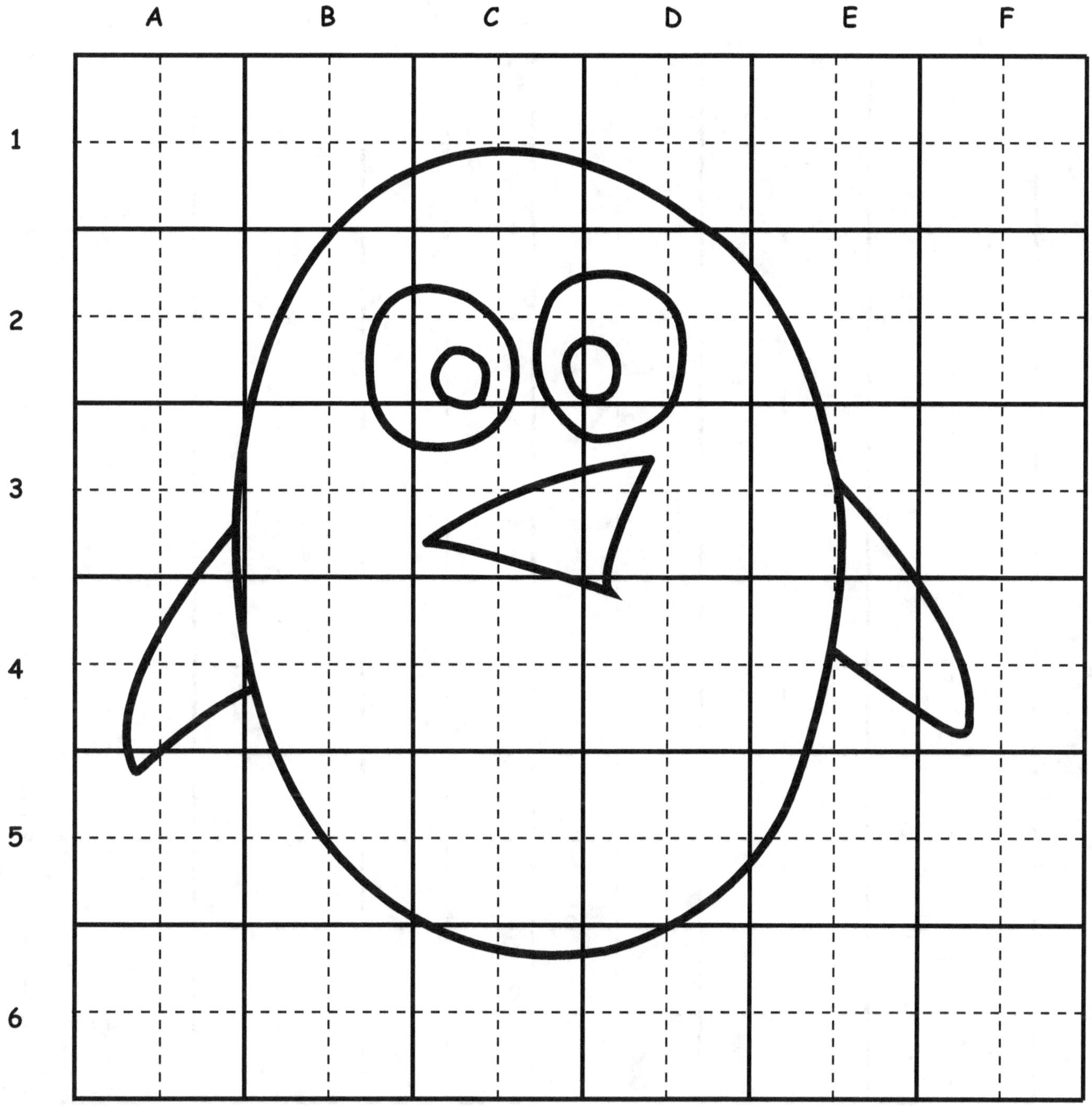

Practice Here With Gride

Add the shape of nose.

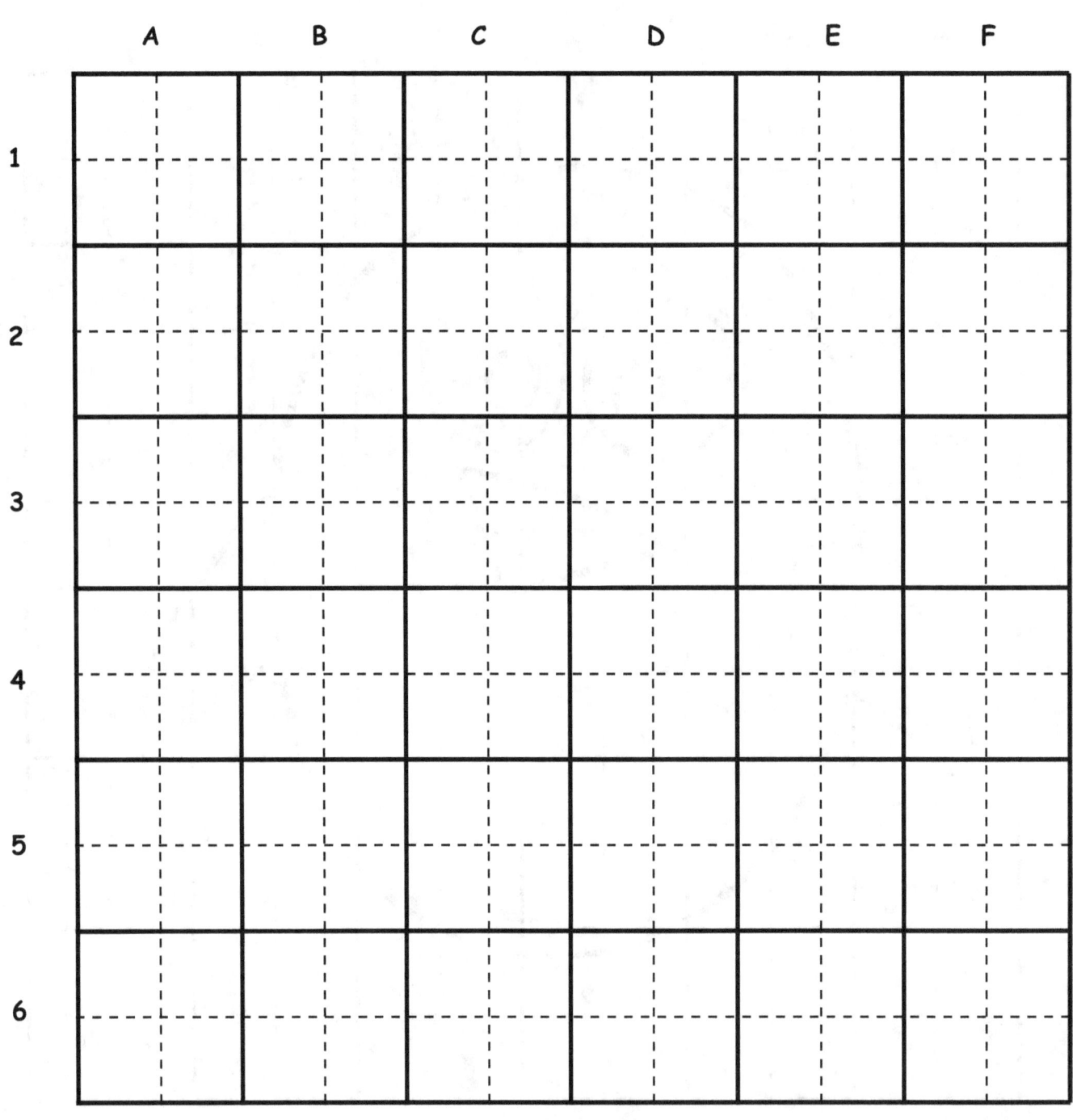

Penguin Art With Grid For Easy Way To Art

5 Add the inner shape of belly and feet and erase all extra and unnecessary lines.

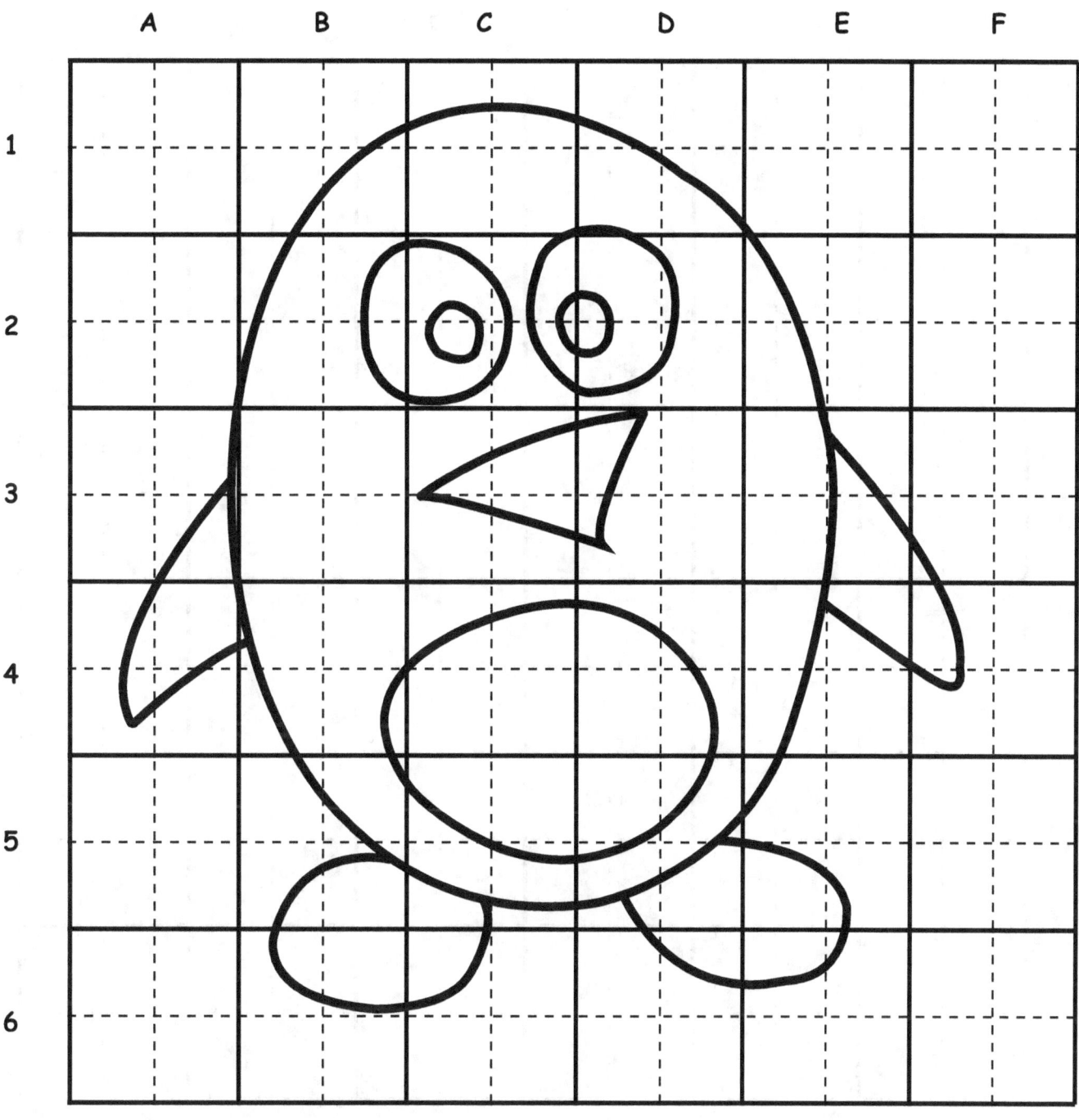

Practice Here With Gride

Add the inner shape of belly and feet and erase all extra and unnecessary lines.

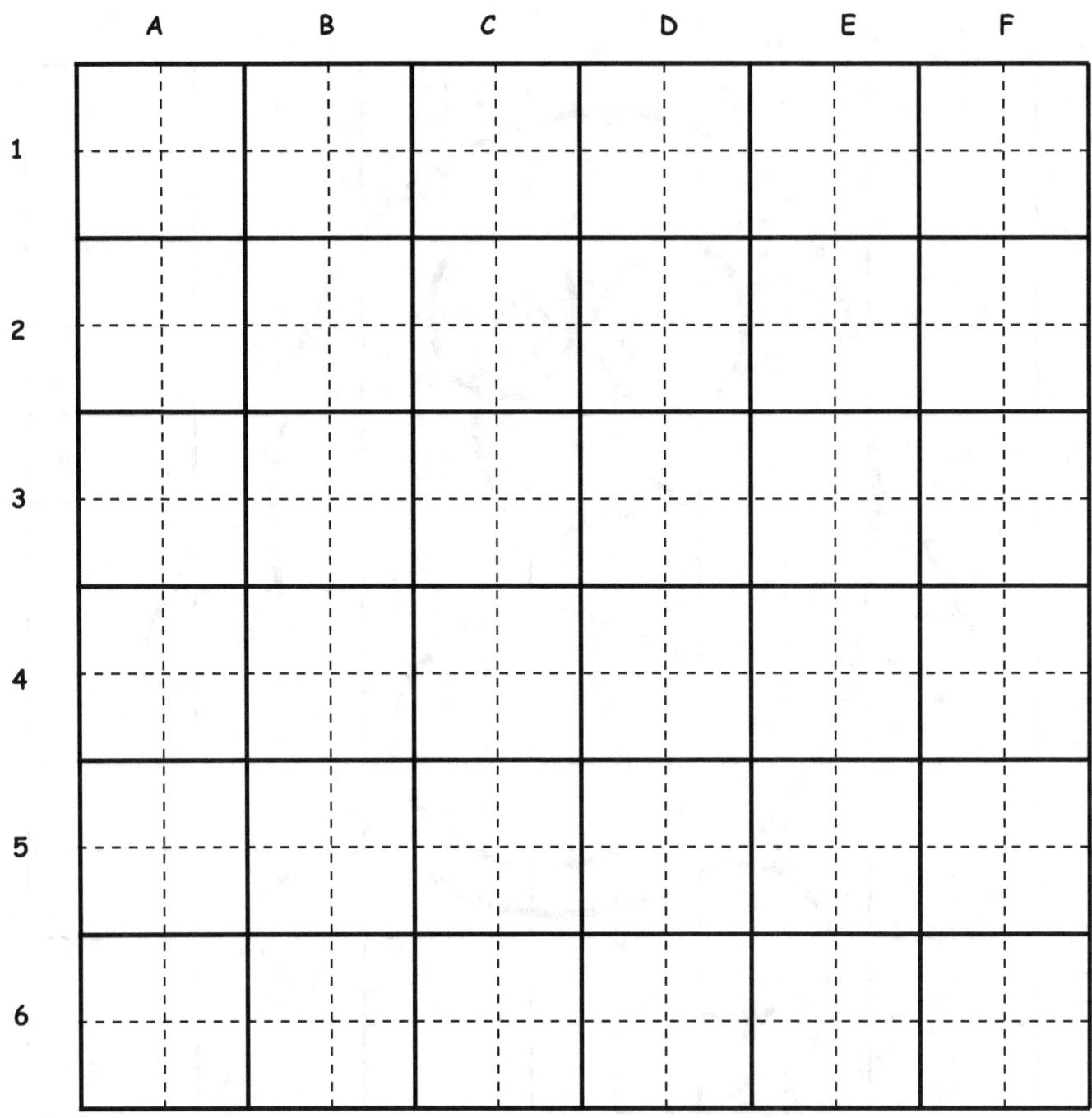

You Penguin is ready to color!

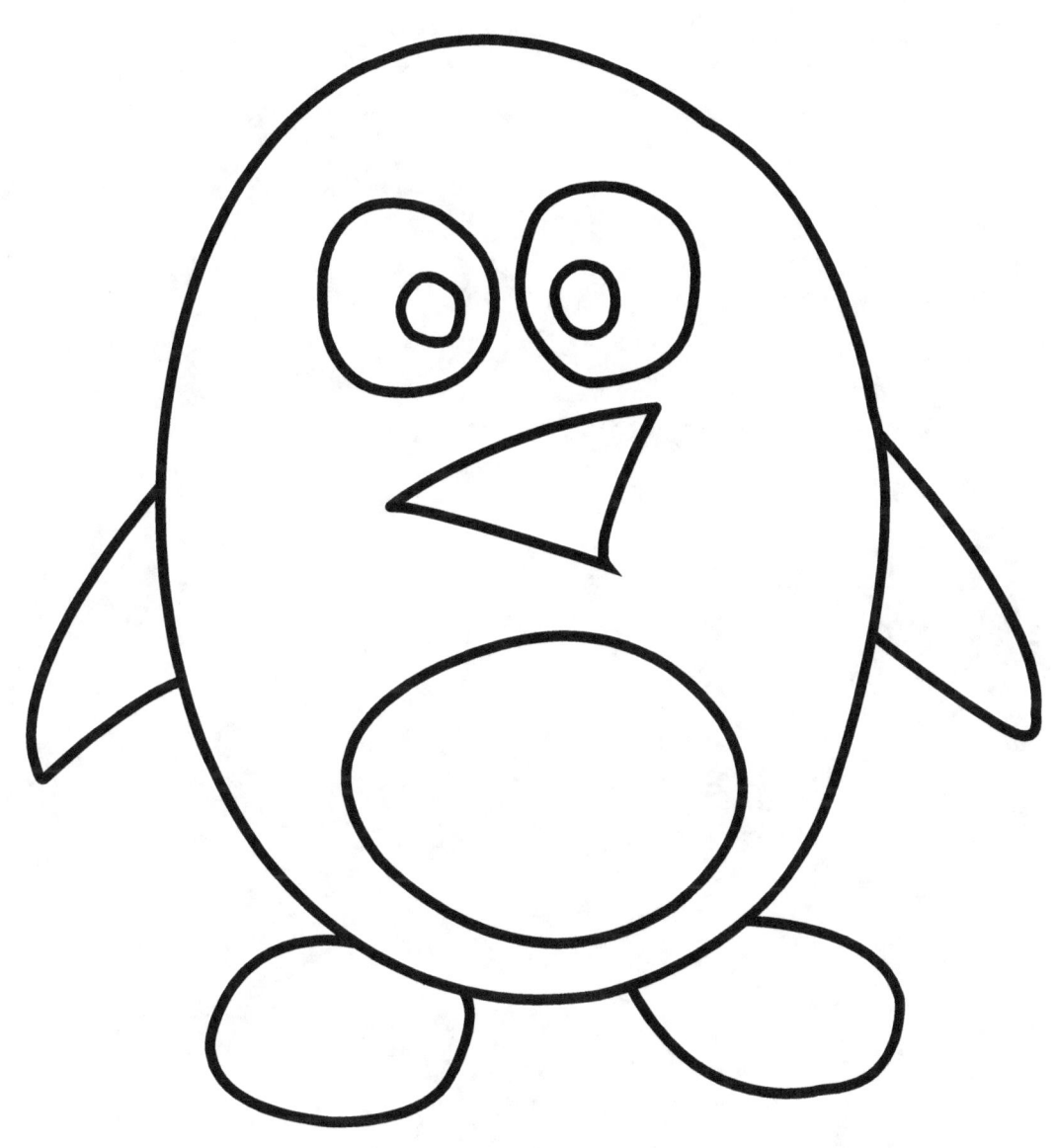

Practice Here Blind

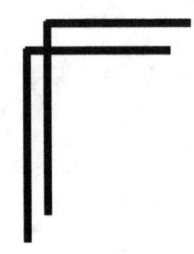

The End